Praise for *You Thought It Was More*

"This updated version of 'You Thought It Was More' revives the fascinating story of Louis 'the Coin', one of the underworld's most intriguing figures. Veteran author and journalist Andy Thibault knows the ins and outs of the New England Mob as well as anyone, and it shows in this must-read true crime book."

— Larry Henry, senior reporter at Gambling.com, "The Mob in Pop Culture" columnist for The Mob Museum in Las Vegas.

"So much sets this book apart — the extraordinary tales it tells, its insider's look at organized crime and Louis Colavecchio's enormous affection for his characters. But the biggest surprise? I was held in total suspense by the technical sections. I never expected to be riveted by metallurgy... but I was."

— Novelist Pam Lewis, author of *Speak Softly, She Can Hear* and *Perfect Family*.

"Ka-Ching! A BIG WIN. Louis the Coin figured out a way to make slot machines pay off, really pay off, to the tune of several million dollars. Much of that went into the coffers of the Patriarca Crime Family, which punched far above its weight as the crime family from the smallest state in the union. Louis, with his co-authors Andy Thibault and Frank Douskey, tell his compelling story well and weave it into a history of the ruthless world of Rhode Island organized crime. This is a world of violence and greed that ensnares public officials and law enforcement and rivals the old-world protestants for power in the Ocean State. Buy it."

— Richard Esposito, investigative reporter and former Deputy Police Commissioner, NYPD

"The Rhode Island mob and the eponymous Patriarca Family have had many chroniclers, but none has captured it better than Andy Thibault in the Louis the Coin memoir. Throw in a heavy mix of Goodfellas and you have a book that will take its rightful place in mob lore."

— Atty. J. Bruce Maffeo, white collar criminal defense attorney and former federal prosecutor for the Organized Crime Strike Force, Eastern District of New York.

"Louis the Coin was the wisest of the wise guys, an inventive manufacturer and casino counterfeiting legend who took pride in outsmarting everyone in his path, especially the authorities. His gaming chips and coins were so good the only thing that could bring him down was his own greed. No wonder mobsters loved him. He's the stuff of movies. His story and this book inspired me to write the feature film screenplay, 'COIN MAN.'"

— Jack Chaucer, screenwriter and author of the four-book *Nikki Janicek* series.

—

"Louis 'The Coin' Colavecchio won a name for himself by being able to make anything, and now he has made a profane and raucously funny memoir of his life of crime. This is a world of hot cars, hot jewels, hot women, a wad of cash in your pocket and a handmade silencer on your Ruger automatic pistol. Bookies and loan sharks, enforcers and counterfeiters, con men and scam artists: 'You Thought It Was More' evokes a bygone era, treating us to a wise-guy crime romance that's part 'Law & Order,' part 'Guys & Dolls.'"

— Rand Richards Cooper, author of *Big as Life*, is an essayist and restaurant critic for *The New York Times*.

"Louis the Coin was an uncannily talented machinist with an appetite for crime. Thibault takes readers along on Louie's wild ride — from Connecticut's tribal casinos to Atlantic City and Vegas — and reveals how the man's ego and connections got him busted."

— Karen Florin, Managing Editor, *The Day of New London*.

"Remarkably crafted. Who would have thought Louis the Coin could be a vivid storyteller? He writes with commanding vigor. Reminiscent of 'Honor Thy Father,' the gracious portrait of the Bonanno crime family by Gay Talese."

— James H. Smith, New England journalist and author of *A Passion for Journalism."*

"Riveting! Raises the bar for all future storytellers in this genre of wise guys and their adventures."

— New York trial attorney Bruce Baron, media commentator on news outlets including MSNBC and Fox News.

"You Thought it Was More is not — thankfully — literary. It is, however, a tale told in a voice that rings true, very much in the aesthetic tradition of our best oral histories. Louis 'The Coin' Colavecchio would probably be right at home in a Studs Terkel book."

— Poet Jon Andersen, Professor of English, Quinebaug Valley Community College, and author of *Stomp and Sing*.

"First off, how can you not love a book written by someone named Louis the Coin? It's worth reading just to enjoy the names of the wiseguys! This is a must-read for anyone who loved Goodfellas, Casino and Bronx Tale! Louis took me so far into the Providence Mob that I thought I was a snitch! I'm still looking over my shoulder!"

— Mickey Sherman, criminal defense lawyer and author of *How Can You Defend Those People?*

YOU THOUGHT IT WAS MORE

New Adventures of the
World's Greatest Counterfeiter
Louis "The Coin"

As seen on The History Channel & The BBC

A memoir of sorts:

Some of this really happened and some names
have been changed to protect the guilty.
See author's note.

Louis Colavecchio

With Franz Douskey and Andy Thibault

YOU THOUGHT
IT WAS MORE

New Adventures of the
World's Greatest Counterfeiter
Louis "The Coin"

VINDICTA

Vindicta Publishing

Las Vegas ♦ Chicago ♦ Palm Beach

Published in the United States of America by
Histria Books
7181 N. Hualapai Way, Ste. 130-86
Las Vegas, NV 89166 U.S.A.
HistriaBooks.com

Vindicta Publishing is an imprint of Histria Books and a joint venture of Histria Books and Creative Destruction Media. Titles published under the imprints of Histria Books are distributed worldwide.

Library of Congress Control Number: 2024931044

ISBN 978-1-59211-427-6 (hardcover)
ISBN 978-1-59211-442-9 (eBook)

Contents

About Louis 7

Organized Crime in Rhode Island, A Primer..................................10

Louis Sentencing Report 25

Introduction..37

Foreword...38

Author's Note 39

Chapter 1 – Sherwood Manufacturing Company 40

Chapter 2 – Dean Sales Co..57

Chapter 3 – The Office 73

Chapter 4 – La Fantasia...81

Chapter 5 – Breaking The Lease..91

Chapter 6 – Mona Lisa Jewelry 104

Chapter 7 – The S&S Bar 110

Chapter 8 – Beating Ma Bell 125

Chapter 9 – Dairy Land Insurance 134

Chapter 10 – Foreign Car World 140

Chapter 11 – 'The Bust Out' 174

Chapter 12 – On The Run..182

Chapter 13 – Trop Jewelry Company...191

Chapter 14 – The Counterfeit King 208

Chapter 15 – 'Silence Is Golden' 234

Chapter 16 – Vegas Junkets..239

Chapter 17 – Getting Caught..243

Chapter 18 – Atlantic & Gloucester City Jail 255

Chapter 19 – Fighting My Case 270

Chapter 20 – Fort Dix...286

Chapter 21 – 'You Thought It Was More'..298

Epilogue 316

About the Authors..320

About Louis

Louis the Coin was a genius in metallurgy whose estimated haul from producing counterfeit slot tokens and chips easily exceeded $3 million to $4 million from casinos around the country.

Some casinos admitted it, and many — most of which were in Nevada — didn't.

Louis sat at the right hand of New England Mob Boss Raymond Patriarca — one of the most powerful gangsters in U.S. history — with direct access to his family members. Louis was a friend of theirs and a talent, though not a made man.

He was neither your average jeweler nor your average mob associate. He began his criminal career as a teenager and went on to earn a business degree from Providence College.

In the years before his death, Louis attended community college in Rhode Island because he loved learning. His expertise ranged from making jewelry and fixing printing presses to orthotics and of course, counterfeiting slot machine tokens and currency.

Colavecchio could duplicate or create almost anything made from precious metals or stones. All he needed was a sample. The samples were analyzed professionally for content, weight, and availability.

Foxwoods had been booming for about five years when Colavecchio set his sights on Connecticut. Mohegan Sun had just opened.

Colavecchio never talked about his friends — at least to police. But one of the important numbers in his personal phone directory was for Louis "Baby Shacks" Manocchio, then the reputed Mafia boss of Rhode Island. Manocchio lived in Providence's Federal Hill neighborhood, where he once operated the Café Verdi restaurant. He was convicted of a mob hit in 1968, but that was overturned by the Rhode Island Supreme Court. In 2015, Manocchio was released from federal prison to a halfway house after serving five years for his role in an extortion plot.

Before Colavecchio could move on the casinos, he needed to do some homework. He also needed some serious equipment. Colavecchio's expert analysis revealed he needed the following: precious metals including copper, zinc and nickel, a 150-ton press from Italy, and laser-cutting tools to cut, shape and create dies to stamp out the coins.

The coins were tokens, to be used in Las Vegas, Loughlin, Atlantic City, and the Tribal Casinos in Connecticut. When state police brought a sample of Colavecchio's product to Foxwoods, the experts did not believe it was counterfeit. Some called it a masterpiece.

State police advised the casino to keep track of inventory; the token counts were bound to be off because of the surplus. Meanwhile, the inventories at Atlantic City casinos were multiplying like rabbits.

"We know that he hit Vegas hard," an investigator said. "But since many of the directors of security there were former FBI agents, they denied it. The problem did not exist. It never happened."

Evidence mounted. A surveillance team comprised of detectives from Las Vegas, New Jersey and Connecticut waited for Colavecchio to hit New Jersey or Connecticut again. He chose New Jersey. This time he used only $100 tokens. It was easy. There were fewer machines to watch.

Colavecchio was arrested in Atlantic City in late December 1996. The pinch did not make the papers for about a week.

In his car, Colavecchio had 750 pounds of counterfeit tokens, a fake police ID, disguises, a handgun, maps of casinos, and various casino documents.

The FBI, Secret Service, three state police agencies and Providence police took inventory at Colavecchio's Providence operation. The government had to rent two storage facilities to store all the loot that was seized.

Everyone took their turn arresting Colavecchio. He hired a former Rhode Island attorney general and a respected New London attorney as his lawyers. Foxwoods and Mohegan Sun acknowledged finding a total of at least $50,000 in fake tokens.

Investigators borrowed microscopes from local high schools to inspect mounds of tokens. It took them weeks just to determine that Colavecchio hit one Mohegan

Sun jackpot for $2,000. Worked out by Connecticut based detectives, Secret Service, and prosecutors, Colavecchio ended up in a conference room and getting VIP treatment at Mohegan Sun. His lawyers had worked out a deal.

Colavecchio showed law enforcement how he did the job and promised to help the casino tribes and the state ward off any future raids.

They say he was a hero in Providence as well. Colavecchio served a relatively short federal sentence at Fort Dix in New Jersey and did not "rat out" any of his friends. The New York Times and Providence Journal also reported Louis was hired by the U.S. Mint upon his release from federal prison for the token scheme a couple decades ago. That was because his dies in coins were of better quality than government production. The U.S. government paid Louis about $18,000 to be a consultant.

Louis died on July 6, 2020 at his daughter's home in Cranston, RI. He had gained a compassionate release from federal prison weeks earlier after serving time for counterfeiting $100 bills. He was 78, as noted in his New York Times obituary.

He counted among his friends the detective who arrested him in Connecticut. The Connecticut State Police Museum, in cooperation with The Mob Museum in Las Vegas, is developing a traveling Louis the Coin exhibit.

Andy Thibault

Organized Crime in Rhode Island,
A Primer

The history of organized crime in Rhode Island is chock full of colorful characters, comical and tragic stories, violence, and greed. It is an underground version of politics. They share the element of constantly seeking money to support their operation.

The difference is often blurry.

To understand organized crime in New England, in particular, Rhode Island where the link to politicians was an open secret, one must understand two realities:

• First, those involved in organized crime were ruthless, sinister, greedy, selfish, violent, and brutish — but with interesting nicknames.

• Second, many people in Rhode Island adored them and believed life, at least on Federal Hill, the unofficial headquarters of the wise guys, was better, safer, and more enjoyable.

To this day, people who recall the days of mob dominance wax nostalgic over those decades.

Back then, the bodies of the whacked bookies or suspected rats rated only passing indifference.

They never resulted in any witnesses. This is the mythology of the mob, with a sizable number of Rhode Island citizens religiously devoted to the fable.

One man's reputation was so well established that all anyone had to say was "Raymond" or "The Old Man" and everyone knew who you were talking about-Raymond Loredo Salvatore Patriarca.

Beginnings

The mob in New England, dominated for many years by Providence, RI, is the story of the rise of "traditional" organized crime in the United States, controlled extensively by Italians. Joining the immigration wave, the Mafia, a primarily Sicilian phenomenon, arrived in the United States.

In the US, the Mafia became known as "Cosa Nostra" or "La Cosa Nostra" translated variously as "Our Affair" or "This Thing of Ours." From its beginning in the 1800s, the hallmark was secrecy and brutality. The very existence of the organization was denied until the first of the made men — men admitted as full members of the secret society — to cooperate with the government. Vincent Teresa, an associate of the Rhode Island mob, testified about its existence.

As the five main families rose in New York, other groups rose in Chicago — known as the Outfit — as well as in Las Vegas, Kansas City, Buffalo, Milwaukee, and other cities. Boston was the birthplace of what would become the Rhode Island mob.

In the 1930s and 40s, Phillip Buccola ran the family in Boston. At the same time, Raymond Patriarca, born in 1908 in Worcester, began his rise within the organization. A hint of Patriarca's future dominance within organized crime and influence with political figures happened early in his criminal career.

In the 1930s, the Providence Board of Public Safety named Patriarca Public Enemy #1. His rise to power was in full swing. In 1938, he was sentenced to five years for armed robbery, yet only served four months.

An inquiry into the circumstances of Patriarca's release revealed he was blessed with special, if not truly divine, intervention.

Executive Councilor Daniel H. Coakley, a close associate of Massachusetts Gov. Charles F. Hurley, drafted a parole petition based on the appeals of a "Father Fagin."

There was no Father Fagin, just a fictional character Coakley had fabricated. The governor granted Patriarca's parole. The news leaked out and an uproar occurred. In the end, Coakley would be dismissed from the governor's office.

Patriarca remained free.

It would underscore Patriarca's reach into political circles and enhance his standing among the wiseguys. It wouldn't be the last time a priest worked to help Patriarca, only the next one would be real.

In the 1940s and 50s, Patriarca rose to head the New England Mob. Buccola, under indictment for tax evasion, fled the country back to Italy. Patriarca stepped in and assumed control of the family.

His stellar reputation — for brutality and ruthless control of bookmakers, loan sharks, hijackings, and any other lucrative mob business — was unmatched among the national organized crime groups. Most notably Patriarca's special connection with The Five Families in New York put him firmly at the center of power. His reign would run from 1950 until his death in 1984 — of a heart attack while at the home of his girlfriend.

During his reign, the fabled level of his influence both within the criminal world and in the political arena grew exponentially. His reach contributed to the defeat of an incumbent governor because of the perception of his influence.

The late John A. Notte Jr. was the 65th governor of Rhode Island, from 1961-63. The late Col. Walter Stone, a former Providence Police Chief, was the Superintendent of the Rhode Island State Police and a sworn enemy of Raymond.

Reports circulated that Notte fired Stone at the behest of Patriarca. This generated many rumors and innuendos. During the campaign for governor in 1962, The Republican candidate, the late U.S. Sen. John Chafee, promised to reinstate Stone.

Notte lost the election by a mere 400 votes. Chaffee reinstated Stone as promised. Stone would remain Colonel until 1990, the longest serving head of a State Police agency in the country.

Information corroborating the alleged influence over Notte became public because of a Freedom of Information Act request to the FBI about a bug placed illegally in the office Patriarca maintained at his vending machine company, Coin-O-Matic.

The building, on Atwells Avenue in the heart of Providence's Federal Hill, would become known as "The Office."

The bug recorded many conversations between Patriarca and other mobsters, including a discussion about a $25,000 bribe allegedly paid to Notte.

In 1981, a meeting of law enforcement agencies, including the State Police, FBI and the New England Organized Crime Strike Force, discussed an individual who had cooperated with the State Police.

Excerpt, FBI Patriarca Files:

"SOURCE became very emotional, stating that he would not testify and would not consider entering the federal witness protection program. On April 15, 1981, a meeting was held at the offices of Colonel Walter E. Stone, RISP. Present were representatives of the State of RI Attorney General's Office, the New England Organized Crime Strike Force and FBI, besides the RISP. Stone advised that even though the source had become uncooperative and is refusing to testify in this matter, a responsibility exists on the part of the RISP with respect to the safety of the potential victim. Stone advised it is the intention of the RISP to, at the very least, confront the subjects in this matter."

Nothing ever came of this "confrontation."

Ruthless

Soon after Patriarca took over, bodies started showing up with various bullet holes, knife wounds, bludgeoning injuries or ligature marks. Some bodies bore evidence of a combination of all these various methods of execution.

One the more brutal hits was on George "Tiger" Balletto at the Bella Napoli Café on Federal Hill. This was near Patriarca's vending machine company.

Balletto, a tough guy who posed a challenge to Patriarca's control, was shot several times in the back. Urban legend has it the rounds spun him around, but he never fell from the stool, dying with his head on the bar.

There were more than a dozen patrons in the bar at the time of the shooting.

Not one would provide the Providence Police with any information. This witness-amnesia phenomenon would repeat itself in several incidents connected to Patriarca.

Patriarca's reputation among the New York families led him to become involved in one of the most notorious hits on a mob figure in New York. Recorded on the illegal bug planted in "the office," Patriarca claimed the Genovese family reached out for assistance in the Albert Anastasia hit. Patriarca sent one of his most violent enforcers, Jackie Nazarian, to New York. Anastasia was shot while sitting in a barber's chair. No one was ever charged with the murder.

Nazarian himself would become a murder victim when he made the mistake of bragging, he was taking over for Patriarca when the "old man" was ill. It proved a fatal mistake.

Nazarian would be killed in 1962 by Louie "The Fox" Taglianetti who also would also become a murder victim in 1970, along with his girlfriend — which did not sit well with Patriarca.

Patriarca was even said to be involved in a plot by the CIA to use the mob to kill Fidel Castro. Vincent Teresa, revealed the story during one of his court appearances.

Teresa said Sam Giancana, the Chicago mob boss, reached out to Raymond's consiglieri Henry Tamaleo and Patriarca for a hit man. Patriarca selected Maurice "Pro" Lerner, a one-time baseball star, as the man for the job.

Revelations would corroborate the efforts of the CIA to recruit the mob for the Castro hit.

Lerner would play a part in another murder, along with John "Red" Kelley, that would ensnare Patriarca in a web of lies spun by corrupt FBI agents.

In 1968, a bookie and his bodyguard were shot to death in a Silver Lake variety store, an area close to Federal Hill. The bookie, Rudolph Marfeo, and his body-guard, Anthony Melei, were targeted because Marfeo refused to pay a percentage of his gambling operation profits to Patriarca. The triggermen were John "Red" Kelley and Maurice "Pro" Lerner.

But this wasn't just a simple hit. It was an All-in-the-Family continuation of Patriarca enforcing control. In 1966, William "Willie" Marfeo, Rudolph's brother, was killed in a phone booth for similar reasons.

The Rudolph Marfeo murder would put Patriarca in prison until 1974.

Patriarca's conviction, along with Henry Tamaleo, for conspiracy to murder Willie Marfeo was based largely on the testimony of one of the first mob witnesses to be put into the witness protection program, Joseph "The Animal" Barbosa, an exceptionally brutal Boston-based enforcer.

Another mob witness, John "Red" Kelley, a convicted bank robber, testified in the Rudolph Marfeo murder trial against Patriarca and his fellow gunman, "Pro" Lerner. He testified about meeting Patriarca on Palm Sunday two weeks before the murder and that Patriarca wanted Rudolph Marfeo killed. Kelly said Patriarca told him, "I want him dead."

Kelley's testimony was corroborated by the notorious and disgraced FBI agent. H. Paul Rico. Rico would be convicted of conspiracy to murder Roger Wheeler, an Oklahoma City millionaire, on the orders of James "Whitey" Bulger.

The first trial resulted in a hung jury. The second, with defense counsel armed with more information to discredit Kelly, resulted in Patriarca's conviction. Despite the trial judge's warning to the spectators on the day of the verdict—most of whom were there in support of Patriarca—to refrain from any outbursts, the court erupted when the verdict was read.

Years later, details of the Bulger case and the attendant FBI involvement in criminal activities with Bulger became public. Authorities uncovered evidence that both principal witnesses in the Patriarca trials, Barbosa and Kelley, committed perjury. The FBI knew about it and let it or made it happen.

There was another twist to the Rudolph Marfeo murder trial, involving the real, aforementioned Catholic priest. Father Raymond Moriarity testified he was with Patriarca when Kelley claimed the meeting to kill Marfeo took place. Father Moriarity testified he and Patriarca had gone to the Gates of Heaven Cemetery in East Providence to pray at the grave of Patriarca's first wife.

Through the investigative work of determined Providence Police Detective Bobby Stevenson, and then little-known Rhode Island Special Asst. Atty. General Vincent A. "Buddy" Cianci — who went on to a notorious career as mayor of Providence — the public learned the priest lied. He later testified that he confused the date.

The investigation determined the priest was in Virginia performing a baptism when he claimed to be in Providence. This attempt at Divine Intervention failed and Patriarca was convicted, albeit on perjured testimony.

Patriarca's time in prison, and the perceived treatment he received by those still out on the street, would set in motion the largest robbery in the history of Rhode Island, called Bonded Vault.

Bonded Vault

One problem of being a successful criminal is storage. Where does one keep the ill-gotten gains to keep them from the eyes of the cops?

Depending on which legend one believes, Patriarca either conceived the idea or controlled through the usual methods a place that became known as Bonded Vault.

Hudson Fur Storage was a commercial storage facility at 101 Cranston St. in Providence's West End. Inside the former church building, there was a large safe with 146 safe deposit boxes. Access to these boxes was by invitation only. One had to have underworld connections to get a box, but there were no limitations on what you kept there.

Stolen goods, cash from illegal activities, weapons, jewelry reported taken for insurance claims, anything that you couldn't put in a legitimate safe deposit box you could put there.

Here's the story as recounted by Jerry Tillinghast, one of the men charged — and acquitted — of the robbery.

An abridged excerpt from the book, *Choices: You Make 'em You Own 'em* by Joe Broadmeadow and Jerry Tillinghast, follows:

"It was a hot morning on August 14, 1975, when the group of men entered The Hudson Furs Company. They filled duffle bags with cash, gold coins, silver bars and jewelry. Most of the stolen items are loot belonging to mobsters.

Secrets are only safe if no one knows about them. Patriarca knew all the secrets.

Dussault was first in. Wearing a suit and carrying a briefcase, he approached the door. Hudson Furs was closed for vacation on this fateful day. Typically, there would be fifteen employees.

Today, as the robbers knew, there would be fewer people inside. Sam Levine, his two brothers, Hyman and Abraham, Hyman's wife Rosalind and the company secretary, Barbara Oliva, were there catching up on business matters.

The door to the office had a buzzer. Sam Levine looked up at the man and buzzed him in. If the business was closed, and Levine didn't know or expect Dussault, why let him in? Jerry says he often wondered if the timing and cooperation were not just luck, but inside information.

This part of the story is reconstructed from the official court record. While Dussault entered the building, the rest waited in the van. Sam looked at the man. "Can I help you?" Dussault pulls out a piece of paper, ignoring Sam and reads softly. Aggravated by the intrusion, Sam walks to the counter to deal with Dussault and send him away. Instead, Sam feels the cold steel of a revolver pushed against his nose. Dussault warns him not to trigger any alarms or, "I'll blow your head off." Sam follows the command.

"Who else is here?" Dussault demands.

Sam tells him about the other four. Dussault has him call them out one at a time. Within minutes, Dussault has them all gathered. During the trial, some macabre comedy moments came out about those first few moments.

Barbara Oliva, who would be the other star witness at the trial, looked at Dussault's gun, just inches from her face, and said, "Are those real bullets in that gun?"

"What are you, a fucking comedian?" Dussault growled.

Oliva, scared but not intimidated, replied, "I've seen guns before. Get that goddamned thing out of my face."

The standoff was interrupted by the first of the crew, Chucky Flynn, entering the building and struggling to pull on a mask. Soon they are all inside and the work to smash open the boxes starts.

Dussault and Flynn hand pillowcases to the employees, forcing them to put them over their heads — all except for Sam. They need him if somebody shows up. This happens while the work is in progress. Sam's uncle, an elderly gentleman named Max Gellerman, arrives and is quickly added to the group of hostages. Dussault guards them while the robbers go to work prying open safe deposit boxes and filling seven duffle bags.

While the results were spectacular, the process was a chaotic, unorganized conglomeration of yelling, swearing, jostling and raw muscle power prying the boxes open. It wasn't a smooth or well-orchestrated production. It was more a bumbling group of adrenaline-fueled men flailing away, stumbling toward an unimaginable mountain of loot.

Through sheer determination and adrenaline, they emptied 146 boxes. It took 75-90 minutes. They had specific boxes they were to look for but went after as many as they could with brute force, if not finesse.

Despite the stifling heat, the crowded environment and sweat pouring from them, the size of the haul spurred them on. Loading the van and a couple of cars, the combined weight of the men and loot causing the back ends of the vehicles to sag as they fled the scene.

In the last act, Dussault herded the employees into a small bathroom and blocked the door. Waving the gun to underscore his point, he warned them to stay inside, or he would shoot them.

They did, for a while, until they feared they would run out of oxygen. With some effort, the employees forced the door open.

Before them lay an unimaginable scene. Knee deep on the floor were cash, jewels, gold, silver, and other valuable items. The robbers left as much on the floor as they hauled away. Reports have the Levine brothers scooping up much of the stuff left behind and squirreling it away. That would be a risky business if the information from the so-called Patriarca Papers is to be believed.

Many stories arose from this robbery. But the reason behind may all boil down to, besides the usual greed common in these matters, Patriarca's ego.

When a person becomes a "made" member of organized crime, it is a lifetime access to a share of the family's profits. By keeping "Omertà," the code of silence about mob activities, the organization is responsible for taking care of the family of anyone in prison and continuing to pay them their cut.

While Raymond sat in prison, he did not believe those on the outside paid him his due. Thus, on his release, he summoned one of his most trusted lieutenants, Gerard "The Frenchman" Ouimette, and assigned him the task of exacting payback.

Ouimette was an oddity within the organization. Ruthless, brutal and violent like all the others, but in a position normally reserved for a "made" man. Ouimette was Irish and French. He lacked the Italian heritage to be a full member.

His crew was also a collection of mutts, but with a record of success almost unmatched by crews led by capos — captains — who were made men.

The team included the Ouimette brothers — Gerard, Walter and John — Jerry Tillinghast and George Basmajian. Basmajian was murdered shortly after the Bonded Vault trial for running an operation in Connecticut without the local mob's okay. This core group of the Ouimette crew, along with a few others, were feared and fearsome. They were responsible for loan sharking, bookmaking, robbing drug dealers, and other nefarious acts.

The beauty of the plan was the vulnerability of the victims. If you steal from a thief, who is he gonna call? Patriarca knew — some allege he controlled the vault location altogether — stealing from these guys would bring little heat.

Depending on which version one believes, $10 million to $15 million — $75 million to $80 million in today's dollars — worth of gold, jewelry, diamonds and cash came out of the vault. They didn't bother taking small bills. It wasn't worth the extra weight or space. When they left, the floor was covered with fives and ones and knee deep in other precious items.

John Ouimette, Charles "Chucky" Flynn, and Ralph "Skippy" Byrnes were convicted based largely on the testimony of Joe "The Dancer" Danese, another participant in the robbery.

Jerry Tillinghast, Jake Tarzian, and Walter Ouimette were found not guilty. Raymond Patriarca was never charged, nor was Gerard Ouimette. As to the loot, the FBI claims it went overseas. Others claim it went to New York and John Gotti, who had a tight relationship with Patriarca and was visited frequently by Jerry Tillinghast and Gerard Ouimette.

Tillinghast told a story about the reputation of the Rhode Island mob among the New York families. At a meeting with John Gotti and some of his associates in a club owned by Gotti, one of the associates asked Jerry where he was from.

"Providence," Tillinghast answered.

"Providence?" the wise guy countered, "You fucking guys kill everybody."

Public Connections

Patriarca was, among other things, a shrewd businessperson. He knew how and whom to cultivate legitimate business skills and those other skills — the ones you acquire on the street rather than through an MBA — necessary to maintain control of a criminal empire.

Among the more notable individuals associated with Patriarca was B.A. Dario, the owner of Lincoln Downs Racetrack in Rhode Island and Frank Sinatra, the "Chairman of the Board." They co-owned Berkshire Downs Racetrack in Massachusetts with Patriarca.

Frank "Bobo" Marrapese was another notorious enforcer and Capo who ran one of Patriarca's crews. Bobo was a feared and fearless man. He once threw a cement block through the windshield of a Providence Police car when the officer was writing a parking ticket for Bobo's Cadillac.

Bobo would face several murder trials and walk on most, but finally be convicted for the murder of Richard "Dickie" Callei inside Bobo's Acorn Social Club on Federal Hill.

When one of his associates, Richard "Moon" Diorio, complained Bobo wasn't paying him enough to afford a sunroof for his car, Bobo took a saw and cut a hole in Moon's car: "There's your fucking sunroof."

Diorio would turn on Marrapese and testify against him.

One of Bobo's most unusual outbursts happened on his conviction for stealing a truckload of La-Z-Boy recliners. When the judge sentenced him to 15 years in prison, Bobo quipped, "Fifteen years for a chair? What the fuck would I get for a couch?"

Joseph A. Bevilacqua Sr. was a prominent defense counsel and close associate of Patriarca who rose to become chief justice of the Rhode Island Supreme Court.

Bevilacqua would be forced to resign after Rhode Island State Police surveillance photos of him leaving a mob-controlled motel — infamously while zipping his pants as he left the room he shared with a woman — were leaked to the Providence Journal.

Jack Witschi's Sports Arena was a precursor to the World Wrestling Federation wrestling phenomenon. Patriarca had a controlling interest in the business.

George Lincoln Rockwell and the American Nazi Party shared a mindset with Raymond — at least on racism. Patriarca and Rockwell allegedly shared "concerns" of the number of black — then referred to as Negro — soldiers in the military.

The FBI files, from which most of this information is derived, also claimed Patriarca was involved in fixing New England Patriot football games. Some players were also wagering on the games and with trying to recover stolen furs from Rocky Marciano, the boxing champion.

Patriarca's reach extended well beyond the littlest state in the union. His tenure was one of a national criminal juggernaut.

Fueling Mob Business: Private Connections

Much of the money comes from traditional sources — bookmaking, loansharking, extortion, stolen goods, hijackings and prostitution. There are often more sophisticated schemes requiring a high level of skills not normally associated with the mob.

Counterfeiting can be one of the more lucrative activities. Quality counterfeiting requires skill, planning and patience. Patriarca, through the men he had out on the street, would be keenly aware of any such individuals and make sure he received a significant portion of their profits.

One of the more unusual individuals who found himself as an associate of Patriarca, either through attraction to the wise guy aura or compelled to play along, was Louis "The Coin" Colavecchio.

Louis Colavecchio was one of those guys who yearned for the mob life but also was smart enough to see the downsides. Through a series of circumstances and happenstance, Louis ended up working at Sherwood Manufacturing.

He would come to meet many of the hustlers and thieves doing business with Sherwood—the company wasn't above facilitating the fencing of stolen goods — and would develop the skills of a methodical and talented machinist among many other such endeavors.

Spending time at the S&S Bar, owned by Louie "Baby Shacks" Manocchio and his brother, Anthony, Louis was exposed to the world of organized criminal gambling. The bar ran a significant bookmaking operation and, unbeknownst to Patriarca and Manocchio, a drug business.

Over time, Louis migrated to the jewelry business and fine-tuned his skills with this intricate and painstaking work. It would be this combination of skills and his close association with Patriarca that would lead to his greatest contribution to the mob finances.

While Colavecchio's most active period would come after the death of Raymond, his inclusion within the inner circle of those around Patriarca shows just how close he was to the "Old Man" and the trust the mob had in the enterprising Colavecchio.

Louis the Coin, though not a made man, was considered such a great talent he was part of the inner circle of the Providence Office.

Decline and Fall

After his release from prison, untouched by the Bonded Vault case, Patriarca resumed direct control of the New England mob. While he maintained official control of the mob from within the prison, his return to the street brought an added level of stability. That would change soon.

Age and health concerns would take their toll. Some doubted the validity of many of his health claims. When facing indictment on a host of new charges, Patriarca's doctor, a highly respected cardiologist, Dr. Barbara Roberts, testified that Patriarca was too ill to face indictment or trial.

Dr. Roberts wrote a book called *The Doctor Broad: A Mafia Love Story* about her experiences. She was a lover of a man named Louis "Baby Shacks" Manocchio, a convicted killer and a close friend of Louis The Coin.

Patriarca's funeral in 1984 would attract mob figures and organized crime intelligence units from all over the country.

A Succession of Pretenders to the Throne

With Patriarca's passing, and despite the efforts of longtime Boston Mob Boss Gennaro Angiulo to succeed him, his son, Raymond "Junior" Patriarca became the head of the mob with the support of the five New York families.

Junior often was characterized as inept. This was the result of the contrast between his father and himself more than anything else. Raymond Senior made his bones on the streets; some perceived the Junior had it handed to him.

He was not without skills and ran the organization for several years. But in 1989, a well-placed, and more importantly, court-authorized electronic surveillance operation recorded Junior performing the long-held secret "Omertà" ceremony inducting new members as "made men."

Until that fateful recording, the ceremony was the thing of turncoat's testimony and legend. The FBI recording proved it to be a fact.

Indicted and convicted, Junior went to prison.

Nicholas "Nicky" Bianco, who'd spent 11 years in New York after being sent there by Patriarca at the request of New York to settle an internal war, became boss. Some believe he was always the real boss once Raymond Sr. died, but let Junior hold the role out of respect for his father.

Bianco lasted a year before he was indicted and sent to prison where he died of Lou Gehrig's Disease (ALS) in 1994.

The baton then passed to Frank "Cadillac" Salemme.

Salemme, who in 1989 had survived an assassination attempt at a Saugus restaurant where he was shot, had been named underboss when Bianco took over. He now became the boss.

This caused a shift in the power base back to Boston, but Salemme would only last four years and then follow the standard route of indictment, conviction and prison.

Once again, the boss was replaced by a longtime wiseguy, Louis or Luigi "Baby Shacks" Manocchio. The base returned to Providence. Manocchio had been a fugitive living in Italy after a conviction for murder. He returned after a plea negotiation was reached, did his time and, on release, rejoined the crew.

His nickname has several variations: Baby Shanks or Baby Shacks. Depending on who is telling the story, both monikers were used for various reasons. Baby Shanks referred to a small knife, a shank, as in prison weapons. The Baby Shacks handle resulted from his rumored success with the ladies.

One of these women was the Dr. Barbara Roberts, Patriarca's cardiologist. During a conversation recorded by the police on a wiretap, Roberts was referred to as that "Doctor Broad." When this became public, she had the title of the book she would eventually write. The book is a worthwhile and exciting read.

Manocchio would be caught up in an extortion case and forced to step down from the leadership position. The next in line was the underboss, Peter "Chief Crazy Horse" Limone.

Limone and five other defendants spent years in prison for a murder they didn't commit based on the perjured testimony of Joseph "The Animal" Barbosa and Vincent "Jimmy" Flemmi with the tacit cooperation of the FBI agents who were trying to recruit Flemmi as an informant.

Eventually, a judge ordered Limone's release and the government paid him and the other defendants — or their estates as some had died — millions in damages.

With the ascent of Limone to the position, there was less stability. While these machinations are difficult to know with absolute certainty, Limone, who died in 2017, was also facing legal problems that impeded his ability to control the organization.

Since Limone's dethroning, there have been several acting bosses: Anthony DiNunzio, Anthony "Spooky" Sapgnola, and Carmine "The Big Cheese" Dinunzio.

The Big Cheese would eventually get the nod as the boss and is believed to be the current head of the New England family.

Robert "The Cigar" Deluca, a former underboss, rose to the head position running the Providence faction while Limone was dealing with his legal problems. Deluca, who was also facing indictment and a long prison term, became a cooperating witness and entered the witness protection program.

The Patriarca years were characterized by stability within the organization, ruthlessly suppressing any dissent. With the recording of the induction ceremony in Medford, the beginning of the downfall of the once dominant criminal organization in New England had begun.

While the mob still exists, the number of made men has been reduced to a handful. They still ply their trade in gambling and other activities. The urban myth that the mob didn't deal drugs is just that, a myth. If there was money in it, the mob would sell cancer. But the days of being the shadow government in Rhode Island and New England are history.

Joe Broadmeadow, Captain (Retired) East Providence Police

Joe Broadmeadow retired with the rank of Captain from the East Providence, RI Police Department after 20 years. He served in the various divisions within the department, including Commander of Investigative Services. He also worked in the Organized Crime Drug Enforcement Task Force (OCDETF) and on special assignment to the FBI Drug Task Force. *It's Just the Way It Was: Inside the War on the New England Mob* and other stories is the third non-fiction book by Joe Broadmeadow. UnMade: Honor Loyalty Redemption (written with Bobby Walason) and Choices: *You Make 'em You Own 'em,* (The Jerry Tillinghast Story), Joe's first two non-fiction works, were both number one new releases on Amazon. Joe is the author of three works of fiction. *Silenced Justice and Collision Course*, featuring East Providence Police Det. Lt. Josh Williams, and *A Change of Hate*, a spin-off of the Josh Williams series, featuring Defense Attorney Harrison 'Hawk' Bennett.

Louis Sentencing Report

Louis the Coin 2019 Sentencing Report
By ASSISTANT U.S. ATTORNEY GERARD SULLIVAN
UNITED STATES DISTRICT COURT
FOR THE DISTRICT OF RHODE ISLAND

UNITED STATES OF AMERICA

v.

LOUIS COLAVECCHIO, Defendant.
Criminal No. 19 — 030 JJM
Aug. 8, 2019

GOVERNMENT'S SENTENCING MEMORANDUM

I. INTRODUCTION

The Defendant

The defendant, Louis Colavecchio (COLAVECCHIO) is now a septuagenarian and a senior statesman of the criminal justice system. Historically, he is an old-time mobster and counterfeiter of some repute. Anecdotally, he earned his nickname The Coin by counterfeiting slugs used in slot machines at gambling venues. He has reportedly been banned from every casino in the country.

His Presentence Report reads like a badly written crime novel. In 1997, COLAVECCHIO was federally convicted of counterfeiting casino tokens in a massive operation that targeted all the Atlantic City casinos in New Jersey and the Foxwood Casino in Connecticut. At the ripe age of 55, COLAVECCHIO received a 27-month federal sentence from the United States District Court for the District of New Jersey for his first counterfeiting conviction. COLAVECCHIO was also convicted of larceny in 1997 by the State of Connecticut and received a seven-year suspended sentence.

COLAVECCHIO was next convicted by the state of Rhode Island in 1998 for obtaining money under false pretenses, after he was caught stealing $100,000 from his 92-year-old aunt in a septic plot to which he confessed. For that crime, he received a 54-month suspended sentence. COLAVECCHIO has also tussled with uniformed police officers in the past. He resisted a lawful arrest after attaining senior citizen status at the age of 64. For that crime he received a one-year suspended sentence in 2006. COLAVECCHIO even failed to complete that short sentence without incident. He admitted to an unspecified violation five months into the sentence.

Most recently (prior to committing this second counterfeiting crime) COLAVECCHIO was convicted in Providence County Superior Court for cultivating kilograms of marijuana in a sophisticated indoor grow operation. Besides the marijuana, a quantity of cocaine, methadone pills, and cash proceeds of drug sales were recovered from his home. At the time he committed those crimes, he was already 74 years old. In yet another unearned act of judicial leniency, COLAVECCHIO was spared jail again with the award of a seven-year suspended sentence. In fact, COLAVECCHIO was regularly reporting to a state probation officer when he embarked on his latest counterfeiting scheme that led him to this newest conviction.

The Offense

In June of last year, the United States Secret Service opened this investigation into the self-proclaimed "world's greatest counterfeiter" and his efforts to produce bogus United States $100 bills. The facts are reported in the PSR but the essence of the man committing the crime was also captured on tape as haughtiness. During two videotaped undercover meetings, COLAVECCHIO showed-off to the informant, boasting to her that he was going to foil even the newest security features of the $100 bills in circulation. In one meeting, he explained that he was already working on a defense should he be caught. If apprehended again, he planned to claim that he was working as a counterfeit deterrence specialist to fool the investigators. Unfortunately for COLAVECCHIO, that pre-conceived act of deception was caught on tape.

II. ARGUMENT

That criminal history and the facts of this case alone are enough to support and justify a prison sentence within the guideline range. Even for a man of advanced age and failing health. After all, age and health have never stopped COLAVEC-CHIO from committing new crimes. Those factors have just benefitted him in his mission to best the criminal justice system and win lenient sentences. Past acts of judicial tolerance have only permitted him the liberty to move on to his next criminal venture.

Fortunately, this sentencing Court also has COLAVECCHIO's own words by which to judge the man. COLAVECCHIO detailed his life along with his views on crime and punishment in an autobiography. In his own words, he portrayed himself as a life-long criminal who measured his success by his ability to commit, profit by, and avoid punishment for crimes. All the while ridiculing the honorable men and women who have investigated his many, many, crimes and belittling the court system that failed to sentence him to any significant time in prison.

The Autobiography

The offense conduct and the criminal history published in the PSR do not begin to capture a complete picture of COLAVECCHIO's life of crime. Only a few years ago, in 2015, he published an autobiographical book, YOU THOUGHT IT WAS MORE, Adventures of the World's Greatest Counterfeiter, telling the story of his crime-filled life with egotistical panache. The phrase "you thought it was more" marked "a mobster as being with the Providence Office." You Thought It Was More, Colavecchio, p. 21 "The Providence Office" was a reference to the Patriarca Crime family.

Drawing further attention to himself, he touted his criminal notoriety on television. The cover of the book proclaimed that the pages contain his story, Louis The Coin - As seen on The History Channel and The BBC. COLAVECCHIO was the [principal] author. COLAVECCHIO should have waited to publish his autobiography until after he retired from a life of crime.

The Author's Note (dated December 9, 2014) sets the theme:

Did I really sit at the right hand of Raymond in Providence? Did I really soak the sheets with red wine in a week of partying with three young women in Rome? Did that police chief really thank me for fixing my speeding ticket going 140 mph in a Lamborghini — after the event made the nightly news???

The Early Years

According to COLAVECCHIO, his criminal escapades started in his teen years. Over the course of time, he enjoyed the tutelage mobster and businessman, Vincent Miele (who he referred to as Vinny or his Uncle Vinny) and the New England Crime Boss, Raymond Patriarca (The Boss, The Old Man, or George). They were men that COLAVECCHIO idolized. (p. 16). He shared the presence of mobsters and hitmen throughout the account of his entire life. A young mind shaped by such powerful and influential role models holds that shape well beyond the average criminal. He wrote, "I was so fascinated by the wise guy lifestyle, I'm sure I would have wound up in that scene." (p. 18). As a man in his 70's he still admires the lifestyle. He romanticized his role as a wise guy throughout 21 chapters and an epilogue.

COLAVECCHIO started by tricking people into buying his Uncle Vinny's fake luxury brand sweaters. (Chapter 1). He later moved on to creating his own swindles, "Hustling was fun, and before long, I felt confident enough to go out on my own." (p. 39).

COLAVECCHIO was quickly able to devise a plan of his own to steal money from Catholics. He sent rosaries in the name of a reverend to unsuspecting members of the public. With the rosaries, he asked for donations to allow the "reverend" to continue to dedicate his life to missionary work. (p. 42). There was no missionary work and the donations never left COLAVECCHIO's pocket. A postal worker tipped him off that Postal Inspectors were investigating "a scam to bilk people out of money in the name of the Catholic Church." To thwart the investigation and avoid apprehension, he simply abandoned the money that remained in the post office boxes to avoid making a pick-up while subject to surveillance. He reflected, "We had a pretty good run, and neither Vincent or I felt too badly." COLAVEC-CHIO wrote that he had "no moral regrets about what we had done." (p. 43).

COLAVECCHIO was unfazed by his near miss and loss of profits. By then he had established an illicit enterprise that he named Dean Sales, Co. (Chapter Two). His warehouse space "was constantly being visited by wise guys, cops, politicians, judges, hustlers, shoplifters and every type of person imaginable. They bought all types of swag, ranging from jewelry, watches, china, crystal, flatware, fur coats, and all kinds of other stolen goods." (p. 48). On one occasion, he "received a load of five thousand stolen designer raincoats." COLAVECCHIO recalled that before the FBI could strike, "a Providence Police detective [name omitted] — an alcoholic who liked to associate with wise guys" tipped him off. He managed to avoid arrest and profit from the crime anyway. (pp. 48-51). COLAVECCHIO observed, "Circumventing the law was very easily done in those days." (p. 118).

Similarly, at the age of 22, he created cheap models of the Vatican-owned statue "Pieta" by Michelangelo and sold them to avid church members outside the 1964 World Fair in New York. (p. 44).

The Adult Years

Following that larcenous start as a young man, COLAVECCHIO committed mortgage fraud (p. 52) bank fraud (p. 53), insurance fraud (p. 77-78), and staged burglaries (p. 80-81), he also committed robbery (p. 86 - 88) and burglary (p. 98) — to catalogue just a sampling of the crimes to which he laid claim. He even illegally manufactured a firearm silencer. (p. 299). COLAVECCHIO's autobiography rarely advanced more than a few pages without the retelling of some crime in which he participated, from which he profited, or the commission of which he admired. After one burglary, COLAVECCHIO recalled showing his accomplice something:

It was a poster from the Department of Education. It said someone who drops out of high school will earn approximately $240,000 in their entire lifetime, while someone with a high school diploma would earn approximately $320,000 in his lifetime. The poster was urging kids not to drop out of school and those that did drop out of school to go back and get their high school diploma. I remarked to Vincent that we had just made more money in the last couple of hours than two high school graduates did in their entire lives.

COLAVECCHIO took pride in duping any system at all, including "Ma Bell." (Chapter 8). In the age of pay phones, COLAVECCHIO made and sold "black boxes" a device that allowed users to place long distance calls free of charge. He reflected, "now I knew why the wise guys would pay so much money for some of the things that I made. Not that I ever doubted my workmanship; after all, I'm a perfectionist to the ultimate degree." (p. 140). COLAVECCHIO bragged, "… it fooled one of the biggest corporations in the world." He referred to himself as "brilliant" for his handiwork in that crime.

Often times, while describing his criminal exploits COLAVECCHIO exhibit abject disdain for law enforcement because he thought they were too stupid to catch him or even suspect him as the mastermind behind the crimes. After the unsuccessful execution of a search warrant by the FBI trying to find the load of stolen raincoats, he demeaned the agents writing, "Pissed, and vowing this would not be the end of the matter, the f****** cheap suits left." (p. 51). In one instance, the FBI showed up to investigate a heist in his store. The crime was staged for the insurance money. COLAVECCHIO mocked their inability to figure out he was behind the crime, "I lit up a Muratti and made it a point to smoke it with my left hand [injured in the crime]. I flashed the bandages right under his f****** pointed nose and he never asked me what caused me to be bandaged up." (p. 103).

After being caught with 800 lbs. of counterfeit tokens in his car, the arresting agents transferred the contraband from COLAVECCHIO's Honda to a government vehicle. The sheer weight of the evidence of COLAVECCHIO's guilt caused the agent's Buick to sustain under carriage damage on a speed bump as it drove away. He remarked:

• The f****** jerk didn't realize that he didn't have enough clearance to pass over the speed bumps. Couldn't he feel the steering? It must have felt light as all hell.

• [He] looked like a real jerk.

• You could see the surprise and anxiety in [the agents'] faces as they waited for the second car.

[For the sake of propriety, the United States will redact COLAVECCHIO's oft-used expletives. His literary style makes almost juvenile resort to profanity.]

• I have to admit it was funny.

• They held my car for six weeks, at a cost of $971 … for storage alone trying to figure out what I had done to the Honda so it didn't do what the Buick did. They had experts examine the suspension, springs, axle, shock absorbers but no one noticed the three-quarter inch piece of plywood lying quietly under the trunk's rug. (p.329).

In many of his criminal escapades, when COLAVECCHIO came face to face with law enforcement, he accused them of being corrupt, incompetent, and intimidated by his genius. However, on one occasion while attempting to aggrandize himself, COLAVECCHIO spoke glowingly of a State Trooper who was impressed with his criminal talents. "The New Jersey trooper, who had tried so hard to make my life intolerable, now had a whole different attitude. He called his wife and said,

'I'll be home late honey, I'm with Big Lou.' He turned around, and asked if I would mind saying a few words to his wife." After joking with the Trooper's wife, COLAVECCHIO acquiesced to "say a few words" to other friends of the Trooper, apparently to impress them that the Trooper really was in the presence of an accomplished and notorious criminal. COLAVECCHIO graciously accepted the Trooper's apology for doing his job, "Nothing personal." (p. 330).

Even with his head filled with the arrogance that he accrued over the years profiting from crime and outsmarting law enforcement, COLAVECCHIO still found himself in shock when he realized that other people committed crimes that he did not know about and from which he was not getting a cut. During the time he owned a car dealership, he was fraudulently securing loans to purchase luxury sports cars imported from Italy. When the loan officer in charge of his account was found to have been stealing, COLAVECCHIO lamented, "Sh**, if I ever knew this a** - hole was stealing, I would have been first in line to grab money and not just a lousy hundred grand. I had no idea he was robbing from the bank. I felt like a moron, and a moron with real bad timing." (p. 213-214).

The First Counterfeiting Crime

In a chapter that COLAVECCHIO entitled, The Counterfeit King, he recounted the crime that led to his first counterfeiting conviction. (Chapter 14). In this chapter, COLAVECCHIO devoted many pages to describing in great detail the technical processes of minting coins and the obstacles he encountered in duplicating casino chips and tokens. Of course, in the retelling, ever flaunting how clever he was at the art of counterfeiting.

"As soon as possible, I began taking chips to casinos everywhere … It was a thrilling life." (p. 271). COLAVECCHIO even found some solace in his arrest. He proudly observed, "All the coins they bagged from several of the machines we played came back either genuine or uncertain. Four f****** labs came to the same conclusion. The retired agent said they were wondering if I was for real or not. They took a chance when they finally decided to arrest us." (p. 288). COLAVECCHIO still believed, "Lots of casinos today are playing with chips I made my garage!" (p.271). His lack of remorse was even more apparent as he wrote, "Can you imagine that? I felt guilty if I didn't have the machinery working night and day, but felt no guilt about what the f*** I was doing with that machinery." (p. 292).

COLAVECCHIO was convicted of using the counterfeit chips and slugs in Connecticut and New Jersey. However, those were not the only venues he polluted with counterfeit. He shipped thousands of pounds of tokens to Las Vegas. (p.361). And, casino tokens were not the only items that COLAVECCHIO copied. He boasted, "Making counterfeit items must have appealed to me in some way that I didn't understand. Between the Gucci line of belts, the Charles Garnier jewelry, the Barry Cord Kieselstein silver alligator belt buckle made famous by the tragic death of Nicole Simpson, the slugs, the casino chips, and my last project, the casino slot machine tokens, I must have counterfeited more items than anyone alive." (p. 271).

The account he gave of his prosecution [was] as self-aggrandizing as the rest of the story of his life. He claimed to get a sweetheart deal for a variety of reasons and to beat the system even at that:

I had to pay $90,000 restitution as part of my plea agreement, but I only paid $75 per month. Since I was on suspended release three years and didn't begin paying until four months into the three-year period, I paid only $2400 in total. Technically, that was a violation of my release, and I could have had my supervised release extended until the $90,000 was paid in full, or I could have gone to jail on a violation. Instead, Anne E. Thompson dismissed my supervised release and my restitution early and sent me a refund saying that the court considered it paid in full for the month before and sent the $75. No doubt about it, the chemistry was there. (p.374).

COLAVECCHIO had earlier explained what he meant by "chemistry." He wrote, "When the judge entered the room, I wished I was on the other side of the podium, because I would have asked her out on a date. There was a chemistry between us that you could cut with a knife. I loved her instantly and I haven't had this feeling too many times in my life. Her name was the Honorable Anne E. Thompson, and she was the chief United States District Judge. When our eyes met, I could feel the chemistry penetrate the distance between us. (p. 370-371).

Violent Crime

Aside from a conviction for resisting a lawful arrest (at age 64), the PSR does not include any convictions for significant crimes of violence. However, COLAVECCHIO admitted to committing several in his autobiography. Both for business purposes and as a thug COLAVECCHIO revealed, "I never went anywhere without a gun." He described paying a visit on a man with whom he had a dispute. COLAVECCHIO detailed, "I had a small Colt Jr. .25 caliber automatic in my right pants pocket. The bullet was chambered before I went in the house.

The gun was set to fire. I needed only to cock the hammer and pull the trigger." (p. 60).

COLAVECCHIO bragged of a number of instances in his life where he enthusiastically resorted to violence. On one occasion, a man wrote him a bad check. COLAVECCHIO observed "If I didn't get my money, I'd beat him to a pulp" then recounted how he brought the man to his mother's house and demanded that the man's mother pay the debt. (p. 87).

One time, COLAVECCHIO used a strong-arm (that he called "Paddy") to viciously beat a man for "a f****** lousy $3,500 that he was owed. Not satisfied to simply send the enforcer to inflict a beating COLAVECCHIO went himself because, "this one was personal ... he was making a f****** fool out of me." (p.172). He portentously reiterated, "I went along on this collection because I wanted to see the mother f****** 's face when I showed up at his place." (p. 173). The victim was beaten so savagely "the guy's nose was spitting blood like Old Faithful." When the victim fell silent, COLLAVECCHIO coldly instructed his enforcer, "Don't kill the a** - hole. I want my f****** money." (p.174).

With the victim bloody and beaten, COLAVECCHIO told of how he "casually" strutted around the man's office to find the money he was there to collect. When the victim did not cooperate in efforts to open a safe — another round of beating began, "you could hear the guy's f****** nose breaking in a couple of places and the familiar sound of a broken jaw." (p. 174). He stole the man's cars to make up for the shortage of cash in the safe. COLAVECCHIO paid the enforcer $400 for beating the victim so badly. They suffered no repercussions. It was a fact of which he was proud, "No mention of what we had done or consequences were ever brought and Paddy and I actually felt we helped him a lot." (p. 177).8 That sort of experience undoubtedly nurtured COLAVECCHIO'S sense of being invincible. That theme ran through the life he recounted in his autobiography.

This self-told account of COLAVECCHIO's life history paints the picture of a man whose devotion to criminal pursuits absolutely prevented him (and will prevent him) from leading a normal life. He is effectively unable to enjoy life without conceiving new criminal ventures. It is who he is and what he does. The world's greatest counterfeiter is proud as a peacock, "I never appreciated or recognized the multiplicity of talents and skills I possessed until I began reading about them in my pre-sentence investigation and other legal documents the government presented after my arrest." (p. 272). Criminal pursuit forms the fabric of his life and his sense of identity. In fact, COLAVECCHIO purports to hold a "Doctorate in Crime." (p. 400).

Prison Life

During his brief time in prison for his first counterfeiting conviction, COLAVECCHIO enjoyed prestige as a notorious criminal and powerful inmate. He met new inmates with a familiar greeting, "Hi, I'm Lou." (p. 393). Apparently, no last name was necessary. A man nicknamed "The Sarge" a former Army Ranger and a "trained assassin" paid him homage, "Yeah, I can see you're the boss around here." (p. 393).

Throughout his entire incarceration, he described prison life as surrounded by friends, criminal colleagues, and guardians, who did his laundry for him, gave him haircuts, cleaned his room, and protected him day and night. "What a f****** beautiful crew we had. It was non-stop laughter from then on." (p. 397). Eventually, he was surrounded by such servitude that prison became a real home for him. (p. 409). Correctional officers, however, held a lower station than other members of law enforcement who were merely incompetent. He opined, "I think it was a job requirement that a CO be inbred and illiterate to get his job." (p. 386). COLAVECCHIO figured that, "I gave the government two years of my life, but I got back experiences that make it more than worth the two years I lost." (p. 425).

Epilogue

COLAVECCHIO felt no remorse for a lifetime of criminal activity, "Do I feel guilty that what I did was wrong? No, I don't." (P. 423). He measured his success by calculating how much he benefitted from his crimes against how much he had to suffer from them with mathematical precision, "… When I was first sentenced to 27 months — that as a former math teacher, at my age, middle 50's, 27 months was around four percent of my life. That's a small percentage to pay for living as well as I did. If I can make it to 100 years old, I will have lived my lifestyle and spent only two percent for doing it my way. Cool, huh? " (p. 421).

III. CONCLUSION

COLAVECCHIO's autobiography portrays him as an adrenaline junkie who will always climb a higher mountain, jump from a higher cliff, and dive deeper into the depths to get his next fix. Only, COLAVECCHIO commits crimes to get his next fix, his next brag, his next triumph. He seemingly has to have the last laugh at the criminal justice system. His identity hinges on successfully playing the system and getting away with it.

COLAVECCHIO should receive a prison sentence because he has an incurable desire to claim the upper hand on the criminal justice system. He also has a criminal appetite undeterred by age, health or incarceration — and perhaps more importantly, by attempts at judicial leniency. Each suspended sentence, each dismissal of a charge only fed into his sincere belief that he is smarter than everyone working in the criminal justice system. He has, by his own boastful admissions, committed vastly more crimes than he had ever been caught committing, often while on conditional release. In fact, even after being awarded pretrial release in this case, COLAVECCHIO tested positive for cocaine.

At 77 years of age, with a variety of medical conditions that he claimed are debilitating, and after being granted pretrial release, COLAVECCHIO soon tested positive for cocaine. When confronted about his drug use by his supervising probation officer, he denied addiction, refused treatment, and explained that the drugs were just for sex.

Throughout his autobiography, COLAVECCHIO took great pride in his criminal achievements and his ability to avoid punishment. He shamelessly bragged about his life choices; it was as though manipulation of the criminal justice system was half the fun for him. COLAVECCHIO profited from a lifetime of criminal exploits, he relished in the notoriety of his crimes, and nourished his sense of self by walking down memory lane over the course of 426 pages — ending the book in 2015 with the possibility of more crimes to come. He ended his story, "…I still have some possibility to change the ending, the final chapter. The matches are pretty much burnt out now, but maybe I'll get just one more light, just one more chance. That would be nice. 'You thought it was more.'" (p. 426).

And so it was. This newest counterfeiting crime began after he published those final words in 2015. He lit one more match even as he served probation for a drug trafficking offense. A crime that he committed at 74 years of age. Now in 2019, he once again stands before a United States District Court poised to marshal wit and charm, age and health, to try to avoid jail and mock the system one more time. COLAVECCHIO will never change, and society can only be protected through his incarceration. Without a guideline sentence, we all become his final triumphant chapter.

IV. RECOMMENDATION

The United States agreed to recommend a sentence within the guideline range as determined by the court. The PSR calculated COLAVECCHIO as a Level 13 - Criminal History Category II offender. His guideline range is 15 — 21 months of imprisonment. The high end of that range is lower than the 27 months that he received for his last counterfeiting conviction. That sentence did not deter him from making bogus $100 dollar bills.

The United States therefore recommends a sentence at the high end of the guideline range, 21 months, as closest to the sentence he received for his last counterfeiting conviction. By COLAVECCHIO's math, that is again a small percentage of his life to pay for a lifetime of committing crime. However, unless he lives to be 100 as he boasted he might, this time it may be a larger percentage of the time he has left, but still a low price to pay.

Respectfully submitted,

/s/ Gerard B. Sullivan

GERARD B. SULLIVAN

Assistant U.S. Attorney

U.S. Attorney's Office

50 Kennedy Plaza

Providence, RI 02903

CERTIFICATION OF SERVICE

On this 8th day of August 2019, I caused the within "Government's Sentencing Memorandum" to be filed electronically.

/s/ Gerard B. Sullivan

Introduction

I first heard of Louis Colavecchio in my former life as a Connecticut State Police Detective Sergeant. Assigned to the State Police Casino Unit, one of the duties was keeping intelligence flowing between law enforcement agencies throughout the country and my own regarding criminal activity in the casino industry.

A routine call from a colleague with the New Jersey State Police started me on a two-year-long case involving dozens of casinos, half a dozen states, and a lot of overtime. He told me a story of counterfeit slot machine tokens, the suspect, and a Connecticut connection.

When the case was wrapped up by numerous jurisdictions, I saw a face I had seen many times before. This was a very unique crime involving an even more unique individual, Louis "The Coin" Colavecchio.

Louis grew up Italian as I did. He loves to eat. So do I. At some point in our younger days, we both made choices about which road to take.

Louis loved developing a scam described to me by a U.S. Secret Service agent as the largest counterfeiting case in their department's history. I loved having a hand in solving it.

Louis came up with a brilliant plan. We, the cops did, too. I do not condone his criminal behavior, but I understand it; he was very creative, an artist. I assisted in some small way with him going to jail and he served his time... After spending time together after the case closed, we have developed a friendship. That's OK with me. I am no longer a trooper, having retired in 2003.

He's retired, too, right?

Jerry Longo

Connecticut State Police Detective Sergeant (Retired) Jerry Longo is now a senior investigator for a major casino. As a trooper, he was assigned to several barracks and the Bureau of Investigations. He received five medals, one for Valor, two for life saving, and two for meritorious service. His commendations included one for arresting 125 drunk driving suspects in one year.

Foreword

Louis The Coin had to learn how to survive the high and low-life existence.

He chose to live on the streets of Rhode Island. He learned by going to 'college' in Ft. Dix, and knew a guy or two who did his time in Danbury, and I ain't talking about the college on White Street.

It is fortunate that he did, too, because he lived to tell the tale in this compelling, insider's account of the Providence underworld he knows because he sat at the knee of The Old Man, watched the code of the old 'Fellas' broken when young scum like Baby Corsino sold drugs right under the Old Man's nose on Federal Hill, and learned to smile when headlines in The Providence Journal screamed out things only an insider like Louis The Coin could know.

In this book, Louis The Coin offers the novice the genuine article when he promises to take his readers on a stroll through the streets of the Providence only an insider knows — DelSesto's Bakery, inside to the cutting tables of Sherwood Manufacturing on Eagle Street.

You can add the name "Louis The Coin" to that stellar list of characters — Brando, Mario Puzo, and Francis Ford Coppola.

What?

"You thought it was more?"

Lionel Bascom

Lionel Bascom is Professor of Writing at Western Connecticut State University and author of *Rubouts* (Avon 1991) and *A Renaissance in Harlem: The Voices of a Lost American Community* (Harper Trade, 2001).

Author's Note

I often feel like I'm dreaming, especially when I'm awake.

Did I really sit at the right hand of Raymond in Providence? Did I really soak the sheets with red wine in a week of partying with three young women in Rome? Did that police chief really thank me for fixing my speeding ticket going 140 mph in a Lamborghini — after the event made the nightly news?

What?

Hey, You Thought It Was More ...

Louis Colavecchio
Providence, RI, Dec. 9, 2014

Chapter 1
Sherwood Manufacturing Company

What a fucking pickle I got myself in this time. I'm sitting on a concrete bench in DePasquale Square, not far from where it all began some 45 years ago: broke, cold, depressed, dressed like a bum, a convicted felon collecting a lousy $489 a month social security, and wondering what the fuck happened to that sharp, college graduate, wise guy businessman who earned millions more than any 30 average working stiffs earn in their entire dull, fucking lives.

It all began in June 1959, when I drove my T-bird to DelSesto's Bakery on DePasquale Avenue in the Federal Hill section of Providence. This area was Mafia central of Rhode Island, ran by a small but ruthless family. Raymond Patriarca was an aging mob Boss, so respected nationally that he sat on the Commission, a group consisting of about 45 or 50 members of Family Bosses throughout the country. Some of these members included mobsters like Tony Accardo, Joe Bonanno, Joe Colombo, Carlo Marcello, Joe Profaci, Carlo Gambino, Albert Anastasia, as well as successors to Lucky Luciano's and Al Capone's crew.

Raymond was a big man in the mob scene, and in New England, his word was supreme. I always remember him smoking his fat cigars, dressed in a cheap pair of slacks and shirt, and standing in front of his office, on Atwells Avenue, Providence. This was home to one of his businesses, the National Vending Company. National Vending was a lucrative business whose vending and pinball machines occupied the most profitable locations throughout Rhode Island. This business allowed Patriarca to launder an incredible amount of cash from other activities, as well as the vending business itself. It was a perfect cover for someone in his profession.

In his younger days, Raymond Patriarca used his balls and a Thompson machine gun to break two of his friends out from a local prison. He was caught after a shootout, sentenced to a lengthy prison term, and pardoned a few months later. He had a way of making problems disappear, and his power extended to local politicians, law enforcement agencies, and judges.

Raymond's modest lifestyle — living in a small house on Providence's less affluent part of the East Side, with his son Raymond, Jr. and wife Nancy, a practicing nurse, and his lack of a flamboyant lifestyle allowed him to keep as low a profile as his position of authority would allow. He was one of the fairest people I ever met. He meted out justice in an almost mechanical way, not favoring anyone, and his decision was final. No one fucked with this man.

Years later, I was to intervene in a dispute between him and a small vending company that my cousin Cosmo owned, concerning a prime location at the Rhode Island Adult Correctional Center. I was so influential with Raymond by this time, that I got him to leave Cosmo alone and let him keep the A.C.C location. This was a real plum because the inmates and CO's working there had to purchase their butts from Cosmo's machines. So what does the fucking bum — my cousin — do, but fill the machines with contraband cigarettes, which had no federal or state tax stamps. This was a felony! Cosmo got away with this for a long time until he was finally caught, arrested, and convicted. He served 60 days in the same jail where he was selling cigarettes just a short time earlier.

So, after all my influence, he goes and makes a fucking jerk out of me, and loses the location to National Vending anyway.

But, for the time being, all I was interested in was buying a couple of loaves of warm Italian bread with a burnt crust from DelSesto's Bakery on De Pasquale Avenue. A young girl with big brown eyes, brown hair, full lips, and a gorgeous figure showing through her white uniform — whose age I guessed at 16 or 17 — waited on me. I fell in love in 30 seconds flat. Her name was Ann and she lived on Metropolitan Road, just a few blocks away from my home.

I ate more Italian bread in the next six months than I had in all my life. Soon, we were dating seriously and I met her parents.

Her father was an insurance agent for John Hancock Life Insurance Company, and in those days, agents went from house to house collecting on policies that carried weekly premiums of 50 cents to one dollar each. He was a handsome man with white hair and a mustache. He had a deep voice that made it seem like he was always yelling when he spoke. He was an honest, hardworking, middle class stiff. His wife Susie was a petite, attractive woman.

Susie was a floor manager for a small company called Sherwood Manufacturing Company, which made sweaters that appeared to be cashmere, but were actually a type of cheap fiberglass cloth. A year or so earlier, the material used in these sweaters came under the close scrutiny of the government because it was highly flammable and caused the tragic death of a young girl in a kitchen fire.

The first time I entered Sherwood Manufacturing Company — which occupied a large part of the second floor of an old mill building at 75 Eagle St. in Providence — there were sweaters and vests hanging from clothes hangers everywhere and were being sprayed with a material to prevent them from catching fire.

Sherwood's owners were Vincent Miele , whom I later referred to as my uncle, and his friend from Worcester, the powerful crime Boss, Raymond Patriarca. Their office was always filled with wise guys that hung out and played cards and talked about their business.

As a young man I found this all very fascinating. Vincent and I grew so close that I don't think either of us ever realized that we were at least 25 years apart in age. As Ann and I continued dating, my friendship and admiration for Vincent grew.

Vincent was 45 years old and 5'10" tall. He was quick witted, intelligent, and could easily have become a very high level mobster if he desired, especially with all the connections he had. He chose to become a businessman instead, who would supplement his income with an occasional illegal score or two.

When he was a young man, Vincent started out by hustling whatever items he could buy cheap and then sell for a profit. Later, he began a manufacturing business that sold primarily to street hustlers. I was so fascinated by the wise guy lifestyle, I'm sure I would have wound up in that scene. Vincent always told me that the smartest move was to run a legitimate business, pay taxes, show income, then make scores on the side. Never use a score to pay your mortgage. Let it buy your vacation or other luxuries. Somehow, I never grasped this concept. He constantly kept reminding me that the Old Man, his friend and partner, Raymond, would give his right arm to be out of the rackets.

Vincent was a skilled hustler, but had a soft heart, and let many marks escape, because he knew they needed the money for their families' food or rent. On the other hand, he could be fearless and he knew how to take money from his mark. He was a businessman with a very practical attitude. If he extended credit to a hustler and the hustler beat him by not paying, he would ask me to prepare another order for the jerk. When I asked why, Vincent was quick to point out that he had already lost the money, and it would be doubly foolish to lose a customer as well. So we shipped to the guys who beat him C.O.D. and continued to keep them as customers. Vincent never took a loss personally. It was part of being a businessman.

Vincent dressed like a successful businessman would have in those days. He was a member of the Jewish Community Center on Elmwood Avenue, and took Ann and me to numerous functions there. He had lots of Jewish friends and sometimes, using his great sense of humor, would explain that while Gentiles prayed to God for good health, the Jews prayed for more money.

"What's so bad about that," he would quip. "A God should help you make money."

Vincent's wife, Tina, loved these affairs. They provided her an opportunity to dress up and mingle with successful people. One day, in Sherwood's office, a sheriff served Vincent a letter from an attorney. It was Tina demanding that Vincent spend more time with her, and less time at the office. Vincent and Tina had been married for years, and they were still very much in love. He thought the idea of her going to a lawyer to tell him to spend more time with her was cute, and laughed profusely. They had a nice marriage.

Some people believe that certain animals possess a sixth sense, and know immediately if someone should to be feared or trusted. I don't know if that is true or not, but I'm absolutely positive that Vincent possessed an uncanny ability to make an evaluation of someone's personality immediately, and he would sometimes tell me things that no one could know on a first encounter. One such time was when a young, thin man in his early 30's, came to Sherwood to apply for a job. He said his name was Billy Hill, and that he was a good sewer and could operate other machines as well. He said he had just left his last job because there wasn't enough work for him and the other employees, and he didn't have seniority. The first thing Vincent asked him was how long ago he had been released from jail. The man was shocked, and replied "just a few months ago." Vincent told him he could begin work the next day. I was awed.

I can't remember a single time when he commented on someone's personality or their character and he was not right. It was uncanny. He never judged anyone's lifestyle. He accepted everyone, but always knew, instinctively, where to draw the line on their loyalty and trustworthiness. He frequently reminded me that, "Everybody's different." These two words stayed in mind all my life. He lived by those words. I try to also.

Another of Vincent's statements that has proven accurate so many times in my lifetime is, "That which you think is going to happen, inevitably never does." This statement was used in reference to times when some part of a plan or scheme failed, and one might begin to imagine all sorts of things that would surely follow, like an imaginary domino effect. He was right. Rarely, did one failed step ever lead much further in the anticipated direction.

There was one last expression that Vincent used that was a regionalized slang for wise guys from the Providence area. It makes no sense to anyone not brought up in this environment. He would say at the end of so many statements, "What'd you thought it was more." The shorter version was even more popular. "You thought it was more." It was used at the end of practically every sentence. I suppose you could say there exists a similar phrase made popular by the very successful wise guy TV series, *The Sopranos*, in which they constantly command "Forget about it" in an elongated verbalization. We used this phrase often too, but long before it was made popular by a TV show.

Wise guys usually introduce another wise guy as being, "Our friend," or "He's with us," or if the guy has ranking in the mob, a "made man." You might say, "This is John, he's a 'good fellow,' " and its slang version would be, "he's a good fella." Using the phrase, "You thought it was more" identified him with the Providence Office.

To show you what a small world this is, in 1998, I was incarcerated in a fucking rat hole, Fort Dix, New Jersey, which was the largest Federal Correctional Institution in the country — housing some 4,000 inmates. I wound up with two roommates, one a young man from Connecticut who worked for the Boss there, Bill Sabia. I knew Sabia well, often making many trips to his office located downstairs in the Brass Rail, a restaurant he owned. The other was the nephew of a high level New York mobster, Andrew Giannino, nicknamed "The Sarge," because he was a Ranger during the Vietnam War. Guess what he said after the first time we introduced ourselves. "I'm Andy, but everyone calls me The Sarge. You thought it was more." I freaked out, and asked about his using that expression. Turns out, he was a close friend of both my uncle Vincent and his brother Tony, who lived in New Jersey. Now, talk about a small world. We all knew the same people.

I spent two of the best years of my life there.

Before long, I was working part time at Sherwood and attending classes at Providence College. I couldn't wait for classes to be over to get to work at Sherwood. I was told by Vincent that I was the fastest cutter he ever had. The material was cut with a large electric knife held in a vertical position on a stand with small wheels and was capable of cutting through all of those layers at once. One slip by the operator during this process could result in the loss of one or more fingers in an instant. It was a common accident, in the days when OSHA required no safety devices on such a dangerous machine. Appropriately enough, the machine was manufactured by a company called "Mamin."

I knew I was fast, I always had good mechanical skills, but the praise from my "Uncle" always made me feel good. He would complement my "never spoiling the cut", as the process was called, by winding up with two left or two right sleeves, and how he never had to check my work, he just knew it would be perfect.

I had another motive for wanting to finish the cut quickly. After it was finished, the scrap cloth baled and the table cleaned, I would be in for the thrill of my life.

The sweaters were packed together with a matching vest in a fancy box that bore the name of either Park Lane, Esquire, Dunn Hill, Playboy, or some other designer name from that era, indicating that its contents were from some upscale boutique or store. A label on the side of the box had small squares to indicate sizes: small, medium, large or extra-large. If one of the squares were checked, one would know the box's contents at a glance. Of course, since all the sweaters were the same size, none of the boxes were ever marked, leaving the seller total discretion to make them whatever size he wanted them to be. In addition to the size, another square contained the suggested retail price of the product. These were marked with a rubber stamp and the amounts generally used were either $39.95 or $44.95. Inside the box were the sweaters and vests, which were packed in a clear plastic bag with an oval white area, on which was printed the name, Dunn Hill, and below the name in a script type font, "The Casual Look." On the bottom of the bag was another white section on which was "For All Seasons, A Fashionable TWO-PIECE Combination Set." Below that it read, "Made In U.S.A." There was also an impressive gold foiled guarantee which read, "Guaranteed Made In America By American Workers,".

The hustlers that bought these boxes had their preference as to which price would be stamped on the product. Each had their own style of selling to his mark, but humor was always popular, and some of the hustlers would have made great comedians. I remember one who, if told by his mark that he didn't wish to buy anything, would point to a stack of boxes in the back seat of his car, and ask, " If you don't want them, what the fuck am I going to do with them?" As if they were the potential buyer's problem!

The cost to these peddlers was $2.25 per set. Most customers bought two or three cases per day, each case containing approximately 30 sets. A good peddler could easily sell 50 to 100 sets each time out. Some hustlers were so good that one wondered when the market would be saturated and everyone would become wise. After all, it wasn't possible to wear these things more than once, as they would either fall apart, cause an itchy rash, or if washed, shrink to the size of a postage stamp.

But, the market never did dry up. So, as PT Barnum once said, "There's a sucker born every minute, and at least two to take him."

The irony of selling these is that they sold best to people who had a touch of larceny in them. I remember an old hustler by the name of Carlo DeFrancesco, nicknamed "Garlic," because he believed eating and wearing garlic was a cure for all kinds of illnesses. He was a great peddler, but obviously a little nuts, at least that's what we thought at the time. When he decided to finally quit hustling, he actually wanted to sell his "route." This included truck stops, bus stations, and other locations where sales were easy. The asking price was $25,000.

Eventually "Garlic" wrote a small paperback book called "Diet or Die," proclaiming the use of garlic as a cure-all for cancer and other diseases. He cited numerous articles to add validity to his claim, and also said he himself was cured of his cancer by consuming large amounts of garlic. Of course, he never had cancer, but that was a trivial oversight on his part.

He then applied for a grant to the U.S. government to start a research center to study the beneficial effects garlic had on a person's immune system in helping fighting cancer and diseases of the intestines, as well as other diseases and viruses. To everyone's amazement, he received a check for $100,000, an absurdly large amount of money in those days. I guess he turned out to be an even better hustler than anyone ever realized.

There were lots of other hustlers in and out of Sherwood Manufacturing during that period. One I remember vividly was Morris Sparks, whom we nicknamed "Sparky," from Sherman Oaks, California. He couldn't pronounce the letter V and constantly called Vincent "Wince." He was a frequent visitor. Later, he came very close to getting whacked, making what is usually a fatal mistake of taking wise guys' money and spending it foolishly. One of the wise guys he took money from was Raymond Patriarca himself.

Several wise guys were gathered at Sherwood's office one afternoon. Included in this gathering were Raymond Patriarca — whom we never referred to by his correct name, but either as the "Old Man" or "George", Henry Tameleo who ran the Office for Raymond in Boston, several hit men including Rudolph Sargenta, Bobby Almondi, Eddy Latio, Rocco Andreoli, Andy Marino, numerous other wise guys, Sparky, and my Uncle Vincent.

The purpose of the gathering was to purchase additional land in Las Vegas, which at that time was slightly more than a desert city with eight or nine small casinos and legalized gambling. No one ever stopped talking when I entered the room. Each of the players in the room, with the exception of Sparky, had an envelope containing at least $50,000, and in some, much more. Because Sparky was from California and would be returning the next day, the envelopes were all placed in one of Sherwood's plastic bags, and handed to Sparky.

The old man made it brutally clear that half this money was to be used for the purchase of land on the Las Vegas strip and that not a dollar was to be spent on a teaspoon of land that was not directly on the strip. The other half of the money was to be given to Bob Rosati, from Providence, to increase his ownership of the now defunct Dunes Casino to 12 ½ percent. Everyone agreed and left the office.

Sparky was now holding hundreds of thousands of dollars of wise guys' money in a plastic bag and was expected to depart the next day, head to Las Vegas before going home, purchase the land, and give Bobby his money.

But that's not exactly what happened.

Instead of going to Las Vegas first, Sparky went home, where he discussed these plans with a friend who told him it was absolutely ludicrous to buy land in a desert. The friend was a geologist who worked primarily for a large oil company called Calso Supreme. He presented confidential blueprints from his company to Sparky that showed a 50-mile strip of land containing numerous oil rigs, profitably producing oil. The next day, he brought Sparky to the location of the oil rigs, lined up in a perfectly straight rows, separated by less than a mile between each. He told Sparky that this was the most lucrative oil-producing area that the company owned and that plans included buying several more miles of land in that area.

Of course, this was not public knowledge, which would have driven the price of the land way up, but he was sharing the information with Sparky in order to make a deal where they could both make money.

When Sparky saw the many rigs all pumping oil, he saw dollar signs and his eyes lit up. He was so excited that he purchased as much land and oil rigs as the combined money would allow. He told his friend to set up the oil rigs and begin digging immediately. He thought they would bring in money so quickly that he would be able to replace the money long before he told the wise guys about the oil rigs.

There were several problems with this plan, the first being the fact that the land wasn't on the strip, it wasn't even in Las Vegas, but in California.

Within a very short period of time, the oil rigs went dry.

Bobby Rosati, the Providence connection in Vegas, never got his money.

Sparky began to worry. The geologist assured him that there was nothing to be concerned about, and that since all the oil rigs were in a straight line, and his were between lucrative producing rigs, all he needed to do was dig a little bit deeper. He was sure that money would be rolling in soon. Each hundred feet of digging deeper took several days and thousands of dollars. Before long, there was no money left. The geologist said that he couldn't understand it, but he still had faith that they could produce oil.

At this point, Sparky panicked and decided to fly back to Rhode Island and tell his friend Wince, aka Vincent, what he had done. Vincent asked if all of the money was gone, to which Sparky answered yes. Sparky tried to convince Vincent that digging deeper would produce the oil he had expected to make their fortune. Vincent told him that if the Old Man ever finds out, Sparky would be dead. He asked Sparky how much he would need to dig a little deeper. He gave Sparky an additional $12,000 to return to California to continue digging. He did this out of concern for his friend's life.

After digging about halfway to China, with no success, Vincent decided to break the news to the Old Man. Fortunately for Sparky, Vincent pleaded for his friend's life, insisting that Sparky was stupid, but not greedy, and that he himself had kicked in more money of his own in an attempt to make the plan work.

Another meeting was held in Sherwood's office for the same purpose of buying additional land on the strip. More money was collected and this time given to a reliable purchaser, Joe Sullivan, who was Raymond's front man for many years. Ultimately, the wise guys got their additional land on the strip of Las Vegas, and increased their holdings in the Dunes, except for Vincent who had used up all his cash to save his friend's life.

Another very interesting hustler was Frank Corsino, who sold counterfeit watches, bearing the name of some famous manufacturers such as Tiffany, Rolex, Patek-Philippe, Vacheron Constantin, Mathey Tissot, Cartier, and many others. These were wind-up watches with a cheap mechanical movement, and were referred to as "one lungers". The phrase stood for the fact that they contained only one jewel, even though the movement would have been stamped that it contained 17 or even 23 jewels. Quartz movements were not available at that time. The average life of these watches was about a week before they fell apart, and the most expensive part of the whole item was the box, which was a copy of the of the one that contained the genuine product.

Along with the box was a platinum and gold foil price tag which had embossed on it a price of a thousand dollars or more. They cost about the same as the sweaters, $2.50, but were a far better item for a hustler to sell because they were smaller, carried a much higher retail price, there were no sizes or colors to deal with, and, after all, everyone needs a watch or two.

Frank only worked the downtown Providence train station, and many times Vincent and I watched as he worked his magic on some sucker. Watching him make his pitch was a true joy. I think I would be accurate in saying he sold to almost half the marks he worked, making a nice living and doing very little work.

Since selling watches was so lucrative, I asked Vincent why we didn't sell watches as well as sweaters. The only person selling watches wholesale to the peddlers was Louis Raffanello from Olneyville Square, a run-down section of Providence where Louis and his wife Virginia owned a small store whose window was full of stuffed animals and junk items. Inside the store were some cheap showcases, and these contained the watches the hustlers would sell. A small back room held some watch bands, boxes, watch links, price tags, lifetime guarantee labels, and other items necessary for the sale of these counterfeit products. It was a very busy and profitable operation, and every few weeks or so, Louis himself would go on the road to hustle, staying away a week or so, and returning with $10,000 or $15,000 in cash. He set his brother Eddy up in a small sandwich shop, just around the corner, but Eddy had a fast developing cancer and died less than a year later.

President Kennedy had been elected in 1960, and only a short time after his election he instituted a new tax, called the Kennedy Rounds, which was a tax on luxury items, such as fur coats, boats, jewelry, and, of course, watches. Every sale of any of these items had to be reported to the government, and tax had to be collected in the amount of 10 percent of the sale. To not report these sales was a federal crime, punishable by a fine as well as prison. Since Raymond was a 50 percent owner in Sherwood and his sister Betty was employed there, he was adamant about not selling watches because he believed it would draw the attention of the Feds for sure. Hustlers selling the watches were committing a federal crime, because obviously they didn't pay the excise tax, nor could they collect it. They were working from their cars, and were not licensed to sell these or any items. It seemed almost ludicrous that we couldn't sell watches, because Raymond didn't want trouble at Sherwood, when, in fact, we were doing so many other illegal activities. What the hell difference could another one make? It was stupid, but Raymond was the Boss, and we didn't sell watches.

Frank Corsino was Ann's cousin, and lived in the same house that Ann had lived in on Ridge Street a few years earlier. On every major holiday, we made the rounds, as Ann's parents called them, visiting all the relatives and exchanging gifts and other social activities associated with visiting relatives.

Ann and I couldn't wait to get back to her house, where we could make out in the cellar. Frank lived on the second floor with his wife and two sons. One of them, whom Raymond nicknamed "Baby Corsino," was to be assassinated gangland style a few years later. He was a likeable young man, with a handsome, boyish face and a quick smile. That is what most everybody saw.

The real Baby Corsino was a drug addict who turned young girls onto heroin, then used them as prostitutes to earn him money. He was committing a cardinal sin against the wise guys policy of no drugs, and doing it under the nose of the Old Man, right on Federal Hill. The wise guys learned of his activities and took notice of him. His name came up often in the S&S bar, a bar that was directly controlled and owned by the Patriarca Family and operated by Andrew (Andy Shacks) Mansolillo, and his brother Louis (Baby Shacks) who was Raymond's right hand man — and would likely succeed Raymond.

The prime source of income for the S&S was gambling. It was the largest illegal gambling operation in New England.

It was also within walking distance from Sherwood Manufacturing, and throughout the years I was there on a daily basis. Soon, I became a major player, helping plan many illegal activities there. Some of the most ruthless gangsters in the country came from this bar, as well as from all of Providence, simply because the state is so small and the pickings are so thin.

For example, in New York, If you missed one score to another wise guy, rather than start a war and kill him, you simply moved on to another deal. Scores there were, and are, plentiful.

Rhode Island is a difficult environment for any wise guy to survive in, and if someone fucked with your score, most likely kill him. A wise guy from Rhode Island would rather kill than relinquish a score.

Knowing that there were any number of hit men available in the S&S, I wondered why someone didn't do something about Baby Corsino. Vincent and I were driving on Academy Avenue towards Atwells Avenue and Sherwood when we met Baby Corsino crossing the street in front of the A & P supermarket. When he saw us, he came over to greet Vincent and me, and it was immediately obvious that he was either drunk or fucking high on drugs.

After we left to continue back to the shop, I remember turning to Vincent and asking him how they could possibly allow him to live, knowing what he was doing. His flagrant drug use and other activities would have made any one else the target of a bullet in very short time. Vincent's answer was quick and to the point and still rings vivid in my mind: "He won't be around too much longer Lou, let's get back to the shop."

The next morning, the headlines in the *Providence Journal* read that Baby Corsino's body had been found a few hours earlier with one bullet to the back of his head. He had been killed gangland style, and his body was dumped on Croom Street. It was at the bottom of a small hill, near the railroad tracks, and was a popular spot where wise guys either dumped bodies or whacked someone, as several other killings had occurred there before Baby Corsino's.

For years, on the anniversary of his death, the *Providence Journal* ran a front page story: "Who killed Baby Corsino?" His killers were never found.

When the murder first occurred, his brother Anthony, nicknamed Tex, because he worked in Texas for B.A. Dario, a rich old man with a five dollar wig who lived to be about 100 years old. Dario owned Lincoln Downs, Rhode Island's only horse racing stadium, known throughout the country as the easiest horse racing track to put in a fix. Tex watched B.A.'s other financial interests, and it was part of Tex's job to keep furnishing the old man with a constant supply of young girls. Tex was very good at his job, but his reaction, while predictable, was stupid, and his father told him to let it go, or he too would be killed. Tex was not a wise guy, and he did as his father told him, so it wasn't necessary for the wise guys to kill him also.

As I said earlier, I had my own reason to complete the cut and my work in the shop as quickly as possible. I knew that after I was finished, I was going to get the treat of my life. Vincent and I were going to load up my car with sweaters. I was going to be the hustler, and Vincent would teach me the lines I needed to know to sell this shit. I was always fascinated every time we went out on a selling trip.

We usually headed towards Boston, and Vincent was a master at sniffing out places that could be lucrative selling locations. If he were a fisherman, he would have been the envy of all the others, as he had a second sense leading him to his prey. I too, soon learned how to spot good locations, but I was drawn more to transient, outdoor locations, maybe because I was new and not too sure of my skills, or perhaps felt safer there. I loved road construction sites, with lots of workers had money in their pockets and were easy marks to sell. Vincent taught me to look for two or three guys who were obviously together, smoking, chatting, or eating, then put down the window on the driver's side, and begin by yelling, "Are you three guys together?" Here were three guys obviously together and you're fucking asking if they are together.

The next step was to single one of them out, and it didn't matter which one. You would call him over to the car, and if the three began coming over together, point to one of them, making the one you singled out feel somehow special.

"Put your head in the window," I'd demand. Nine out of ten times the sucker came over, and the other two, feeling left out, would ease their way over also. This was exactly what you needed. Three suckers instead of just one. Still shouting for the original mark to put his head in the window, you would explain that you didn't want to yell, because you had to keep this quiet. Between the yelling and the shouting to get their attention, you couldn't have made more noise than if a Barnum & Bailey parade was going by.

The pitch could have any number of variations, but a popular one would be, "I have a couple of boxes left over and they're your size." Immediately, one of them would ask what was in the boxes.

"They're a two piece set," would be the reply, without identifying the contents. This would be followed by the statement that, "I'm the fitter for the company, and that I wouldn't waste your time if I knew they wouldn't fit." Usually, the statement that the boxes were not hot, was said repeatedly. They're not hot, I'm telling you, while looking back and forth, as if nervously fearful that a cop might drive by.

This tactic sped up the sale, and always made the items for sale more desirable. "Don't be afraid, it's just that the shipper packed a few extra boxes by mistake, and I'd be a real asshole if I took them back. My boss is a motherfucker, and I'd be the laughing stock of everyone in the whole place, coming back and saying the shipper gave me too many boxes."

Again, the question of what's in the boxes might be asked. What the fuck difference does it make, I'd reply, they're $45 and there's two pieces in every box. They're a two-piece set. I don't want no $45, give me $15 and let's screw my fucking boss. I don't give a shit anymore about him than he does for me. Vincent showed me how to control the conversation right from the first word, until the money was in your pocket.

Most times, the sucker never really knew what he had bought, unless Vincent wanted to tell him. On some occasions, he would open the box and then close it so fast that all you could see was a camel colored item. If someone recognized it as a sweater, he might ask to see it again. Once more the box was opened and shut so fast, it was unidentifiable. The sale had to close as quickly as possible, so looking back and forth, again as if for cops, it was time to get the money. People with larceny in their heart ate up this kind of deal, and the more you proclaimed they weren't hot, the more they felt they were.

"Look, I gotta get out of here fast. Give me $15 a box and let me get the hell out of here, will you?" Some marks would reach into their pockets, only to come up with $12. In that case, you told him he owed you $3, took the 12 bucks and went on to the other two, who were following every word that was spoken. A typical sale to two or even three of the suckers was not unusual, with each of them paying different prices for the same item. Some bought more than one, because, after all, this was a once in a lifetime deal, and there were only a few boxes left.

I've seen and sold this shit as men's sweaters, ladies sweaters, vests, raincoats, and once, I watched Vincent working a crew of road construction workers on a 90 degree day, with several men gathered around in a manhole, purchase them as sun umbrellas. I think a good hustler could have sold them as rocket engines if he wanted to. The back seat of my car was usually loaded with 30 or 35 boxes, and we would generally quit when they were either all sold, or almost all had been sold, or we made sales for unusually high prices, and decided to call it a day. I remember one guy we stopped who needed two extra-large, two large, one medium, and two small sizes. He wanted seven boxes, and I quickly turned to the back seat, marked the boxes' sizes according to his order with a pen, and collected our money. I was a little nervous turning to mark the sizes, not because the mark was there, but because we were stopped in the middle of a very busy street in Boston and had traffic backed up for blocks. The sucker couldn't pay fast enough, as he was nervous that a cop might walk by, and get caught purchasing hot goods. We called it a day after that sale, and went to enjoy a nice juicy steak, a glass of wine, some fun conversation, and to count our take, usually $250-$300 was our reward for our few hours work.

One real scary event happened in a small bar in South Boston. Vincent made the joint out as a wise guy hangout immediately, part of South Boston's Irish mob. He ordered me to stop the car, park, and grab as many boxes as I could carry. We were going in the place. I thought Vincent was nuts, but I did as he asked. The dirty little bar reeked of foul odors l cheap cigar smoke and stale beer. It was filthy. There was a group of 10 or 12 low-life characters who were playing cards at one of the tables, and I kept thinking that the further into the bar we ventured, the more risk we were assuming.

Vincent walked right up to their table and told them he had some swag, slang for stolen goods. Insinuating that an item was stolen was not needed with this group. That's all they would ever consider buying, I'm sure. He said they cost $45 a box, and that they were two in a box, but didn't say what they were. He said he needed $15 a box. One of the assholes smirked and then laughed and I thought I would be swallowing my teeth soon.

One of the dumber looking morons said, "You want $15 a box, no fucking way. I'll give you $10 or fuck off, assholes." These morons didn't care if it was tuna fish they were buying, as long as they could buy it right. Usually, swag brought about 1/3 of the retail price tag, but these guys were being smart assholes by offering $10. Vincent made a halfhearted plea for $12, but I knew he was just perfectly happy with the $10. We had sold lots of boxes for $10, so that wasn't an issue. He was just trying to make these jerks feel they were putting something over on him. Vincent told the guy that if he wanted them for $10, he should take them all.

"No fucking way, asshole. I need 15 boxes, and you'll take ten dollars a box." I counted out 15 boxes while Vincent took in the $150 in cash.

We left quickly, and I felt comfortable when I started the car and began driving away from that fucking dump. But it wasn't long before I became aware that we were being followed by someone from the bar we had just left with $150 of wise guy money. I said, "Vincent, we have a problem. Someone from the bar is trying to catch up with us." I jammed the throttle to the floor, and told Vincent not to worry, I'd lose the guy in a couple of blocks.

Vincent shouted to immediately stop the car, and pull over to the side of the road. Now I was sure he was nuts, and told him we should get our asses out of there as fast as possible. The best case scenario I could envision, was our giving the money back to these inbreeds, and getting away without a beating. Maybe. But Vincent insisted I stop the car.

As it turned out, I was wrong, and learned a lesson early on never to give back money from a score. I asked Vincent if he knew what the hell he was doing, and he responded that the guy wanted to buy more sweaters. The response shocked me. I pulled the car over to the side of the road, but left the motor running, the doors locked, and my window only halfway down. A big Neanderthal of a man leaped from his car and ran over to my side. By now, I was even more convinced that we had made a very serious mistake. Vincent reached over, and put my window down all the way. The guy put both his hands, which were the size of steam shovels, on my door sill, and I was sure the action was about to take place. He was gasping for breath as he asked, "You guys got a sweater that will fit me?" I breathed a sigh of relief, and had difficulty not bursting into laughter.

The mark wanted to buy a sweater for himself. Vincent was right again. He told the guy to come over to his side of the car, and asked him to turn around, his back toward Vincent, so he could fit him. He grabbed a sweater from a box, and holding the sweater in his right hand, put his left hand on the guy's left shoulder. I mean, this guy had shoulders the width of a football field. With the sweater hanging down the guy's back, Vincent put his right hand on the guy's right shoulder, and asked him if it felt too large. The jerk said that it didn't feel too large, but just right. Vincent told him he was in luck, because we only had two sweaters that size, and for him to take both of them. The guy agreed, and pulled out a wad of money two inches thick, peeled off a fifty dollar bill and handed it to Vincent. Vincent only gave him back a twenty dollar bill, telling him that sweaters this size were hard to come by and $10 wasn't going to buy these. The guy offered no resistance, but took the twenty, and ran to his car. He thanked us all the way back.

When this jerk tries to put on the sweaters we gave him, they won't make it over his fist, never mind fit him. So, now we had another $30, and a few more laughs, and decided to try some new place to eat dinner. We wound up at The Hilltop, a famous steakhouse in Saugus whose lawn was decorated with full-size artificial cows. We both had two giant filet mignons, a bottle of wine, and some great conversation talking about some of the stops we made on this trip out.

Of course, the last one was the freshest in my memory, but the funniest was a stop we made to gas up our car. A guy with a strong accent came out of the station's office, and Vincent immediately tried to sell him some sweaters. He told him if the guy took three boxes, we would save him more than $90. The poor slob told us that earlier in the day he had saved several hundred dollars on an oriental rug he purchased from a peddler, almost another hundred on a watch, and that if he saved any more money, he would be broke. "I can't afford to save any more money he said, almost sobbing, I'm going broke saving money."

Seeing that the guy wasn't going to buy three or four sweaters, Vincent exchanged our tank of gas for a box of sweaters. One never knows what to expect on the road, and we finished our meal, divided up about $125 each and went home. Not bad for a kid still in college, and we did this at least twice a week.

Hustling was fun, and before long, I felt confident enough to go out on my own. I was very good at it. A lifelong friend who I was going to college with often accompanied me. I taught him the business, and he went on to medical school, and later became a surgeon, all with money he earned from hustling our sweaters. We remained friends until his retirement in late 2004. One time, while he was performing a colonoscopy on me, I made him laugh by saying "Mike, did you ever think, when we were going to school that someday you would be looking up my asshole with a scope the size of a garden hose?" He told me to shut up, that this was considered a surgical procedure and not to make him laugh. He was my doctor for many years and I was sad when he told me he needed to retire for health reasons.

Chapter 2
Dean Sales Co.

I never got paid when I worked at Sherwood. I was happy to work there, and the opportunity to make money by being there was more than most adults working full-time jobs could earn.

Then, in 1962, I built my own office inside Sherwood's space and began a small company which I named Dean Sales Co.

At that time, Rhode Island was the jewelry center of the United States, and I had lots of contacts where I could buy costume jewelry cheap. My cousin ran a small job shop, a type of business where you drop off jewelry parts, and they assemble them for you according to your designs. We gave the assembly work to people, mostly housewives, to take home with them. When the work was completed, we picked it up. It was very profitable, since you paid piecework — that is, the amount of work they had finished, and not based on an hourly rate. Also, there were no taxes, benefits, or other job-related expenses associated with this type of operation. Everything was under the table.

I wanted to make rosary beads, of a nice quality, and sell them by mail order. With some advice from Vincent, we decided to see if we could mail them out with a letter from someone whose name sounded like that of a Catholic priest. We ended up with a self-proclaimed minister whose name was the Reverend Jesse L. O'Connor. He was an alcoholic who was connected to some Mickey Mouse religion. We visited him at his house on Prairie Avenue in South Providence. We brought him a couple of bottles of cheap whiskey and a twenty dollar bill. He began shouting to his wife in the next room to come over quickly. The Lord had just arrived, and he was bringing gifts galore.

After he calmed down, we began to talk business. What we needed was a letter saying that the Rev. J.L. O'Connor, a catholic, spelled with a small, non-capitalized C, did missionary work, and that he needed money to continue his efforts. It was like pulling teeth, but we finally came up with a program. It was the fact that he did visit, on occasion, friends who were hospitalized for various illnesses, stabbings, drug overdoses, accidents, or other reasons, so he was indeed doing "Missionary Work." We described what we wanted to do, and that he would receive a percentage of our sales. By this time, he was so fucking drunk, he never asked how much, or how he would be paid. We presented a letter outlining his Missionary Activities, and he signed it. We left before he passed out in a drunken stupor. We never saw him again.

The rosary beads we were sending to people were a nice quality, and the letter was very convincing. The Reverend J. L. O'Connor seemed like a real, dedicated person with a mission to help people. All he asked was a small donation to continue with his work and left the amount completely up to the recipient of the rosary beads. If they could not afford to pay anything, they could keep the rosaries, and he would say a prayer for them anyway. Then wish them to go to hell.

I rented 10 or 12 post office boxes around the state, and the money began pouring in. Some people sent as little as $1, while others sent $5 or even $10. Others asked for more rosaries and made generous donations and wrote beautiful letters praising the Reverend for his work, as well as saying nice things about the rosaries. Within a few weeks, we knew all the fertile areas to send the beads, and it was a full day's work to drive to the post office boxes once or twice a week to collect the cash and count it.

Of the numerous types of people who frequented our hangout, the S & S bar, there were always those who were fascinated to be in the company of wise guys. Wannabe wise guys, I suppose you could call them. One of them was a nice man who worked for the post office. One afternoon, he called me aside, and asked if I had rented post office boxes around the state, in various fictitious names. I asked why he would ask me that question. He told me that his office was investigating what they believed was a scam to bilk people out of money in the name of the Catholic church. He said that a postal inspector deliberately broke a box, claiming it was damaged in delivery, and that the post office was trying to determine the sender or the addressee in an effort to deliver the package. This was all bullshit, of course, but it gave them a major lead to look in the Providence and surrounding areas. So far, all they had was a flimsy case, but they were staking out the boxes for the next pick-up. He said it was possible that I was the subject of an investigation, but without a pick-up by me, prosecution would be difficult. I thanked him for the information, and decided to keep away from the boxes. I abandoned the cash. But we had a pretty good run, and neither Vincent nor I felt too badly. *After all,*

Dean Sales was like a bus stop. Wait a little while, and another bus would soon come along. I had no moral regrets at all about what we had done: the rosaries were worth the money we got, and besides, I rationalized, we made a lot of people feel really good. Some bastards didn't pay for them or return them, so we figured anyone who would rob a rosary had to be a real prick, and that we were far better than they were. Amazing how one's mind can rationalize anything.

Dean Sales had lots of other activities going on, and I wasn't about to let the rosary incident influence its potential. There was going to be a World's Fair held in New York City, in 1964, and I began to wonder how I could make money from this once in a lifetime opportunity. The Vatican had given permission to allow their famous statue, Michelangelo's Pieta, to be displayed at the Fair, and millions of people would be interested in seeing it. It was, and is, one of Italy's most famous attractions to this day, so the opportunity to view it without going to Italy was certainly a great one for all Americans. I began to study pictures of the famous sculpture, and then finally decided that I would reproduce it in miniature, as a tiny pendant, approximately three quarters of an inch tall, and made from sterling silver.

Since I had inherited my father's skills as a master tool and die maker, I knew I was capable of doing this. I worked on the model more than two weeks before I was satisfied that I liked what I had made. It was a very detailed replica of the full size sculpture, and I had captured the expressions of Christ and his mother, the grief a mother feels for her dead son, each and every muscle tone was perfect, in every detail, including the veins in Christ's hands. It was awesome and it was accurate to the original in scale. Next, I had to figure out a way to manufacture them in volume, as they couldn't be priced so high that no one could afford them.

I decided to experiment with different methods of mass producing them, until I finally settled on a process known as the "Lost Wax" process. In this type of production, a silicone rubber mold is made from the original model, in this case my handmade model, then melted wax is injected in the mold and allowed to harden. There existed, even then, many different types of waxes, each with different properties for me to experiment with. Some waxes were better for large castings, others for smaller items. Some were capable of handling more detail, others melted at different temperatures, and usually, the various waxes were color coded to indicate which was which. I'm simplifying the description of the process, as there were many other variables to consider, such as injection pressure, which, if was too high, would distort the wax and temperatures as too hot a temperature meant that the wax would take too long to solidify, slowing up production, and might even cause excessive shrinkage. Too cool an injection temperature would result in the mold's cavity not being completely filled, and detail would be lost. None of these results were desirable. When I finally made a decision as to which wax to use, the process was quick and very accurate, but now there was only a wax replica of my hand-made model.

The next step was the investment process, in which numerous wax pieces were made and joined together, to form a tree, with each of the branches being a wax of the statue. The tree was then placed in a container, and a substance, similar to plaster of Paris, was poured over the wax tree. The whole container would then be placed on a vacuum table, and the vacuum would remove any air that might have been trapped during the pouring of the liquid investment material over the tree. Sometimes, I used a vibrating table, which would also do about the same thing as the vacuum: allow trapped air to escape, and the investment material to penetrate every small nook and cranny on the wax pieces. The investment material hardened enough in a few minutes to allow the container to be placed upside down in an oven, at approximately 1,750 degrees. The wax would melt and run out of the investment material, leaving a cavity which contained the female counterpart of the wax pieces that it was poured over when it was a liquid. This, as mentioned, was called the lost wax process, and it could be done very quickly and cheaply. In one form or another, this technology existed for many centuries.

The next step was to take the investment material, and place it in a centrifugal casting machine. One side of this machine held the very hot container where the wax had just been melted out of, and the other side a porcelain crucible into which silver had been placed, then melted in an oven at the same temperature as the other side with the plaster of Paris cavities. A button activated an arm which was holding both of these hot items, and swung around and around, forcing the liquid silver to flow into the cavity on the opposite side of the arm. In seconds, the liquid silver filled the cavities, flowing into every fine detail that the plaster of Paris cavity had, and within seconds the silver solidified, and the machine's arm stopped moving. Of course everything was still very hot so using copper thongs to pick it up, it was then dropped in a bucket of water. The piece would sizzle and then crack into a thousand parts, revealing the silver tree containing the silver statues. They were all attached, of course, but a small tool, called a sprue cutter, was used to cut the various statues from the sprue. After a dip in boric acid, the parts appeared bright and shiny. Now, the sprue marks had to be removed, generally by grinding or filing, and the individual statues would he hand polished to a brilliant luster. The process yielded about 20-22 pieces each time it was repeated, and a good operator could produce hundreds of pieces per hour. The silver that made up the tree, the part which fed molten metal to each cavity, could be recast over and over as long as fresh virgin silver was added to make up the weight needed to make another casting. Total cost of materials and labor was around $2.50 each, and they would retail at $25-$40 easily.

There was no one who had such a fine product, and its profit potential was recognized immediately by Vincent. We considered ways to market the item to realize its full potential.

Finally, we decided it should be sold in the World's Fair grounds, as close to the original statue as possible. We knew this would not be an easy thing to accomplish, and that we would need some sort of imprimatur or blessing from the church to get such a prime location. After all, the Vatican had lots of its own items within striking distance of the Pieta, and our item would present competition. Vincent, with his sixth sense, said he only hoped they would not demand such a high percentage from our sales, that we couldn't afford to pay it. As it turned out, once again, he was right.

Full of energy and enthusiasm, I approached a priest from our local church, the Holy Ghost Church, located directly across the street from the S&S bar. We were given a brief lesson on what procedures would have to be followed, and several names of higher-ups whose offices were in New York. A week later, after making an appointment, Vincent and I found ourselves waiting in a plush office for an introduction to a small commission of priests, who could make decisions on what items were to be sold at the World's Fair.

Once inside the meeting room all hopes I may have had of selling my item inside the World's Fair vanished instantly. Both Vincent and I looked at each other, neither of us saying a word, but both understanding that we didn't stand a chance. These guys made our crew from the S&S look like a group of Boy Scouts.

The meeting lasted only a few minutes, and we left without an agreement. We realized we were going to have to find the best possible location outside the Fair Grounds, away from the original statue, and began working toward that end. Since the Fair was being set up by union members, it wasn't long before we had a prime location near the entrance where everyone entering the World's Fair had to pass. I think the location probably did more business than if we were inside the Fair itself. We sold hundreds of these pieces, and gave everyone an order form to purchase even more if the wished after the Fair was over. We sold two or three hundred pieces in the weeks after the Fair ended. The item was beautiful, the buyers were happy, and we kept all the profits. It doesn't get much better than that.

Dean Sales also had huge added value. It was located inside Sherwood's vast space, and was constantly being visited by wise guys, cops, politicians, judges, hustlers, shoplifters, and every type of person imaginable. They brought in all types of swag, ranging from jewelry, watches, fine china, crystal, flatware, fur coats, and all kinds of other stolen goods. The general rule was to pay about one third the legitimate retail price, but when you entered the realm of Sherwood and Dean Sales, that was not the price. Some jewelry was too identifiable to sell as is and required extensive re-cutting or remounting to sell safely. Of course, Dean Sales was always happy to do this work for a small percentage.

On one occasion, we received a load of five thousand stolen designer raincoats from a New Bedford manufacturer. The fucking raincoats were everywhere. Dean Sale's small office couldn't handle another coat, so I placed them throughout Sherwood. They were going to a buyer in New York in a few hours. The only problem was that the FBI had followed the coats from the moment they were stolen, based on some asshole's tip, and they were waiting in their cars, just outside our shop. They had not seen where the coats went after they were put on the loading dock and went up the elevator, and they had decided to wait and obtain a legal search warrant. They weren't worried about the coats disappearing because they never left the parking lot while they waited to locate a judge to issue the warrant. But the mill complex was a large one, with several loading gates, and there was always some activity going on in the various businesses that rented space there.

We had no idea the FBI was staking out the shop until a Providence Police detective, named Eddie Carroll — an alcoholic who liked associating with wise guys, and who before his divorce, lived right next door to Ann — called me and told me to carefully go down one of the service elevators, but not the one servicing Sherwood, and look to the left. He said I would find four police cars there, one was from the Rhode Island State Police, another from the Providence Police, and the other two belonged to the FBI. They weren't bothering us, because they were still waiting for a search warrant to be issued. He estimated that it would take them about an hour and a half to obtain the necessary documents, then we would be raided, and anyone on the premises would be arrested. I told Vincent the news immediately, and he called Saul Friedman, our criminal attorney. Saul said to get the coats out as quickly as possible and dispose of them. He would try to get us an additional hour by delaying the issuance of the warrant.

I told Vincent to leave the building by the back door, where there were no cops, and I would handle everything. There were only two of us now in Sherwood, me and my future mother-in-law Susie, and I knew we needed more help and a truck. I called Vincent's nephew, Anthony, who was said to be mentally slow, although I always thought he was fine. He borrowed a truck from one of our neighbors in the mill complex and then placed it in front of the other company's loading dock, its ass end almost in the elevator. The Feds were sitting in their cars, smoking and laughing while we were busting our balls loading up the truck with the swag coats. There was no fucking way on this earth I was going to drop the load off at a fucking lot and lose five thousand coats. Vincent was safe, and I could handle the beef if necessary.

It took two hours to load the fucking coats in the truck, and we drove the truck to a parking lot down the street and left it there. The lot belonged to Uncas Ring Manufacturing, and I put a sign in the windshield that read delivery. Then, Susie and I walked back to Sherwood and entered by the rear of the building. I told Anthony to dial a number I scribbled on a piece of paper. It was Raymond's office. I told him to ask for Vincent and not to speak to anyone else. Give him the message that the place was clear of raincoats, and he could come back if he wanted. I didn't know if Vincent had told the Old Man or not, but it certainly was lucky that his sister Betty wasn't around, because she was a real pain in the ass and would have told Raymond what we did.

Vincent was back in his office within five or ten minutes and patted me on the back. The shop was so fucking clean, you couldn't find anything out of place. There were no raincoats anywhere. In less than an hour, we heard a commotion outside our large double doors. They were unlocked, but the Feds were just about to break them down with a ram, when I opened the doors. The doors were tall and wide, but had little strength. They would have crumbled in a second.

The FBI was pushy, as they usually are, and presented a search warrant. They shoved it at Vincent, saying they knew there was a stolen shipment of raincoats in the shop, and that we would soon all be arrested. Vincent took the warrant and dropped it on the floor, then went into his office, where me and Susie were waiting. The two of us lit up a Muratti Ariston, cigarettes we ordered by the case from Nat Sherman in New York. We read the inscription on the inside of the box "As smoked by royalty and the nobility," and we laughed. Within minutes, the FBI asked where the coats were, and that they knew we had taken delivery of five thousand pieces stolen from New Bedford. Shocked and surprised, said to Vincent that the crime rate was getting to be so bad that from now on we better make sure to keep our doors locked at all times. Life wasn't safe anymore, we quipped. Finally, we told them we didn't have the slightest idea what they were talking about, but if they were finished with their search, we would like to close up the shop. The strain of thinking they could have suspected us was draining, and we wanted to go home. Pissed, and vowing this would not be the end of the matter, the fucking cheap suits left.

The next morning, we took the truck to another parking lot, where we made an exchange of the coats for a tidy profit. I had saved the day this time, and once again the perks of hanging out at Sherwood had paid off. More importantly, I had proven my worth to all the right people. Anywhere I went, I was respected, and the word soon got out to Raymond that I was a "Stand Up" kid. We formed a bond, based on mutual respect, and I was always welcome at his office. One day he said to me, "You're with us now." Several years later, he was to come to my defense and go against the New York Families, by taking my side, and ultimately saving my life.

In June 1963, Ann and I were married. I was a junior in college. I had so much practical experience, and was earning so much money that I wanted to quit school to pursue my other interests. Only because my father wanted me to continue, did I go on to graduate in 1964, with a Bachelor's Degree in Business Administration as my major, and psychology as a minor. School was not difficult for me, and although I studied very little, I passed easily and with respectable grades. I had honored my father's wishes, but now it was time to move on.

Louis Jr. was born on April 29, 1964 and was only a few weeks old at my graduation. Ann and I decided to build a house, and we began the process of looking for a piece of land. Our main criteria was that it not be too far from Ann's parents, as they viewed Louis as their own son. We finally found a piece of land on Hawkins Boulevard, a small street located in North Providence, less than a 10 minute drive from Ann's parent's house. I purchased the land for cash, and construction began immediately.

Later, on the advice of Morris Kaufman, Sherwood's accountant, I took out a small mortgage on the property. Since I had no visible source of income at that time, I visited what we wise guys, referred to as our "piggy bank." I went to see Joseph Mollino, Sr., who ran a mob-influenced financial institution, called City Loan and Finance. There, I gave Puppy Dog, as we called him, some $12,000 cash in an envelope, and he slipped it into a drawer. He then issued me a check for $12,000, along with a payment book, showing I owed $ 43.15 each month for the next 30 years. That was my mortgage payment, and it looked great on paper. No interest was paid on the $12,000 I gave him to secure the loan.

Later, he was to help me, when I needed to show a larger mortgage. Joe (Puppy Dog) Mollino and his wife Ann, were a fixture at my house and my father's. My father, Joe, and Ann were friends for 30 years, but my father had no idea of how City Loan was operating.

In 1990, the failure of City Loan caused the collapse of RISDIC, (Rhode Island Saving Deposit Insurance Corporation) the insurance company that insured financial institutions that did not meet the Federal insurance guidelines. The newly elected governor, Bruce Sundlun, shut down all the institutions that were not federally insured. The reasoning was that Rhode Island law prevented a credit union or other financial institutions from operating without insurance, and since the RISDIC was in receivership, no state financial institution was allowed to operate. The standing joke throughout the country was that if you wrote a check in Rhode Island, the bank would bounce, even if the check didn't.

Everyone who had money in these types of institutions was not allowed to withdraw it, and this lasted almost two years. It was Puppy Dog's son who brought the banking system to its knees, and ultimately, after running away for a year and a half, he returned to receive a 30-year sentence for fraud, embezzlement, conspiracy, and other charges. He served 10 years of his sentence before being released from the Rhode Island Adult Correctional Institution. Even murderers and rapists didn't serve that much time. But it was a political hot potato, and Joe Jr. was to be fully baked.

Since this was, as I mentioned, our piggy bank, all the wise guys had removed their money several months earlier. Even then, we were all investigated. I told my father-in-law to remove his money several months before the bank's collapse, but he didn't because when he attempted to close his account, they offered him an even better rate than he was receiving, which was a couple of percentage points above what a "real" bank was paying. Furious, I ran to the bank, and withdrew my father-in-law's money.

When I gave it to him, he was angry, and asked how I could do this without his signature. I told him "Dad, that's not a bank, it's a fraud, and they will be closed any day now." He realized a few months later what I was talking about.

Now I was totally legit. Or so it seemed, having borrowed money and using it to build a house. The house took approximately six months to complete, and Ann watched every step the contractor took in following our blueprints. One afternoon, she called me to come over to the house immediately, as there was a huge problem. The contractor installed Brodeur windows, instead of the ones listed on our blueprint, which stated the windows were to be manufactured by Anderson Window Co., a premium maker of windows. The contractor showed literature from both companies, and honestly speaking, I liked the Brodeur windows much better. They had the ability to be removed easily, for cleaning, or in the event a broken glass needed to be replaced. But he also said he tried to get the Anderson Windows first, before installing the substitutes, and there would be at least a two-week delay. He took it upon himself to make the exchange.

Ann was furious, and both her and the contractor were going at it like cats and dogs. The contractor finally made a threat. "If you don't accept these windows, and let us finish our work, I'll see you don't move into this place for two fucking years."

Now I was furious. I took the guy over to the side of the house and told him that his truck would be stolen with him in it, and sent to the crusher where it would make a nice package about three feet square, and if his wife put a glass top on it, it would make a great coffee table. He knew I wasn't kidding, and apologized for his mistake in substituting the windows without first getting Ann's permission.

The Brodeur windows were replaced the next day by Andersons. The rest of the construction was eventless, and we moved in by the end of the year.

Ann's parents were heartbroken. They were so in love with Louis Jr., who was several months old by now, that it was like taking a child from his adopted family.

Some guys are always talking about their in-laws, making jokes and demeaning them in various ways. Susie was my mother-in-law, and to tell the truth, I couldn't say one bad word about her. The only thing I didn't like is that she spoiled Louis terribly, and this went on all throughout her life. My only complaint was that I disciplined him for something, she would go over to him and undermine my punishment. She loved him to death.

One afternoon, all the wise guys were in Vincent's office, playing cards. I was there too, smoking and talking with the guys. The radio was on and we heard a startling announcement. President Kennedy had been shot. It was around 11:30 a.m., and the day was November 22, 1963. More news on his condition was to follow, the announcer said.

Most of the wise guys were thrilled. They said Kennedy and his father were both phony pieces of shit, and that JFK had betrayed them, especially when he appointed his brother Bobby as Attorney General and the asshole made it a personal vendetta to go against the Italian Mafia, as he called it. One of the guys said, "Imagine them going after the Mafia, with their fucking history." The radio was always on in Vincent's office, and in mine, because the playing of an FM station made it infinitely more difficult for law enforcement agencies to eavesdrop on a conversation.

Then, at around 1 p.m., JFK was pronounced dead. The country would soon have a new president.

Politics was never a subject that I had any interest in. But, as luck would have it, something happened in the Rhode Island political climate upon Kennedy's death, and my cousin, Lee Magiacomo, wound up becoming the head of the Rhode Island Department of Welfare.

He called two of my cousins and me, and asked if we wanted jobs as social workers. I declined immediately, telling him that I wouldn't have the time, since I had other business interests going. I had just started another business, selling 18k Italian gold jewelry with the price based on its weight from a showroom I built in my house.

Lee said that he had three positions vacant, that the pay was only $125 or thereabouts per week, but that I didn't have to do anything, just come in on Fridays and pick up my paycheck. I would be working in district 5, which was located on Kelly Street, in the Manton Avenue area of Providence. Supposedly, I was to handle a caseload of elderly and disabled recipients, and nothing much ever changed for them. They required little or no attention. I accepted the job on that basis, and immediately raised the benefits of all the people on my caseload.

Every caseworker had a supervisor, and mine was a nice Jewish woman, Mrs. Rosalie Reizen. She and her many friends were constantly at my house, and were some of my best customers.

I was handed a folder from Rosalie Reizen, who asked me to determine if Mrs. Guglielmo and her daughter were eligible to collect welfare. In those days, a social worker also determined a person's financial eligibility to collect money. So, I visited the house one morning, and the three of us, Anselmo, his mother, and me sat at a small, round table in his kitchen. Anselmo's sister was in another room, with the door tightly closed, coughing and coughing. I heard her and knew she existed and that was enough for me. I didn't need to go into the room to see her. I could hear her.

According to his mother, Anselmo Guglielmo was a nice boy. He moved from Italy to the Silver Lake section of Providence, along his sister and mother, just two years before I met him. He purchased a home and was doing his own repairs to it. He had a talent for carpentry. Mrs. Guglielmo didn't speak any English beyond, "He's a nice boy" in a strong Italian accent. She was applying for welfare along with her daughter. The son had called and requested this visit. I spoke enough Italian to be understood them and for them to feel they had a friend in the welfare system.

"Is she eligible"? Anselmo asked me.

"I think so," I said. "I mean I can't see why she wouldn't be, she isn't working, and probably is too old, and doesn't speak English, and so, my quick reply would be, "Yes."

"What about my sister"?

"What's wrong with her"? I asked.

"She is sick" was the reply.

"Yes, I know that, but with what?"

"She coughs all the time. I think she has some lung disease."

"Did you take her to see a doctor?"

"I don't have money for doctors, and she doesn't have any money."

"She should see a doctor soon," I said.

"We'll see," he replied.

"I know they will want more medical information on your sister, so get her to a doctor … Your mother, I think, I can probably slide right in."

"You better," he threatened, or I'll throw her out."

"He's a nice boy" the mother repeated. I knew better, so I took sides almost immediately.

"Mrs. Guglielmo, do you understand what your son is saying?"

"He's a nice boy" she replied. Then she added, "*Vorrei una tassa di café?*" She asked me if I'd like a cup of coffee.

"*Si, prego*, Yes, thanks," I replied.

My curiosity was getting the better of me, and I wanted to get a clearer picture of this scene. Normally, I would just have okayed her and sent the sister to a doctor before signing her on.

"Do you know your son wants to throw you out?"

"He's a nice boy," was the only response.

"Not just her," the son chimed in, "but my sister too. Both of them in the street."

He pointed to the street as he said this.

I would have loved to have talked to the sister, but I am glad I didn't. She might have had tuberculosis or something contagious. I could hear her. A doctor could qualify her.

"Why do you want to throw them out?" I asked. "It's your mother and sister you're talking about, not some strangers."

"They pay or they go," was his reply.

My coffee was strong and was served in a tacky, colorful, Italian cup. I've had espressos that were weaker. I put in lots of milk and four or five sugar cubes just to make it drinkable. Still, it was a nice gesture. I finished my coffee and had to leave. I had an appointment to show some jewelry at 2:30.

When I said I'll come back in three or four days, Anselmo shouted, "If there're not eligible, they're out. No money, no house."

"Don't do anything foolish before I come back," I told him. "I mean it. I'll have someone go over your taxes for this house. With all the repairs you've made, it's probably worth more now than when you bought it. So, do the right thing. I'll be back us soon as I can."

I shut the fucking door behind me. I could hear the mother repeat: "He's a nice boy," as I left.

Two days later, I returned to the house. Nothing had changed. The son and his mother sat at the kitchen table. The son asked me, "Do you have the money?"

I said, "No. I need more information for my supervisor. Things like the town your mother was born in. If she's still married, does she have any sources of income, any assets. It is very simple, and it'll take only a few minutes."

The mother looked at me and repeated: "He's a nice boy."

I said in Italian, "He wants to put you out on the street. Do you understand that? I only need a little information from you, and then I will be able to process your request, and get you some money. It's not going to take weeks. Whatever you tell me, I'll accept as the truth."

Anselmo was furious. "And my sister?" he shouted.

"Your sister needs a doctor. What kind of person are you that leaves his sister locked in a room coughing and doesn't call a doctor? I want to see her."

I told him to open door. The woman was in bed, coughing and didn't like my being there. She resented my presence, and I'm sure, she didn't have the slightest idea who I was or what I was supposed to be doing.

"So," Anselmo said, "do you want to see the whole house? You wanted to see the bedroom badly enough."

"Absolutely," I quickly replied.

He said "Follow me." He took me through the kitchen where we had been sitting, and off to the side was a small bathroom with an old-fashioned West porcelain tub, a broken-down vanity and a sink, some towels, soap, a plunger, and a lot or filth.

Then he said, "I'm working to remodel upstairs first, then I'll begin down here. Follow me."

I never went anywhere without carrying a gun. I was in the jewelry business and had a permit to carry in all the New England states. I had a small Colt Jr. .25 caliber automatic in my right pants pocket. The bullet was chambered before I went in the house. The gun was set to fire. I needed only to cock the hammer and pull the trigger. I put my hand in my pocket. He took me to the second floor. Part of the room was sheet rocked and the remainder was prepared to receive its new walls. On the left side, there were two rooms which were finished, except for paint.

Then we went into another small room, maybe 10 feet by 10 feet. I don't know what that room was going to be, maybe another bathroom. There was another room to the right side.

He said, "Here, I'll show you what I'm building." He opened the door and said, "Go see."

I grabbed the wall on the side of the opened door. The door swung out to nothing but a 15-foot drop to the ground. The motherfucker was trying to set me up for a real fall. But I was prepared. Before a second had passed, I was back in the room with the door closed. I looked at him and said, "You asshole."

I walked down the stairs, and he followed quickly. I cocked my pistol, but kept it in my pocket. He hollered, "A check tomorrow, or they'll be on the street."

But it didn't turn out that way.

I didn't return to the office that afternoon, or the following morning. I got in at 2 p.m. on Friday afternoon to pick up my check. Joyce Moretta, a co-worker, whose father was a well-known psychiatrist, and wrote articles for the *Providence Journal*, came up to me in a panic. "Lou, where have you been?"

I said, "Hi Joyce."

"Lou, the police are looking for you. They're asking everyone where you are. Rosalie called your house all morning."

"What the hell do they want with me Joyce," I asked,

"You didn't see the papers this morning, did you."

"No, I don't read the news. Why?"

"Your client's mother and daughter chopped up Anselmo. They're finding body parts all over Silver Lake."

I smiled and said, "No kidding. Let's take a ride, Joyce. Let's get down there."

We stopped just short of the house. There was a machine with steel claws boring in and out of the sewer. The cover had been removed and the claws came up and emptied its filthy contents into a barrel in a waiting truck.

"Anselmo must have lost his head," I told Joyce. She said that the largest part of his torso was still in the bathtub. I wanted to go in, but the whole area was sealed off and there were cops everywhere. And lots of onlookers, neighbors probably, but who knows, it was front page news.

Joyce and I returned to the Kelly Street office, and as I turned onto Kelly Street, I could see at least two police cars parked in front . When I got in, I was immediately called to the supervisor's office where two cops were waiting. They introduced themselves and began asked me lots of questions. As it turned out, I was the last person to have seen Anselmo Guglielmo alive. Lucky me. They asked me what I could tell them that might be of any help.

"He was a bad guy," I said, "He wanted to collect checks from his sister and mother, or he was going to throw them in the street. Looks like they beat him to it," I commented with a smile.

I didn't know too much about him, because he wasn't applying for assistance. He pushed his sister and mother to apply. But he didn't want to be asked any questions about himself. As for his sister, she had a bad cough, and he wanted me to come back when it got better. I wrote in my evaluation that she needed medical attention and we should send her for a complete physical. What I saw of her, she was probably eligible for temporary disability at least.

The police were impressed at my thorough and accurate assessment of the Guglielmo family. So was I. It was all bullshit, but turned out to be right on the money. So the investigation continued, and I followed its progress in the papers. Anselmo's head was found in a sewer one street over from his house on Union Avenue. An arm was also found at that location. Another arm and one foot were pulled from the sewer that Joyce and I had been watching, one foot was lodged in the toilet, and whatever parts were leftover were still in the bathtub. It turned out that Anselmo had been sexually abusing his mentally retarded sister for years, both here and in Italy. In the final disposition of the case she was sent to an institution for the criminally insane. The mother, on the other hand, was not charged with any crime but was sent back to Italy. Somebody told me that on her fight back to Italy she was heard to say, "He's a nice boy!"

The welfare job lasted about two and a half years, during which time I would drive to Kelly Street every Friday and pick up my paycheck. Sometimes, I had eight or nine in a stack before I deposited them.

Then, one day, things changed, and Lee was no longer the director. The agency had plans to increase everyone's caseloads, and was going to be moved to Fountain Street in Providence, so no more individual districts would be necessary. Everyone would work out of the Fountain Street facility. I resigned that week. I never liked politics anyway, since everything depended on someone's getting re-elected.

Chapter 3
The Office

I found it very hard to believe that anyone would spend several hundred thousand dollars or more to obtain a job that paid $45,000 a year other than that it was an opportunity for an elected politician to make that money back, plus a whole lot more.

Sure, a handful of people in the country might have been interested in becoming a politician for humanitarian reasons, but let's be realistic, they are few and far between. I never sucked up to a politician for a favor. I didn't need to. I could afford to hire the best lawyers in the country, and let them do the ass kissing routine. They were the ones that needed to suck ass, not me.

I was aware that we controlled certain politicians and enough of them came into the S&S Bar for one favor or another. Several of these assholes actually became judges, and one is still very active. For the most part, they were hanging around looking for money for favors they had granted, ranging from simply fixing a speeding ticket, or getting someone's bail reduced, to some pretty hefty things like sentence reductions and felony violations reduced to misdemeanors or even dismissed. I despised their deceptiveness, passing themselves off as upstanding citizens of high moral character, then scurrying to collect their bribe money. This was not only the case of politicians, but also of numerous law enforcement officials who were in a position to see that critical parts of a criminal case might suddenly become weak, such as the disappearance of evidence crucial to the prosecutor. Who knows, maybe they both were working on the same fix, collecting twice as much money.

Almost no one in the Family seemed to care. It was just a part of the cost of doing business, and, one might say, passed along to the ultimate consumer.

Only Raymond took a different point of view. The cheap, purple-lizard-lipped mob Boss never wanted to spend a dime on lawyers, judges, politicians, or cops. I guess his position could allow him to be that way. The local cops were glad he was the Boss on the Hill, as no crime involving civilians ever took place there and the general feeling was that Providence was much better with him than without. If some Cowboy, or Independent, a non-connected tough guy, did something he shouldn't have, he was dealt with immediately. No cops were necessary. Anyone could walk the streets at night without fear of harm. And, if by chance, the cops knew that something was going to go down, sometimes they got word to Raymond to let it happen elsewhere. It made the local lawmen look like they had crime under control.

When Tiger Baletto, an enforcer for the Mob in the late 50s, got out of control and started to knock on the doors of civilians who lived on the Hill — then told the husbands to disappear while he fucked the guy's wife — it wasn't long before he was shot. That ended that problem.

He was shot by Jackie Nazzare, another regular at the S&S. Jackie was a short, seedy character who walked with a cane. He was respected for his ability to collect money for wise guys from non-paying gamblers and stiffs who were being shy-locked. Everyone, including the cops, knew Jackie killed Tiger. The streets were better off with Jackie than his predecessor and nothing was made of this assassination. No one cared as long as it didn't conflict with their interests. But, soon it did.

It was Jackie's job to collect money not only from local people who were paying juice from 5 percent to 10 percent a week. He also was to keep things under control for the Old Man in other areas like Boston, Revere, and Somerset. Jackie was also sent to New York to help in the killing of Albert Anastasia.

Jackie had some plans of his own, and they involved screwing the Office — activities that were sanctioned by the Office — and were run by Henry Tameleo in Boston. The Office received a percentage of each and every one of these. Jackie wanted to take them over and run them for himself. Jackie was getting out of control.

I remember being in Raymond's office one afternoon when two wise guys entered. They were there to pay him his percentage of last Saturday's game held in the Ebb Tide bar in Revere Beach.

The Old Man refused the money repeatedly, saying, "No, no, I don't want it. You boys make some money. It makes me happy to see young fellows get ahead. I admire your energy."

After three or four times of their insisting that he take the money — which they referred to as his end — he finally relented and said, OK, but it isn't necessary. He took the money and put it in his drawer. But the wise guys knew better. If they hadn't shown up on their own with the Old Man's cut, they would soon have more trouble than they could handle. A beating, or worse, much worse, was a certainty. No one cheated the Old Man out of his cut.

It's a funny thing about gambling. One could have a winning streak and defy the odds against him, or just the opposite, suffer from a losing streak, and the House wins more than normal. But over time, it all averages out somehow. The Old Man knew exactly how much he had coming from any activity he was involved in. I don't know if it was his intuition, something about Henry Tameleo, or if he had someone at each game keeping him informed, but the fact remains the same. He knew how much he was due. God help anyone who fucked with that money. And several did. Usually, a beating was all that was necessary, but I would need to count on both my hands and feet the number of persons killed for this reason.

Jackie Nazzare was different. It was his job to collect the money and deliver it to The Office. He was also responsible to collect from the slow payers and deadbeats. The Office depended on him.

Raymond felt something wasn't quite right. The numbers from the games didn't seem to add up correctly. Jackie was called into the office. Unlike today, where someone might get killed over a ridiculous dispute in a gas station, in those days, killing someone, even if he had committed a major mistake, was not taken or carried out lightly. It was always considered a last resort, one to be used when all other efforts or solutions had been exhausted.

By this time, Jackie felt invincible because he had committed the ultimate deed for the Old Man, and that he had earned the supreme right to do anything he wanted to do. He was a made man. And he had made friends in New York. Still, Raymond worked with him, trying to get him to "do the right thing" as he would put it.

Jackie was a hardheaded son of a bitch and defied Raymond. He actually told people he would like to take over The Office. There was no reasoning with him, he was totally out of control. Raymond finally made the decision: Jackie had to be whacked. In some other state, the killing of Jackie would have required the permission of all the Family Bosses, since Jackie was a made man. But here in Rhode Island, things worked differently and Raymond was supreme over his Family.

"Breaking an egg," as Raymond called someone who committed murder for him was not enough to allow the shooter to do anything he wanted in defiance of the Boss, and skimming money from Raymond was one of the ultimate sins. There were many people in the S&S who would be capable and more than glad to whack Jackie, as no one liked him. Raymond would choose the hitter wisely because he knew this would be an important one, elevating his choice to a higher position in his Family. He didn't want to make the same mistake that he had made when Tiger Baletto was killed, only to be replaced by another out-of-control asshole.

Most people think that a hit carries a price tag and that a Boss pays someone to do a hit for him. This is rarely the case. Hits are rewarded in several ways, the most common being an elevated position within the Family. The status of being a made member brings perks with it that are recognized throughout the country. Even more frequently, a hit man received a larger percentage of a take from all sources or just a designated one as his compensation. Raymond made his decision with the utmost diligence.

It was a drizzly night in Providence, and the furniture store directly across the street from the S&S closed early. The store was called J.O.'s Furniture and its owner was an old man named Joe Orabona. He sold Italian immigrants tacky furniture at high prices and then financed the buyer's purchase. Since few of the customers spoke English, he would be able to grant them credit on terms that were very profitable to his store. Still, he remained in business for 40 or more years.

The store had two large showroom windows, one on the left side of a huge double door entrance, set back from the sidewalk a few feet, and the other to the entrance's right. Around 8 or 9 p.m., Jackie would finish making his routine stops on the Hill, collecting money, and would enter the S&S for a drink before returning to his cheap apartment on Spruce Street. His route was always the same: He would start at the S&S, walk all the way down to Angelo's Restaurant, then cross the street, and return on the other side. By the time he reached the furniture store, he was finished with his business, and would cross the street again and enter the bar for a drink and to count his take.

This night was to be a little different.

As Jackie moved under the front entrance of the furniture store, seeking temporary shelter from the drizzle to light up his Parody, a man approached him. It was obvious they knew each other, as Jackie continued lighting his cheap Italian cigar. The second man reached into his overcoat and pulled out a .38 caliber snub nose revolver and fired six shots into Jackie's body. Jackie spun around as the shooter continued to empty his gun in Jackie's body. It was over in seconds, and the shooter put his revolver back in his pocket, and walked up the side street, slowly disappearing into the dark night.

Jackie Nazzare was dead. The gun shots drew lots of attention, and windows opened in several houses to see what had happened. A man in one of the apartments hollered to his wife to, "Shut the window and mind your own business." Soon, all the windows were closed. No one wanted to get involved, and I can't blame them. Identifying the killer meant certain death for the witness.

Only one problem existed. An ambulance arrived on the scene in minutes and the EMTs didn't cover the body. Instead, they wheeled Jackie into the ambulance and sped off to Rhode Island Hospital, just a few blocks away. Jackie Nazzare was still alive and was now hooked up to all sorts of tubes and breathing apparatus in an effort to save his life. This was a botched hit and could bring the most serious of consequences to everyone involved.

Jackie remained in a coma for a couple of days, then regained consciousness periodically. The state police and the FBI kept him under 24 hour surveillance, and whenever he was conscious they tried to question him. The local police knew Jackie well, as did the FBI. Both questioned him, but all he would say was, "Fuck off and leave me alone." His periods of consciousness grew shorter and shorter each day and it was obvious he wasn't about to tell anyone who shot him.

Then, the FBI got a bright idea. One agent dressed up as a doctor and one as a priest and told him that he would not live through the night. Wouldn't it be nice to clear your conscience, and also bring justice to the man who shot you?

Jackie signaled one of them to come a little closer. The agent — now thinking Jackie was going to reveal who had shot him — bent over close to Jackie. Jackie spit in the FBI agent's face, calling him a mother-fucking piece of shit. Jackie Nazzare died the next afternoon, seven days after he had been shot and never revealed the name of the man who shot him. Even though the hit didn't go exactly as planned, Raymond was pleased with Rudolph Sargenta's work. He would be handsomely rewarded.

But Rudolph's work was nowhere near finished. I don't know much about gambling, but gamblers are a breed unto themselves, and the wise guy wannabes who gambled with the wise guys were always losers, even if they won. Sure, the suckers would get paid for their winnings, but on the other side was the bookie, who worked for the House, or Family, and the S&S was the House. It was capable of laying off bets taken by other bookies, at ridiculous odds. Laying off bets was simply a way to even up the odds on a baseball, basketball, football team, boxer, or anything else people gamble on went too far to one side or another. It could put a bookie out of business. The S&S was a place to run if a bookie took too much risk.

The thing about running an illegal bookie operation, or other crimes, for that matter, that made them so lucrative, was that you could prey on people who couldn't call the cops. For instance, if someone borrowed money to gamble, or open a business, or whatever reason, it was for something that wasn't legal. Therefore, he was an easy target to extort money from, to threaten, beat up or make money with any way possible. Someone with larceny in their heart was a good mark for hustlers, and these suckers were prime marks for all kinds of wise guys.

So the world spun around and around, and everything had an order, or so it seemed.

One gang of cowboys were running a very profitable, and expanding, floating crap game in Providence, but they were not part of any Family. Christ, there were enough brothers to have their own family, and they were tough. They were bringing a lot of attention to Providence, and the Office, and even the cops wanted it to stop.

Despite numerous warnings of the consequences, they continued to run their own gambling operation right under Raymond's nose, and they weren't going to kick in a nickel. This went on for more than a year. Finally, Rudolph Marsocci, one of the more powerful of the brothers in the group of four, was shopping in Evelyn's Spa, on the corner of Pocasset Avenue and Alto Street in the Silver Lake area of Providence. It was early afternoon. Two men walked into the spa with shotguns in their hands and in wide open view of anyone who may have been in the spa.

They opened fire on the cowboy, who had been causing so much trouble in the Providence gambling scene. He was cut in half by the point blank firing of 12 gauge shotguns. The two men left the spa as if nothing had happened. One of the shooters was my friend, Louis, the other, a dapper man in his late 30s or early 40s named Maurice (The Pro) Lesher, who played semi-professional golf all over the country. He was later tried for this crime, pleaded out to a 10-30 year sentence and did some 10 ½ years at the Rhode Island Adult Correctional Institution. The other shooter ran from Rhode Island and managed to live without detection for 10 and a half years, finally surrendering when the political climate in Providence was more favorable. He returned and made light of his disappearance, almost as if saying, "I didn't know you were looking for me."

Shortly after, another Marsocci brother, Willie, was in Christina's Diner on Atwells Avenue only a short walk away from the S&S. My friend and his wife were having dinner there when a lone gunman walked into the crowded diner and shot Willie while he was in a phone booth. The shooter was not wearing a mask or any other sort of disguise, and he walked calmly from the diner. No one saw anything. Two of the most troublesome Marsocci brothers were dead. The others caused no further trouble.

After he returned to Rhode Island 10 and a half years later, Louis was offered a deal: plead guilty to the first Marsocci murder and serve a year and a half, or go to trial and risk a life sentence. He refused the deal, and went to trial only to be found guilty. He received a life sentence with a minimum of 30 years. We all thought he was crazy to pass on the deal he was offered, but Louis was and is, one of the smartest men I have ever known. He is so sharp, even now at age 74, he can outsmart almost anyone. And he is still in strong physical condition, about 5'10," 160 pounds, a competitor in the Boston Marathon as well as being an avid skier.

So what the hell was someone this clever doing in jail? Louis had an appeal prepared before he was found guilty and now he filed it. His lawyer was Tom DeFusco, a mobbed-up attorney and a powerful politician as well. DeFusco was Rhode Island's Secretary of State for a few years. He argued that Louis's trial was prejudiced, because it didn't contain a single school teacher in the jury. How the hell this could make any difference I will never know. But, like I said earlier, Raymond had a way of making problems disappear, and Louie was Raymond's right hand man. A new trial was granted and Louie was found not guilty. All of this took only a year and a half.

He was a free man, and so was his friend and conspirator in the Marsocci shooting, Maurice Lesher. Louie made a statement to me that rings in my head to this day. He said he'd rather be dead than in jail. I guess you have to believe that of someone who was on the run for 10 and a half years. Louie's trial and acquittal meant he wasn't a convicted murderer. He was free and clear.

While Louie was away, he lived the life of a king. Even just a few years ago, while I was incarcerated in Fort Dix, he filed a brief with the Rhode Island Supreme Court in which he demanded that he not be called the head of a Mafia Family since that was never proven. We all had a great laugh about it. What the fuck difference could it make what he was called. He had beaten the system all his life and was still the Boss.

Like Raymond, Louie kept a low profile, never drawing any undue attention to himself. He drove an old, rust-colored car, lived modestly in his mother's house on Freese Street in Providence, kept a small apartment above the S&S, and never flashed fancy clothes or jewelry. Now here he is not wanting to be called a Mafia Boss and going to court to put an end to the newspapers and other media calling him that because that has never been proven. For someone who avoided publicity, he drew plenty of attention to himself. Go figure. We were so close that while Louis was away, few people knew his whereabouts. I was one of those few people.

Chapter 4
La Fantasia

Running a business from my house was both a good and bad idea. I had built and completely set up a modern showroom, but I was also running newspaper advertisements in the *Providence Journal*, which brought in customers, but also attracted all kinds of weirdoes.

I remember the doorbell rang one evening, and I peeked through the peep hole in the door to see a tall, grubby looking man standing there. I put my hand in my pocket and took a firm grip on my Chief's Special, a small five-shot .38 caliber revolver loaded with hollow point ammunition. Then I opened the door.

He began saying, "Many wars have been caused over rocks." I didn't know what the hell he was talking about, but I was certainly ready for trouble. It turned out that he was just an eccentric character who didn't live far from my house. Even so, I didn't like the idea of possible trouble, especially when my family was in the house and most of my appointments were at night. This went on for two years. I always wondered what kind of trouble awaited me every time I opened the door.

The idea of selling 18 karat Italian gold jewelry by weight was a new and exciting one. People loved buying a beautiful piece of handmade jewelry and paying a price determined by its weight on a scale. This was not only a fresh concept, but the 18 karat and the Italian jewelry origin made it an instant success.

I was doing business with companies that were just getting started or selling only to a local market area in Italy and I watched several of these companies grow to sales of hundred million dollars or more per year. Today, they wouldn't answer an e-mail unless it was from some major jewelry chain in the United States. At that time, I was having dinner and drinks with the owners who were happy to open up a small market in the United States.

The weight of the piece in reality meant nothing since all pieces were marked with a code indicating what price category per gram they would fall in. A chain — machine made in 18 karat gold — would probably be in the lowest price category per gram. An 18 karat, hand-made piece of jewelry might cost five times as much per gram.

Stones like diamonds, rubies, sapphires, emeralds, tourmalines, pearls, and so forth, were marked on a tag by their total weight and were added to the base gram price. This was, of course, only a different marketing strategy. It was new at the time. Today, this is a common practice in most jewelry stores.

After leaving the Department of Welfare, I spent a great deal of time between my various businesses — Sherwood, Dean Sales, and LBC Imports, which was my jewelry business. The jewelry business by itself could have kept me busy.

In 1969, I decided to open a retail outlet in a brand new mall called the Midland Mall which was owned and operated by the Homart Development Corporation, a wholly owned subsidiary of the Sears Roebuck Company. Today, this mall is called the Rhode Island Mall. By now, I knew the jewelry business in and out. With my wise guy connections, I was able to buy swag items and could sell them in the store. The move to the mall would be an expensive one and I would need plenty of cash to put the idea into reality. Since I had been in business for a few years at the house and had a nice insurance policy on my safe's contents, a loss wouldn't have raised any undue suspicion.

The policy covered a burglary from the safe only. Since the room and the safe were protected by an elaborate alarm system, the insurance company issued a policy which they reviewed and I increased every year. The insurance company was comfortable with their investment. The box was a modern Mossler, with a smaller safe located inside which held cash and the most expensive diamonds and jewelry. It had a burglary rating that rivaled the best found in the largest jewelry stores in the country. To me, it looked impenetrable; at least without doing damage to the safe's contents.

I needed a complex burglary — one that could bypass an alarm system and then a very experienced safe cracker to open the safe. Neither the alarm specialist nor the safe cracker posed much of a problem for me as I knew several of them from the S&S bar. I made my choices.

I also asked Vincent to confirm my picks for this job, and he agreed that I had chosen wisely from our crew. A crew is a closely-knit group of wise guys who are ultimately all responsible to the same Family Boss.

In the Sunday *Journal*, week after week, I would place advertisements in the bridal section which would read "From Italy" in bold print," Direct Importer of Hand-Made 18 Karat Italian Gold Jewelry bracelets, charms, earrings, etc. Louis

Colavecchio, 31 Hawkins Boulevard, North Providence, Rhode Island, evenings 7 to 9, 231-0506."

The advertisements in the paper drew attention, obviously, to my business being run from home. Later, they would be blamed for the burglary by the police, with one of them saying it brought too much attention to my jewelry business. This was, of course, exactly what I wanted.

I wondered how fucking stupid could this cop be to make a statement like that. What did he want me to do? Keep it a secret that I sold gold jewelry. Maybe I should have had an unlisted phone number also. That might have helped keep people away.

I set the dates when I would be out of town with my family and I would leave one thousand dollars in an envelope in the smaller round cash safe. This was how they were going to be paid. Everything was now in place. I would not participate in any way with this burglary. It had to be 100 percent iron pipe. No one had a problem with that at all.

The following weekend, Ann and I went on a trip to New York on a Friday. We left Louis at Ann's parents and must have stopped in every fucking designer store on Fifth Avenue. Of course, I was fascinated with FAO Schwartz and spent a good hour or so there, playing with their toys, so I guess I shouldn't complain too much.

It was a great weekend and Saturday night was particularly nice because we ate at one of my favorite restaurants — the Azzura Grotta on Broome Street in Little Italy. Frank, the maître d', knew me well and always had a table ready for me even if the place was fully packed. He was a big gorilla, with a huge gaudy pinky ring with his initials blazing in diamonds. The restaurant was a very busy place, with the kitchen in full sight and waiters running from table to table, almost non-stop, speaking Italian, and bringing orders they had taken only by memory to their customers.

Every once in a while, my mind would wander to the burglary planned for the weekend. Was it over? Did it go okay? Was anyone caught? And, on and on. But, all in all, the short trip was very enjoyable and Ann did plenty of shopping for herself, and also for Louis Jr. It's a good thing, I thought, that I didn't plan on staying any longer, or I would spend all the insurance money that I anticipated collecting.

We came home early enough to make the 11 a.m. Mass at the Blessed Sacrament Church on Academy Avenue. All during the Mass, which seemed to last for hours, I was wondering what awaited me at the house. After the Mass, I wanted to go home, but Ann insisted we go to her mother's house and eat dinner there, pick up Louis, Jr., go to my mother's house, and then return home. Another four hours to wait. Another eternity, it seemed.

When we finally did get home, I unlocked the front door and everything appeared to be in order, neat and clean. Then I began thinking, maybe something happened? Maybe they got caught? Or something spooked them into postponing the job? These were the best guys in their field, and it would take something serious for them to call off a planned score.

I tried to use Vincent's reasoning. "That which you think is going to happen inevitably never does." I took a deep breath and said I was going downstairs to do a little work in the office. The showroom was at the end of the corridor, past the downstairs kitchen, bathroom and laundry room. Everything appeared to be fine. They didn't do the job, I thought. I said to myself, "Something must have gone wrong."

Then, I unlocked the door and the lock seemed to behave in a strange way. The door opened. I was startled by what I saw. There was almost a four-inch deep layer of what looked like powdered cement around the safe. Dust was everywhere and you could write your name on the walls, showcase tops, windows, anywhere. I never saw such a mess, not even when the house was under construction.

The work on the safe was something to behold. It was drilled from the left top corner, over to the right top corner, then down the right side. There must have been 500 holes drilled in the door, and the door was bent back and swung freely on its hinges. Later, I was to learn that this is an old procedure used where noise and damage from an explosive device was not acceptable and that this was known as peeling.

It must have been a hell of a lot of work was all I could think. I didn't touch anything as I knew the police would want to check for finger prints and other evidence. I looked inside of what was left of the safe. The small round money safe was completely missing. That safe had to weigh two or three hundred pounds by itself, and it was gone. I didn't know how the fuck they got it out of the larger safe and out of the house and not make a mess. When I left the room I tracked dust all the way down the corridor, yet when I first entered it the floor looked to have been cleaned after the safe was removed, and I'm sure the guys would want to get out of there as quickly as possible. Then, when they did get out, they still had lots of work to open the smaller safe. The smaller safe was a much more difficult safe to open than the large one. But, again, that's not my business.

The safe had been broken into and it was up to me now to break the news to Ann. So, I walked upstairs and I told Ann that we had a burglary and not to be upset. I told her the room was a mess and of course she wanted to see it right away. Somehow, she didn't seem to be as surprised as I might have expected she would have been, and this was sort of comforting to me. She never asked me if I set this up but she knew I was certainly capable of doing just that.

She called the police and they responded within a few minutes. Several cars arrived at the house. I'm sure all our neighbors were wondering what was going on at 31

Hawkins Blvd. The investigation was a very short one. Their conclusion was that some alarm specialist had disabled the alarm system and the thieves had all the time that they needed to do their work. One cop said everything looked so neat because they sealed the showroom door before working on the safe and probably covered the floor with a plastic sheet when they removed the inside safe. I asked why they would bother to keep the floor clean when they were in a hurry to finish the work that they were doing. They were there to rob the place not to clean it. The answer that I received was that if we had come back in the middle of their work, while they were attempting to open the safe, we would not notice anything wrong until we went into the showroom. By then, they could have put on masks and held us hostage until they finished their work.

"That's how professionals work, you know," one of the cops said.

We told the police that we had left the house on Friday afternoon to spend the weekend in New York City. Again, one of the cops said it could have been any time between Friday night or Saturday, or possibly even Sunday morning since we had a pattern of going to the 11 o'clock Mass and then after that visiting Ann's mother's house for dinner, and after that my mother's house which meant that we would not return home until late in the afternoon. We spent the entire Sundays, generally, away from the house. The cop said there was a rash of burglaries in North Providence in the last few weeks but nothing like this one that he could remember. He said it probably was fortunate that we did not interrupt them because, who knows what might have happened.

"Consider yourself lucky," he said. The police report could be picked up Tuesday afternoon if I wanted to stop by the station. I would need it for my insurance company. All the cops left. Everything had gone as planned.

About a week later, the police found the small inside safe in a field in South Providence. It had been opened and its contents had been removed. I identified it as the safe taken from my house.

The corporate name for the new store was LBC Imports, Inc, but the name on the store front Read "La Fantasia" which is Italian for fantasy or dream. Opening the store was much more costly than I had expected. The Homart Development Company was interested in every phase of the construction. Since it was a new mall, the company even required the building of walls both inside and outside my area.

The outside wall was to have a huge arch with two metal gates that joined in the middle. When the store was closed, the gates would be locked and you would still be able to look inside the store. They were similar to a wrought-iron type gate with spaces in between the bars. They were painted gold. The rest of the outside wall, which was maybe 30-feet long or so, was covered in plush carpeting of red, white, and green — the colors of the Italian flag.

Inside, there was a bright red rug. There were two raised islands, both covered in a bright white rug used to display very unusual and expensive larger items. One of the items I remember was a kid's toy. It was battery operated, round, similar to a golf cart but very cute and capable of holding two children. It had a colorful cloth top with fringes all around. It was a real eye catcher and an expensive toy for its time. It cost just over $1,500. I sold two of them to a flamboyant local contractor.

The other island displayed another elaborate toy, this one a very detailed replica of a Ferrari. The kid Ferrari had headlights, brakes, a horn, two speeds forward, one reverse, independent rear suspension, a genuine Momo Italian steering wheel, bright chromed spoke wheels, and Pirelli tires. It was another expensive toy retailing for more than $2,500. I decided not to sell it and to give it to my two children, Louis and Susan. Louis was about six years old at the time and Susan was four.

Louis would drive it with Susan sitting beside him as a passenger, and generally I kept them to a very close perimeter around the house. But, one time they strayed off about a block or so and caught the attention of a passing North Providence police car who told them to drive the car back to the house and stop in the drive-way. I have pictures of Louis and Susan in their little toy car, four years old and six years old, in our driveway with the police car behind them.

The cop turned out to be a patrolman named Richard Torselli and we became friends almost immediately. Our friendship lasted more than 40 years. Although I haven't seen him in a few years, I'm sure we would both be happy to see each other. I guess it's just that we're both very busy and our paths haven't crossed in recent times. When he finally retired from the North Providence Police Force, he was a captain and took a job as a security officer with Citizens Bank in their head-quarters in East Providence.

Working for me when the store opened was a widow named Teresa Barone, sister to the infamous Dr. Felix Barone. Barone was a heart surgeon who was charged, convicted, and served a five-year prison term for implanting pacemakers in people who didn't need them in order to get kickbacks from the pacemaker's manufacturer and to bilk Blue Cross and other insurance companies out of hun-dreds of thousands of dollars in a short period of time.

Teresa was a nice woman, overweight, and much older than I was. She was constantly embarrassing me by making passes at me and would love to confront me at the end of a row of showcases where I had no way to avoid her. She would remove her shoes and I still remember her strong foot odor. I didn't want to hurt her feelings but, boy, did her feet smell. Her daughter worked for me for a short time and was even worse than her mother. I wasn't at the store too many hours a day, and many days I never went at all. But, thinking back, some of Vincent's instincts must have rubbed off on me.

I remember one incident during which I was out of town for a couple of days, and when I returned to the store, I asked Teresa how it was going. She was so proud to say that she had made three or four sales, all to the same person, a nice young man. She said the man loved the store and kept coming back pondering the purchase of different items, leaving, then returning to succumb to his desire to purchase them.

I don't know why I was suspicious, but I immediately asked how he paid for the items. She said by checks drawn on a local bank. I asked to see them. The minute I saw the checks, I knew the sales were a phony, and the checks were no good. I asked Theresa if she had called the banks to see if the checks were good, and she said she had not. She said the guy was very honest looking, and that she believed he was OK. I said I'll bet you a hundred bucks these checks are phonies. She said she wouldn't take the bet because she couldn't afford to lose any money if she lost, but insisted that I was wrong. I immediately called the bank to learn that the account they were drawn against had been closed a couple of years earlier. They were useless. Teresa was genuinely surprised. She asked how I could know at such a fast glance that they were worthless, and I didn't have an answer. I just knew they were.

The checks totaled about a thousand dollars, not a lot of money, but I was a wise guy and didn't like being fucked. So I asked her some questions about the guy, and she described him. It was no one I knew. The address on the checks was a dead end, and I wrote the thousand dollars off as a bad deal. I told Teresa not to feel too badly about this, that the guy was just a small time con man, and she shouldn't be too upset. I could see how much it was bothering her.

Then, one day, about two weeks later, I was upstairs in my office, and Teresa shouted for me to come downstairs immediately.

She said, " Lou, that's him, the guy who gave me the bad checks."

I said, "Theresa are you sure, really, really sure?"

"Yes," she repeated, "positive."

Boy, did I get a kick out of that. I followed him around the mall, while he went in and out of several stores but didn't purchase anything, telling the clerks the same story that he would think about it, and maybe come back. Since we had never met, the guy had no idea I was following him. I waited until he left the mall, and followed him right to his car.

When he put his hand on the door handle, I hit him with a punch with all my might in his right kidney. He dropped to the ground and was screaming in pain. I told him to shut up or I'd hit him again. He had tears rolling down his face. I told him I owned the store where he purchased a grand worth of items with his lousy checks and to give me my money or I'd beat the shit out of him.

He had no money on him. I searched all of his pockets. I took his driver's license, and said let's go. The address wasn't too far from the store. He said he had no money at home either, at which point I got furious.

"You son of a bitch, I want my goddamn money now," and smacked him across the face, giving him an instant bloody nose. He started to cry and said we could go to his mother's house, and she would give me the money. I said, "If you have any funny stuff in mind, you're fucking with the wrong guy."

If I didn't get my money, I'd beat him to a pulp.

He said, "No, no, I'll get the money from her." We got in my car, and I began driving. A short while later, we arrived at a nice little house in Warwick, and he said it was his mother's house. I asked him where his father was and he replied his father was dead.

I rang the doorbell with my left hand while holding his ear with my right hand, twisting it to the point where he couldn't keep his head straight. He was hurting. A nice woman, maybe 60 years old who could have been anyone's mother, came to the door. She knew immediately what was going down.

"He owes me money," I said, "and he told me you'd pay it. It's a thousand dollars. If you don't have it, I'll leave right now."

"No, no," she screamed." I'll get it right away."

I told the asshole that if his mother calls the cops, he'd be one dead asshole. This was obviously not the first time she had bailed him out of trouble, I thought, as she handed me the money.

"Thank you," I said and left them both.

When Teresa finally left working for me, I felt relieved. Then Vincent asked me to give his wife Tina a job. I was overjoyed because she was a nice person, looked good, dressed sharp and was just fun to be around and I had socialized with her and Vincent at the JCC many times and we got along very well. And, there would be no more passes like from Teresa.

I loved having Tina working at La Fantasia. The store itself never did much business and we would laugh every Monday morning when the rug near the front gate was loaded with popcorn. It was like a zoo we used to say, with all the visitors throwing food at the animals.

Customers used to come in and instead of looking at the merchandise would ask questions about the rugs, they were so plush and so colorful. I felt like I should have been selling fucking rugs instead of jewelry and gifts. But, that wasn't important to me. I had other sources of income to support the store and the store gave me legitimacy.

I was connected with so many sources for swag diamonds that at any one time it was possible for me to fill the top of the desk in my office with diamonds. I even had a guy who worked downstairs, for Cogen's Printers, whose boyfriend worked for a large diamond company and was robbing eight to ten carats of the highest quality diamonds every week. I paid $1 a point for stuff that would cost $6 a point or more, wholesale. He robbed that company for two years before it ended.

I had hundreds of diamonds passing through my hands each week. I didn't mind kicking in a couple of thousand dollars a month to keep the storefront, and Tina worked alone most of the time and was so dependable that some days I never went to the store. I was making money everywhere but at the store. One day, while Vincent and I were talking, he asked me how much Tina was robbing from me at the store. I was shocked he would ask something like that, and I asked him what he meant.

He said, "Lou, Tina's a kleptomaniac, she loves to steal things. Let her steal from you but don't let her pull the plug on the store. Keep it to a minimum and you'll be okay."

He had told me a year or more earlier that Tina liked to take things but now he was telling me right out that she would take things from anybody, including me. But, with his sense of humor, I thought he might be kidding. I asked him if I should say anything about it especially since I hadn't noticed anything missing, but then the store really wasn't much of a priority to me so I probably wouldn't have noticed if almost everything was gone.

Vincent laughed and said just to tell her if she wants anything she could have it. "She'll take it anyway so what's the difference?"

This bothered me a little, so I had built a little diamond cage, as I refer to it, which was a small secured area within the store and whose entrance was protected by a lock which required a key each time you entered it. If someone wanted to buy a diamond or another expensive piece of jewelry, I could take them into that room and show them items in private. Tina was not knowledgeable about diamonds or precious stones and she didn't have a key to enter that area. If someone showed interest, I told her to take their name and phone number and I would call them back and make an appointment. This went over very well and I felt Tina could take the rest of the store for all I cared.

Chapter 5
Breaking The Lease

I was making frequent trips to Italy during this time. I would attend many trade shows in Milano and Florence, as well as travel throughout Italy looking for items for my store.

My driver, Carlo Panzironi, had a run-down Fiat and was just getting started in the business of chauffeuring people around Italy, mostly Rome. He needed business and he took me wherever I wanted to go, waited for me and in many cases stayed overnight while I conducted my business. He couldn't speak a word of English, but I had a private tutor from Berlitz teach me enough Italian for me to get around quite well. The trips were lengthy because in those days to get a decent price on airfare you had to stay a minimum of 21 days. The longer you stayed, the cheaper the ticket price would be. But, usually a flight on Al Italia would cost about $650. Carlo was a fun kid who made the 21 days so enjoyable they would pass quickly.

I called him a kid but he was only a couple of years younger than me and was full of jokes. One time we passed the red light district in Rome. I told him to stop the car so I could watch the girls while they hustled their customers, and he shouted, "No!"

He said, "E multo pericoloso" and then "chi sono tutti homini," which meant that it was very dangerous to do that because *they were all men dressed in drag* and if they thought you were making fun of them, you could be in for some serious trouble.

One day, while driving on the Autostrada, I asked him if he knew of any cars for sale, Ferraris especially, because I was interested in purchasing a sports car for myself. He knew so many people I figured it was almost impossible he wouldn't know somebody. It turns out that he knew not only of dealers selling Ferraris, but also he knew some private people who had Ferraris for sale. I decided to take a look at some of them.

After looking at a few cars, I finally bought a beautiful blue Ferrari Dino. This was a tiny little car, absolutely gorgeous, with a six cylinder motor, tuned and modified by Ferrari. It was so beautiful to look at it was captivating. The name Dino was a tribute to Enzo Ferrari's son whose name was Dino and who died at a very young age.

I brought the car back to the United States and drove it every day for months.

Before one of my subsequent trips to Italy, I sold the Dino at a $1,500 profit. I had bought a Ferrari, drove it, had fun with it, used it as a toy and still made a profit. I began to think maybe I was on to something here.

During my next trip to Italy I concentrated more on finding exotic cars than finding items for the store. I purchased three beautiful Ferraris: a yellow Dino, a silver 365 GT 2+2, and a red 275 GTB-2, the long nosed model.

I had three Ferraris parked in my driveway. Believe it or not, one of my fucking neighbors, an elderly doctor named Sammartino — who was known to be a real whiner and complainer — filed a complaint against me. Can you imagine filing a complaint against somebody that has three Ferraris parked in his driveway? The guy was so bugged that he tried to get me some trouble, but nothing came of it.

Accidentally, I had found something very lucrative. I didn't want the store anymore. This was fun, profitable, and without any overhead. What a nice combination. I continued to carry the store financially until one day, somewhere around mid 1971, I decided I had enough. It was nothing but problems.

I had to figure how to get out of the lease I had signed with the Homart Development Corporation and to close the store. I had lots of contacts in the jewelry business, both with buyers and sellers. And I needed an out. My accountant was so stupid that he said to me, "What you need is a flood." I said, "What the fuck would a flood do? What I need is a robbery, not a flood." What a fucking idiot.

A robbery would be a very difficult task as the store was across the corridor from the Roger Williams Savings Bank which had security both inside and outside their premises. Also, there was an armed guard who patrolled the mall all night until it opened the following morning. In addition, my store was very highly alarmed. It was going to take some very precise and talented mechanics, as they are sometimes referred to, to pull this off.

I discussed the situation with Vincent to get his point of view. "This is going to be difficult but possible," he said.

It would require an alarm specialist, a strong worker to do the sawing and other heavy work — similar to a laborer on a construction project — and also a very good safe cracker. The important items from the store were placed in the safe at night.

The alarm man would have to be in and out of the mall's various stores to check service doors, exits, air conditioning ducts, stairways and every square inch of that mall. Vincent picked a guy whom I didn't know and then said he would like the laborer to be an aging hitman who had 17 hits to his credit. The aging hit man was Bobbie Almondi, who was going broke and maybe had some loose marbles.

I questioned Vincent's judgment about using someone that was going bad to be part of such a sophisticated operation. Vincent assured me that Bobby would be able to follow orders and would be needed only for manual work which he would be perfect for, and that he could keep his mouth shut.

We would save the delicate skills for the other members of our crew. I respected Vincent's desire to help his down-and-out friend. Hey, I trusted Vincent and agreed to use the old guy, but was very insistent that he didn't make a single move unless told to do so by me. This was a big score and I didn't want anyone to fuck it up.

The alarm mechanic was a good fit for the job and would perform his magic in very short order — with the help of Bobby doing the heavy part of the work. Everyone was selected, briefed, and the job was to proceed except for one little hitch.

The alarm expert wanted to know who we had on the inside. A job like this usually required someone who worked in the mall and could provide plans and blueprints of the construction of the mall and could move around, point out things such as the guards' habits, both during the day as well as night, how much time it would take for the security guard to go from one end of the mall to the other, and whether his pattern was dependable. Was he armed? How much resistance would he show if confronted with a dangerous situation and told to remain still and silent? Did he smoke? There were so many questions that I needed to have answered. Since we had no one on the inside, it was up to me to provide as much information as I could. The answers were generally passed to Vincent and he would pass them along to the person who had asked them in the first place.

I provided all the information I could, but, obviously I didn't know everything he needed answers to. I told him I would stay late for a few nights and see what I could learn.

The first thing I found out was that the bank across the way closed earlier than the stores in the mall did. They were required to close by 8 p.m. due to banking regulations. They had no security personnel of their own at night. I gathered a lot of information from the bank's manager, a young woman with whom I sometimes had lunch at the mall. It appeared that the bank would not be a problem. They had elaborate security within their premises but it ended there.

The next thing was the security guard. He was a short, slim, stupid man who reminded me of Barney Fyfe from the Andy Griffith Show. I don't think he knew which end of a gun to point at a burglar. As far as resistance, he was a lazy asshole and wouldn't go out of his way to risk his own life. I'm sure, if confronted with a dangerous situation he would have shit his pants at the first sign of trouble. As the days unfolded, the job looked more and more feasible.

The alarm expert had been in and out the mall many times throughout the week and knew a great deal about the security at Midland Mall. He needed to see my upstairs where all the alarm controls were located. I was there when it was wired and alarmed, so

I told Vincent I would agree to show his friend around. He agreed to come by the store at a preset time and I would take him to see whatever he needed to see to do his work. I was now involved much deeper than I thought I would be but the plan was in motion and I wanted it to continue. This was going to be a real live performance and I was needed as a player. Oh sure, I was concerned about being caught but that was not strong enough to call it off. It would happen as we had planned.

After meeting with the guy, I was sure Vincent had made the right choice. We never introduced ourselves to each other. He didn't ask my name and I didn't ask his. This was strictly business for us. When we were upstairs, the only remark he made was that all the power coming into the mall to supply each one of its stores passed right on the other side on my upstairs office wall. It was a major plus, he said, but I heard him mumbling to himself that the mother-fucking safe was about two inches in the way of a major conduit carrying all of this power and would make the job much more difficult.

The conduit was about 15 inches in diameter. One slip up in cutting this and moving it to get in could mean instant death. He needed to get a look at the other side of the wall and would have to come back with some special equipment.

The following day he returned with a keyhole saw which he had altered to cut on the backstroke instead of the normal forward cutting saw blade stroke. The reason for this was immediately obvious to me. He wanted to cut a hole in the wall but also wanted it to appear as if the wall had been cut from the other side. He wanted the debris from the cut to fall on the inside. He was a very skilled operator indeed. He cut a hole only a foot or so long, where the bottom of the wall met the floor.

Later, the hole would have to be a much larger, either square or rectangle, and that would require a continuation of the cut that he had just made. He gently pried the wall and inserted a folding inspection mirror, through a 1-by-3-inch hole inside the cut. He looked at the other side of the wall, especially at the conduit. It was exactly what he had expected. The other side was wide, long and easily accessible. It was an actual service room and once he found out where it led to, the job would be much easier for him. The fucking conduit, however, would be a problem.

The safe had been in its present position for about two years and it was wired for that exact spot. It certainly wouldn't be possible for me to call the alarm company that had installed the security system and have it moved and rewired to another location. The only alternative was to cut the conduit and hope he could move it about two inches. It was real fucking risky. Still, there was no other way around it. Bobby would cut the wall and he would then cut the conduit very carefully. Since the conduit was long — going from the first floor to the second floor and even a little beyond — he felt there might be enough play once cut to get the necessary two inches for the safe's clearance.

The day of the burglary came and it was a fucking disaster.

First, the bank's door was not securely locked. It was about an eighth of an inch open and even though the alarm indicated that it was safe and secure, the door was not properly secured. When everybody left the mall, maybe a couple of people brushed against the door. It moved another eighth of an inch or more and that was just enough to sound the alarm. Now the alarm went off inside the bank and the bank's security guards were in the bank within minutes. A security guard was placed outside the front door of the bank and was probably going to spend the night there or at least until the manager came in and secured the door properly before leaving.

That was only the first part of the disaster. The second part was that Vincent wanted to come along. I have no idea why. Maybe Vincent thought that it was one last fling. With this, I felt an obligation. I couldn't let him go alone. I didn't want him there in the first place but certainly didn't want him there without me.

So now the crew is Bobby, who would be the laborer to cut the wall, and remove the safe from the building, the alarm mechanic who felt removing the safe was much easier than opening it there, me, and Uncle Vincent. The plan was changed and eliminated the safe cracker coming along . The safe would actually be brought to him to be opened in another location.

All three mechanics' share of the score totaled $5,000, which was placed in an envelope and was locked inside the safe. So now the crew was one man less with only Bobby and the alarm expert, Vincent, and me.

Bobby's job was to finish cutting the wall, cut the conduit, and remove the safe from the building. The conduit cut much easier than I thought but, it still needed to be moved about two inches to the left in order for the safe to slide out of there and into the next room. Bobby got a bright idea to open the safe without moving it. He was going to use a sledgehammer and a chisel to attempt to open the safe. I grabbed him immediately and told him to put the fucking sledgehammer down. The fucking moron would wake up all Warwick if he had his way.

The alarm specialist took the chisel that Bobby was holding and tried to force it into the cut Bobby had made in the conduit. It moved a little bit and by now, he had a bite on it and forced it with all his might.

With all this is going on, we didn't know if there were still guards in front of the bank, so silence here was an absolute must. But the conduit moved more than it was supposed to and I could see it putting pressure on the insulation of the wires running through it. Breaking that insulation would, at minimum, cause a flash fire and sound alarms all over the mall.

The weight and pressure of the conduit's edge was pushing hard into the wire, but it looked as if we would get away with it. The insulation on the wire was holding up. If nothing pierced it, then we had successfully cut the conduit and moved it more than two inches.

The next move was Bobby's. He was still pissed that I hadn't let him slam a chisel in the safe's door, but he got his dolly with rubber casters and placed the safe on it. He had no problem placing the safe onto the dolly and wheeling it from the room. He and the alarm mechanic disappeared shortly after that and Vincent and I were now alone. It was about 2 a.m. and it had been a long and stressful day. We both had a second wind and decided to sit back awhile.

The mall was dead quiet. Fifteen minutes had passed since the two men had left and we heard no sirens. We figured they had pulled it off and that they were well on their way. We smiled at each other and relaxed.

Then I got curious to see what the other side of the wall was like. I peeked in and saw a small service room with tools, electric wires, fuses, switches and everything necessary to do electrical work. It was a service area for the electrical requirements of the mall. I told Vincent to take a look. I wanted him to see something.

It was a poster from the Department of Education. It said someone who drops out of high school will earn approximately $240,000 in their entire lifetime, while someone with a high school diploma would earn approximately $320,000 in his lifetime. The poster was urging kids not to drop out of school and those that did drop out of school to go back and get their high school diploma. I remarked to Vincent that we had just made more money in the last couple of hours than two high school graduates did in their entire lives.

Vincent laughed and we decided to sit on the floor and goof on the poster for a while and light up a Muratti Ariston. We were very careful while we were smoking our cigarettes to put all the ashes in our pocket. When we finished smoking, we put the butts in our pockets. A Muratti butt in that office would have been disaster.

We decided it was time to leave when the chilling thought hit us. Suppose the guards were still in front of the bank. We couldn't take a chance because even if there was no one there, the mall's doors might be locked, or worse, even alarmed. We sat down again and decided to smoke another Muratti while we pondered what to do. We had never planned exactly how we were going to leave the mall.

I went back into the other room and ventured further to find the staircase. It was a short walk and led straight out to the parking lot. It was a real simple move to get out.

Our rented car was parked about a block away from the building where I had noticed cars remained parked all night. Maybe some of the mall employees met for a romantic evening and took a car to a motel or something and left one of their cars there. But, at any rate, a car parked there late at night or all night for that matter, would not have alerted any patrol cars that may pass by, if they even had cars patrolling the mall premises at night.

We had a way out and I went back to get Vincent and leave. When I squeezed through the hole I brushed the conduit gently. Nothing happened. I don't know what made me do what I did next but I pushed harder on the conduit just to see how secure it actually was and how heavy it was with my left hand and in a millionth of a second there was a blinding flash as a burr from the conduit pierced the insulation. Thousands of volts and amps melted the conduit instantly. I was thrown five or six feet back to the floor with a piece of my left small finger and fingernail missing. It was bleeding profusely. When I looked, I saw that even the next finger was split wide open and was also bleeding.

Both fingers were black. I felt I was lucky to be alive. Vincent wrapped my fingers with a clean handkerchief and asked me how I felt. I replied, "Fuckin' lucky."

"Don't worry," he said, "We'll call big Al when we get back on the road and meet him at his office."

Al Picolli was a dentist who had his practice on Mineral Spring Avenue in North Providence. He also did work at the ACI and was a dentist for Raymond when he was incarcerated there. He was a friend to all of us. He was also my next door neighbor.

But first we had a new job. We had to go searching for the parts of my finger and my fingernail and any blood that was splattered on the floor and even look at the fucking conduit that had caused all of this. We were both uneasy but we had to go back through the opening again to the other side and see what was in that office that we could use to accomplish this task. What we found was some orange shop rags and a gallon of lacquer thinner. We went right back into my office. There we were, two grown men on our hands and knees talking to each other while we're wiping up blood with lacquer thinner and searching for body parts.

I was able to find my fingernail almost immediately but that was about all that was left. I told Vincent to stay away from the conduit because it wasn't worth the risk of disturbing it again. Anything that was on that conduit was burnt well beyond any recognition and there wouldn't be of any use as evidence, that's for sure.

Half an hour later, we were quite sure that no evidence from my accident was left and took the rags with us, leaving the lacquer thinner.

There was a strong smell of burnt electrical wires throughout the whole office.

I was quite sure that it was only a small burr that had penetrated the conduit. If it had been anything more than that, the entire mall would have been without power, several of the alarms would have been set off in the mall and the flash, of course, would have been much worse. I was lucky to be alive.

The walk down the stairs was very short and it led to a heavy metal door. We were in the parking lot in a matter of a minute or so. When we were several blocks away we stopped to call Big Al at his house and told him to meet us at his office.

When he removed the handkerchief he said I was lucky that I didn't lose both my fingers. He numbed everything up, stitched up my fingers ,and bandaged them and never asked what we had done. The bandage and stitches he placed on my two fingers were obviously professionally done and there was also a burn on the top of my left hand on which he just placed a gauze bandage, telling me to change it tomorrow.

We were done for the night. It was after 4:30 a.m. and we left for home. It was going to be another long day.

As I was opening the shop the next day, I met Tina and we both went through the front door just about the same time. She noticed immediately that I had a bandage on my hand and asked what had happened. I told her I had a flat tire and I jacked up my car to change it and the jack slipped cutting my fingers and scraping the top of my hand.

I said, "It looks worse than it is Tina, don't worry about it."

Soon, I went upstairs where I discovered that the store had been burglarized. I told Tina to call the police and the mall security immediately. Both numbers were on labels on the phone.

Tina came upstairs first and was shocked. She called security the minute she saw the damage that had been caused upstairs. The security guard arrived quickly. It was the Barney Fyfe look-alike that I had met before. He looked around upstairs then said, "Let's go to my office, file a report for Homart, and wait for the police."

Walking to his office he was quick to say that he wasn't on duty last night or that this would never have happened. He said it looked very professional to him and made a statement that almost broke me out in laughter.

He said, "You know guys that do this kind of thing get their jollies off by watching people's reactions and I'm sure he's watching us now." He likened it to an arsonist who likes to watch a fire that he had set.

I said, "You're probably right."

I filled out an incident report, then met with the Warwick police. They asked a few questions but were anxious to finish and leave. There wasn't any evidence or any clues. They said that the job was done very professionally.

So far, no one asked me a single word about my hand or the bandages on my fingers.

Shortly thereafter, the FBI came into the store. I expected them. I never liked the FBI because they were pushy sons of bitches and they were rude and ignorant publicity seekers who were as crooked as the fucking people they put in prison. They said that this job would require at least three people and that of the three people one of them was fried to death. They were positive that one of them was dead.

By now, the mall's repair crew was ready to examine and repair the wiring and the conduit, which required the power be turned off in the mall. The FBI held back the repair work for about an hour while they examined the conduit, walls, floors and the whole scene. And while all this was happening, one agent stayed behind talking to me about what was taken, how much it was worth, if it was insured and lots of other questions that you would expect the FBI to ask you.

I lit up a Muratti and made it a point to smoke it with my left hand. I flashed the bandages right under his fucking pointed nose and he never asked me what caused me to be bandaged up. I'm sure he thought I had a part in the burglary but knew I wasn't going to say anything and he didn't push me any further. They stayed most of the day, then left and said, "We'll be in touch,", as if that was some kind of a threat.

I said, "Thanks. Get my stuff back as soon as possible, will you, and catch these guys."

A couple of days later, a safe was found in a lot on Cranston Street, a run-down area in Providence. I was called by the FBI to come in and identify it. It had been opened. It was empty. I identified the safe, said it was mine and left. The next day I called my diamond suppliers to inform them of the robbery. I told them I would come to New York in a couple of days and said, "Don't worry, I have an idea."

When I went to New York, I visited all the dealers whose diamonds had been stolen. Since they were my property, as I had purchased them on a series of notes, they were not covered by their insurance.

The solution was simple. "Fill out and back date by a couple of days a memo slip which I'll sign saying I received diamonds for inspection but the title remained with the diamond dealer." The memo clearly stated the property belonged to the dealer and generally was for a short period, usually five to ten days at the most.

If a customer wanted to see three or four stones, the dealer would send them out on memo and the store would show the stones to the customer. If the customer purchased one, the remaining stones would be returned to the dealer and the stones that the store kept would be billed to the store.

Memos are generally reserved for only diamonds and other precious stone dealers covered by insurance. If the dealer had a large deductible, say $5,000 or so on his memo insurance, then we would increase the amount of the phony memo slip for that amount. In some cases, some of the greedier fucking dealers even wanted to make a profit off of the memo and push the prices up another $10,000 or more. So what the fuck did I care. I wasn't going to pay for anything anyway.

The dealer would recoup all his money — not in a series of notes but all at one shot and make a profit at the same time. This worked great for the dealers, but the problem was this type of insurance is so high risk, that only one company would take these risks. That company was called Surplus Lines Incorporated, and company policies were placed with the London Group, Lloyds of London. In the most legitimate of losses that they incurred, there were notoriously slow payers. They couldn't refuse to pay the diamond dealers as the diamond dealers were a powerful group and their business was a large part of Lloyd's business in this field. So even if they thought I set this burglary up, it didn't affect the diamond dealers. They were just innocent victims.

They collected, but then Lloyd's began looking at me. They followed me, investigated me, investigated my background, and considered what to do about what they felt was a set-up job. Still, their hands were tied as the police and the FBI could never find any evidence implicating me as a participant in my robbery. Lloyd's could do nothing about it but pay for the loss.

But that wasn't the same as my insurance company. They had issued me a policy for only $80,000 but somewhere in the fine print, they took away most of the coverage.

I didn't really give a shit as I had so many diamonds and a ready buyer, my friend Leo Lister from International Diamond Distributors. His company was one of only 21 site holders in the DeBeer's Mining Corporation, a South African diamond company which at the time was the supplier of 80 percent of the world's diamond gemstones through their wholly owned subsidiary, the Diamond Trading Company. They controlled and manipulated the diamond market. A site holder had to purchase an amount of diamonds allotted to him in its totality or he would lose his status as a site holder. It was up to the site holder to distribute what he didn't want or need to other diamond dealers and diamond cutters. If prices went too low on diamonds, the Diamond Trading Company allotted smaller packages to their site holders, thereby buoying up prices. If they thought prices were getting too high, they would reverse the strategy and allot larger packages to site holders, thereby increasing the supply and keeping prices from climbing higher than they wanted them to. They were an exclusive monopoly and could manipulate the entire world's market of diamonds as they saw fit.

Leo was my very close friend and throughout the years, we did millions of dollars of business together with never a disagreement. I had no reservations about flying to New York City and leaving him with two or three hundred thousand dollars in diamonds and either getting paid that day or going home if he didn't have the cash on hand, returning a day or two later to get paid.

I took the businessman's flight at 10 a.m. and was back in Rhode Island by 3 p.m. What could be easier than that?

But, as I said, my insurance company refused to pay on a bullshit technicality, so I hired a law firm by the name of Devcof and Silverstein. I wound up with a young junior partner in the company named Max Winston who would handle my case with Lenny Devcof, consulting with him from time to time. It was going to be necessary for us to sue the insurance company to collect. Max and I later became friends and remain so today. Now he has his own law firm, the prestigious Winston and Barylich which is located in downtown Providence.

Money was not the issue in the lawsuit. I was going to place the store in bankruptcy to get out of my lease with Homart Development Corporation. Once I did that, any money collected from the lawsuit would go to the store's creditors. Of course, I was one of the store's largest creditors along with the diamond dealers, but by the time the lawyers got done with their fees, the court fees, the transcription fees, and the bankruptcy fees and everything else was paid, there probably wouldn't be more than $17 left over.

When I told Leo of my plans to go after the insurance company he smiled. He said, "Go after them motherfuckers tooth and nail." I certainly did. Two and a half years later, after a very spectacular two-week trial that made legal history in Rhode Island law books, I prevailed and was awarded $101,100.

The *Providence Journal* ran the news several days in a row and law students from various Rhode Island colleges sat in on the trial every single day. It was me and Max, two young kids against eight old, white-haired insurance company lawyers.

Once for effect, upon entering the courtroom, Max's shabby briefcase fell apart and work notes and documents flew all over the floor. The jury loved us and one old lady had an obvious affection for Max. She had a cough and Max would order the court to give her a glass of water. Max was very smart, quick on his feet, humble but had a way of pounding a witness so badly that at one time it looked as if he may have been pounding him more than he should have. He asked me from where I was sitting, how it looked to me. I told him that I felt that one of the qualities that makes someone a good artist is knowing when to put the brush down. I felt it was time for him to put the brush down now and that if he kept punishing the witness any further the jury would start feeling sorry for him. Max agreed and moved on to the next victim. He was ruthless in a polite way and we turned out to be a real great team.

Chapter 6
Mona Lisa Jewelry

The store closed. For the first time in years, I had some breathing room.

I slowed the pace down and worked on my Ferraris in my garage at home. The world was my oyster. Between the diamonds that I already had, and the few hundred thousand dollars that I purchased of swag stuff, I was in real fine shape.

Through mutual contacts, my exploits caught the attention of an Italian jeweler named Antonio Colomonici. Colomonici owned an upscale jewelry store on the Via Veneto in Rome, which was called Mona Lisa Jewelry. He was a flamboyant character, handsome at age 55 with pure white hair, a $2,000 hand-made suit, a $300 shirt, $700 alligator shoes, and a collection of beautiful women all the time. He later traveled the world with his red Ferrari Testarossa with three or four completely naked women draped over the automobile. The women were beautiful to look at but I felt bad for the car.

He had great connections in Italy and one of them had asked that he reach out for me to go to Italy to discuss some business. He also had requested certain diamonds of specific sizes and qualities that I bring along. In December 1971, I decided to take Ann with me. This was the first trip that she had ever made to Italy. Usually Ann liked staying home when I went away as she could remodel the house without my interference or keeping track of the money.

At this time of my life, I always had $15,000 or even up to $25,000 in cash in my pocket at any given time. If I was asked how much money I had on me, I would never know. But, I had the feeling Ann was taking money from stashes. So, one night I decided to actually count my money and write it down on a piece of paper. I was in my pajamas and my pants were in our bedroom. I had $20,800 exactly. The next morning I counted my money again — $18,800. I must have counted wrong the night before, I said to myself. $2,000 was an even amount and easy enough for me to mistake and certainly she wouldn't take that much money. So, I did the same thing the next night, counted my money. Next morning, an even $1,000 was missing. I had to learn to count better, I thought, or perhaps I wrote the wrong amount on paper again.

On one trip back from Italy, I stayed far beyond the normal 21 days, perhaps three weeks beyond, because there was a strike on the docks in Livorno, a shipping port near Pisa that I used frequently. I was worried about leaving the cars without the proper shipping documents. When the strike finally ended, I arrived home and found the house was completely remodeled with all new furniture. I told her I liked the furniture and asked how much it cost.

"Well," she answered, "The dining room set was on sale and I got it for $6,000."

I asked, "What, that cost $6,000?"

"Oh, no," she said, "that didn't cost $6,000, just the table and chairs cost $6,000. The other pieces were extra ...You fucking jerk, I robbed you every night for weeks. How many other people are robbing you and you don't even know it?"

I laughed like hell. God, I loved her balls. Robbing me, then telling me I was a jerk. But I felt if my wife couldn't rob me, then who in the world could? It turned me on so much I couldn't get enough of her.

We left for Italy and when we arrived, my driver Carlo Panzoroni picked us up at the airport and took us to our hotel in Rome. The next day Carlo took me to look at some Ferraris and I purchased four. I made plans to ship three as soon as possible and then got all the paperwork, title and insurance for one of them since I wanted to drive it throughout Italy with Ann. By now, Carlo was driving a brand new Mercedes Benz diesel and had several drivers who worked for him. He had met and was dating a Japanese girl who ran tours through Italy and she steered so much business towards Carlo that he was now making a fortune. He still would drive for me for many years to come but only because I asked him. When he knew I was going somewhere for something that was illegal, he would make sure that he was the driver. Carlo knew that I had some very powerful connections in Italy and respected me throughout all the years that we knew each other. Even with his own business to run, he always had time for me.

Ann was only interested in shopping. Italy's historic buildings, statues, and bridges meant nothing to her. Just a lot of dirty stones and bricks.

Our first stop in Italy was to Gucci near the Via Veneto. Then, to all the shops and boutiques in Italy. I think we saw and visited every goddamn one of them.

The next day, I had an appointment to visit with Antonio Colomonici in his store, Mona Lisa Jewelry, and Ann came along. Antonio Colomonaci was not only a colorful character in his jewelry business but also a colorful character in his life.

One of the newspapers in Italy stated that he had the largest robbery that ever took place in Rome. The thing that made it so unusual besides the fact that there was so much jewelry and money taken was how the robbery took place. It was accomplished by masked gunmen riding horses down the Via Veneto with machine guns in their hands, stopping in his shop which was just off the Via, holding up the place and then getting away with the horses running down the Via Veneto and onto several side streets. It was impossible for the cops to catch them and they slipped away easily.

Colomonaci was a great character and I remember him very well. He was also a gentleman. Antonio absolutely loved Ann and kept repeating, "Prima Classa, Prima Classa," which means first class. He had jewelry, pearls, emeralds, sapphires, and diamonds. Enough to satisfy anyone's taste.

But first, business. Antonio and I went into his private office. There were pictures everywhere of beautiful girls with see-through lingerie adorning the walls. It was very distracting to say the least. He told me that he wanted me to meet people, connected people who wanted to purchase some swag diamonds of high quality. They had rich buyers throughout Europe and we could all profit from this business deal. A call was made and an appointment was set up for the next day in the afternoon in a store not very far from the Via Veneto. I agreed to return the next day alone and he said, "No, bring Ann, prima classa. She can remain in my store while I go on my appointment."

"Okay," I said, "I'll see you tomorrow."

We went back into the store and Ann was looking at every piece of jewelry in there. His prices would choke a horse they were so high. I was used to paying almost nothing for what I bought so they probably seemed even higher to me than they actually were. We left the store and spent the rest of the day visiting more shops.

The next day I told her I had an appointment near Antonio's store and she could wait for me at the hotel. She didn't like that idea and insisted on coming on the meeting with me. I told her I didn't think that was a good idea. I knew that we were visiting some wise guys and I thought she was better off at Antonio's store or remaining at the hotel.

"No," she insisted. "I want to come along." She had balls, that's for sure.

While I had a Ferrari Dino to use, so far we had only used Carlo as our driver. First to Antonio's where we made a call to confirm we were on our way. He would not be coming with us. He also informed them that Ann would be accompanying me there. When we arrived at our destination, it was a small store on a side street just a few blocks away from Antonio's store. It was about 11 a.m. Carlo waited outside in his Mercedes.

The minute we entered the store, we were shuffled into a small office, and up a flight of stairs. There was an adjoining office and the door was open between the two. We could see characters coming and going and I knew we were in a very active scene with lots of things happening and going on. If I didn't trust the guy who OK'd Antonio and his friends, I would have left immediately. I had Ann with me and I didn't like her being in there.

A very polite man, who was obviously a boss there, greeted us as we sat around a large mahogany conference table. He spoke English quite well and asked if we would like something to eat or drink. I ordered an espresso and Ann refused anything. He asked me if I had brought the diamonds with me from the United States and I replied, yes, I had.

He said, "Do you have them on you?" I said, "Yes, I do." He asked to see them. I reached into my pocket and pulled out a diamond pouch and put it on the table. The contents of each diamond envelope were marked on the outside of the size #1 blue lined diamond paper. They were all 2 carats and up — mostly brilliant cuts, which are round with one or two pear-shaped stones in the lot. All diamonds were at least VVS- 1 quality, and E color or better. The man opened each and every envelope, then placed on top of each of the papers a thin, folding, square chrome metal piece to keep the diamond envelopes open and the diamond on top of the paper so he could identify it.

The stones are all in clear view now and with the Bausch and Lomb 10 power loop and a small color corrective diamond lamp, he held each piece in his tweezers and looked at them as if he were a kid in a candy store.

"Buono, buono, molto buono. Belissimo, buono, buono," he kept repeating. He loved them and wasn't afraid to show it.

"How much for the whole lot?" he asked.

I said, $300,000." He answered, "Too much, $250,000."

I said, "No, not enough." We finally agreed on splitting the difference at $275,000.

I wanted cash. He said to wait a few minutes and left the room. This was decision time now. Take the stones and get the hell out of there or wait to see if he returns with the money. I kept reasoning that my friends would never put me in a situation like this, unsafe for me and now even for Ann, but I could see the action still going on in the next room and I really didn't think this place was capable of purchasing $275,000 worth of goods.

After what seemed like an eternity but was probably only a few minutes, the man returned with several stacks of money bound by elastics. They were all hundred dollar bills. He handed them to me. The first thing I did was examine a couple of the bills to see that they weren't counterfeit. The fucking money was real. Ann grabbed the money from me and began counting it. I had dealt with deals like this so many times before I knew what $275,000 in hundred dollar bills looked like. I told her to stop counting and just fan the bills to make sure they were all hundreds. She did so. They were all hundreds and I was sure that the count was correct. She stashed the money, my money, in her fucking Gucci pocketbook and within minutes we were back in Antonio's store on the Via Veneto, only this time with $275,000 in cash. I began thinking if I had taken them to Leo in New York I would have gotten $50,000 less. At least $50,000 less.

But this fucking trip was probably going to cost me more than the fucking $50,000 I would have lost with Leo because I needed to pay tribute to Antonio who set this whole thing up. I told Ann that I needed to give Antonio money. She was holding the money and I told her that it would have to be a minimum of $20,000 for his end. Ann came up with a different idea. A very novel idea.

Give him lots of business and pay all the money for everything, in other words, retail. Pay the long price for all the jewelry and give the jewelry to her. What a clever idea she had. Buy her more fucking jewelry. Before long, she had on an 18-carat yellow gold belt which must have weighed about half a ton, a strand of pearls, not cultured but natural Mikimoto pearls, 9 mm. Perfectly formed oyster secretions with an 18 Karat gold and diamond clasp. The strand was so long you could tow a car with it. By the time I left Mona Lisa, I had spent $35,000 and there was almost three weeks left for us to be in Italy. This was definitely going to be more than a $50,000 trip.

We went back to our room which was located in one of the better hotels in Rome and immediately when I turned the light switch on, the light bulb blew out. I had pushed the round button on the solid brass antique style switch and Ann was very sure that this was a bad sign, that we were going to be robbed of our money.

"It's a set-up," she said. I clutched her pretty face and said, "Ann, the light just blew out. No big deal. Let's take advantage of the darkness."

We made love for two hours before I called the front desk and within minutes, the light was repaired. If anyone wanted to kill us or rob us, this certainly wouldn't have been the place to do it. It would have been done in the office that we had just left. She realized I was right and laughed. She had scored more jewelry in an afternoon than most people could afford in a lifetime.

Up until now, we had been driving everywhere in Carlo's car. By now, my Dino was ready and I wanted to use it for the remainder of our trip. Boy, was I dreaming. Ann had so much luggage, packages and other kinds of stuff that it was necessary to load the small trunk first, then get in the car, both of us, and have a hotel employee put the rest of the luggage in Ann's lap.

We ultimately put about a thousand miles on this car driving without a fucking square inch of room to spare inside the car. The trip took us to Florence where Ann bought more jewelry on the Ponte Vecchio, known as the old bridge, which spans the Arno River and is renowned for its fine, handmade, gold jewelry. There were probably a hundred small shops in that area alone and I think we visited every single one of them. We were within walking distance of the Old Bridge, right down the street from Harry's Bar.

When the trip was finally over, I knew every store in every major city in Italy. This would be the last time Ann would make a trip to Italy with me.

Chapter 7
The S&S Bar

The S&S bar was practically my second home. I spent time there every day, hanging with the wise guys, doing some business, and enjoying the company of other people with whom I had lots in common, either on a personal basis or business related.

The bar was an extremely active place with very few people if anyone, who came in that we didn't know or that didn't have some business there. It was like a private little club open to a select group of people connected to the Patriarca family.

Everyone speculated that when off track betting became legal, bookies would go out of business, like when Prohibition was repealed, the mob lost its largest source of income. But this was not the case with legalized off track betting for two important reasons.

The first, was that a person could bet more than just horses or dogs with a bookie. He could bet all sports events, plus a whole lot more. But more importantly, a bookie could extend his sucker credit. And that credit was an incentive for the bettor to bet beyond his means. If the mark got in trouble, the money he bet soon turned into a loan at 5 percent or more a week. This was a tremendous source of income for the Mob, and especially the S&S bar.

Sure, our Family was into all the rackets: gambling, extortion, arson, prostitution, shylocking, and all the other money makers, except, supposedly, drugs. But, believe me, more fucking drugs went through some of our guys hands than water down the Mississippi, but it was kept quiet. As long as Raymond didn't see anyone using, selling, or getting busted with drugs, everything was OK.

The main source of income at the S&S was from gambling, and gambling-related activities. Andrew Mansolillo, (Andy Shacks) was Louie's (Baby Shacks) brother, and most of the time Andrew handled all the S&S business. The nicknames Shacks came from the fact that both men attracted lots of women. Andrew was a heavy set man, rarely shaved, rough talking, but very intelligent, with his biggest asset being that he was Louie's brother.

The owner of record for the bar was Etta Mansolillo, Andy's wife. Andy was a felon and couldn't own a liquor license. This was not a major factor for anyone with a felony conviction who needs a license to operate a business that required its owners to have a clean record. Circumventing the law was very easy in those days.

His marriage to Etta was always shaky. All he did was give her a couple thousand dollars a week in cash and stayed away from his house. He couldn't stand her. His brother Louie was never married and was an up and coming mobster who now is considered the head of all organized crime in New England. His brother and Louie were to become two of my closest friends.

The bar itself was a simple joint. There were double doors that led directly to Atwells Avenue. There was an old mahogany bar and was still in very good condition despite its many decades of service. The back of the bar was also mahogany and Andy would always say that he was going to have it refinished but that day never arrived. It wasn't a fancy place but it was certainly comfortable.

At the end of the bar was a rocking chair which was mine. If someone were sitting in it and I came in, they would relinquish it to me immediately. Next to the rocking chair was a table on which I could put a glass of wine. Before long, two or three people would come over and join me and we would talk. The conversation would almost always eventually turn to business because that was one of the purposes of the bar. It was a meeting place for various types of business activities.

At the end of the room to the left was another small room. This room was like a kitchen with a refrigerator and a stove. Something was always cooking in this room. Usually a sauce in a huge pot would contain meatballs, sausage, braciola, and pork. There were always several types of pasta on the stove. We had the best and I can say that everything was delicious.

We had a contact with a pilot who flew frequently to France. He owed a great deal of money to the shylocks as he was a heavy gambler. He had fresh bread delivered from France to the bar every single day. He did anything that he could to keep himself in favor with the guys there. None of us ever left hungry, that's for sure.

There was always someone who frequented the bar or gambled through the bar and who owned a restaurant, especially the 1025 club, so food was constantly being sent over, complimentary of course. At night, say 11 or midnight, we would send out for Chinese food to a downtown restaurant called Luke's. We would call in our order and then one of us would usually go pick it up. The average bill that we would run up would be anywhere between $95 and $100 and we would usually leave a $25 tip. Of course, everything was paid for with stolen credit cards, including the tip.

I recall one occasion when one of the cards was declined for a little less than $100. The bill was paid for by another stolen credit card. Andrew was so pissed when this happened that he looked in the phone book to see if he could find the guy who owned the card. He wanted to call the guy a fucking bust out, and get his address. He said he needed money more than we did and wanted us to send the asshole a $100 bill. Things like this happened often at the S & S, but we had lots of credit cards and more stolen credit cards went through that bar than any other business or any other place in Rhode Island.

Ultimately, one of the regulars that hung out there all the time, Joe Meglio, (Joe Meg), was involved in an $11 million scam with credit cards which involved most of the New England states. It was the largest credit card fraud in United States history. It went on for years. One day the FBI questioned the owners at Luke's. Boy, they turned out to be a bunch of stand-up guys. They never gave us up. Who knows, maybe they were afraid of us, but I don't think so.

The bar was a fun place to be and I remember one day when an old man was mouthing off some bullshit. He was wearing a straw hat and Andy set it on fire. The fucking hat was blazing on his head and he didn't have the slightest idea what we were all laughing at. After a couple of minutes, someone flipped the hat off his head and doused it with water before he got burnt. Then the guy put it back on his head. The water dripped all the way down his face and he was startled when he took his hat off and saw it was half burnt. The look on his face had us all laughing.

Andrew ran the bar until Louie came back. Louie had a small apartment above the bar for his entertainment. Ann's uncle, Carmine Ruzzero, who we called Minniestew, was a 10-percenter at Lincoln Race track but was always around the bar. Andy's uncle Watso, an old man in his late 80s and still a tough guy was always there. Another one who was always around was Rudolph Sargenta, one of the highest level enforcers in the Family. The crew also included Eddy Latio, another enforcer, Rocco Andreoli, Eddie's counterpart, Joe Meg, a great con man, my uncle Vincent and George Bashaw, another enforcer. On occasion there was Frank Corsino and his son Baby Corsino, Louie Tortelli — Louie the Fox as we called him — who was later executed gangland style for holding back on paying his end of a gambling operation. Unfortunately, Louie was having a relationship with a woman he visited every Friday night, and when he was shot leaving her house, she ran out and got a glimpse of the shooters. She was also killed.

Paddy Reese, an ex-boxer who has been featured in The Ring magazine as a super lightweight, was constantly there. Paddy was my friend and acted as my personal bodyguard for many years. Andy Marino, (called Muzzi), was another constant figure at the bar. Joe Timpani, a gambler who owned The Leopold Lounge in the Silver Lake area of Providence, would come in sporting two or three diamond rings and in the winter a full- length fur coat. He was another flamboyant character, sharp as all hell, and a very heavy gambler, who bet thousands of dollars daily on sports events. He owned a plastering business, Timpani Plastering and helped me obtain a $5,000 interest free disaster loan in 1978 when President Carter declared Rhode Island a disaster area after the Blizzard of '78. Joe died at an early age of a heart attack. He was one of the more colorful characters at the bar.

Then there was Sal Lisi, Louie Mansolillo's, partner in a jewelry and loan business called the Geneva Watch Company. We used to call Sal either Salite or "The Horn" because he had his voice box removed when he was diagnosed with throat cancer. He spoke with a battery-operated device held against his throat. I was to work with Sal for many, many years and we made a good deal of money together making counterfeit quarters.

Tillio was another regular at the S&S. He was a small, meek man who lived a short distance from the bar with his mother. He would constantly be talking about what a great cook his mother was, until, finally one day, Andrew blew up.

"What the fuck does your mother know how to cook?" he screamed. "Pasta fagioli, braciola, sausage, meatballs. What the fuck is that. The best chefs are me... Does your mother know how to cook Beef Wellington, Oysters Rockefeller, Pheasant Under Glass, Duck L'Orange, or Chateaubriand?"

I don't think Tillio even knew what these dishes were. Tillio bowed his head, and said, "I guess you're right, Andy."

There were many, many people who hung at the bar just because they liked to be in the company of wise guys. Anyone walking into the bar that we didn't know was suspected to be an undercover cop from one action or another, and on many occasions we were absolutely right.

Every once in a while, we would see a wrinkled old coat hanging in the far corner of the bar. It belonged to Steven Saccone, who ran a gold buying business in Cranston. This was really a front for a drug laundering scheme for one of the major drug cartels in Columbia. He was warned by some cops that he was being watched, his phones were tapped, and there was a video camera monitoring his movements 24 hours a day and the FBI was building a case against him. In spite of all of this, he kept his deals going. He was earning so much easy money that he just couldn't quit.

Eventually, Saccone was grabbed by Interpol in Germany, along with his wife, Donna, carrying $19 million in cash. He was trying to clean out some of his hidden accounts. His brother-in-law was a quiet, respectful young man who worked for Steven and he was also arrested. His name was Mickey Healy. Steve received the longest sentence in United States history, 660 years or 1 year for every million dollars that he laundered. His wife Donna, received eight years in Danbury, Connecticut and Mickey, his brother-in-law received 12 years.

Mickey was with me in Fort Dix. By that time he had been incarcerated for six or seven years into his 12-year sentence. He was sporting a long ponytail and studying the stars. He had lost touch with reality and the outside world. He asked me to pass messages to his sister, in Danbury, since my co-defendant was also incarcerated there. I was glad to help.

During my time at Fort Dix, I read a newspaper article that said Mickey's father's house had been seized by DEA agents. His father put the house up for sale and then was seen digging in the flower garden taking out packages. A neighbor called the police, and they dug up several hundred thousands of dollars' worth of gold from the yard. You wonder how anyone could be so stupid.

But, no one got in trouble when these three were arrested, even though their connection to the S&S and the old man was obvious. The charges of money laundering stemmed from dealings with the highest Columbian drug lord and this was a supposed taboo in our Family. Nevertheless, I saw many drug deals go on in there. It was so obvious that The Horn was dealing, but no one ever spoke of it, and I kept my mouth shut. It was none of my business. And everybody loved and respected Steven.

Then, there was Alfred Gelfuso. Alfred was Vincent's brother-in-law.

Following is a conversation we had, with others included.

"Lou, the house is on Oaklawn Avenue in Cranston, number …"

"No, I interrupted, I don't want to know the fucking number, Just tell me what you want."

"It's alarmed, but there are three windows on the side, all in a row, and I can plainly see the alarm's hardware. This is an easy score, two guys can clean the place out in 15 minutes. The guy's rich. I see his wife coming out of there with diamonds, fur coats, you name it. They have a silver Cadillac, and I think they go to Florida a lot, because it's January and she's got a tan."

"So what do you want to know?"

"I want to jimmy the window, but I need to disable the alarm. If I get our friend to do this, he'll want a cut. You know what you get for this stuff, when you move it? Can I cut the glass? And if I do, then what? What do you suggest?"

"I'm no fucking alarm expert, but if you take a piece similar to the part of the magnetic hardware that's on the bottom half of the window, cut the glass and put the part on top of the stationary piece, not the piece that moves up with the window, it'll keep the magnetic switch engaged when you lift the bottom half of the window up. It'll keep the magnet in place. Yeah, that will work. But that will get you in, nothing more. If they have motion detectors, or pressure mats, or sensors, you'll set off the alarm."

"The guy uses a round key to set the alarm, I saw him. A light goes from green to red.

Before he opens the door, the light goes from red to green."

"Well, that makes a difference. No keypad. It's a simple system," I said. "Real cheap, but still there could be a mat or other sensors in the house."

"We'll take that chance. If we trip the alarm, we'll screw out of there fast."

"If you trip the alarm, you might not know it, it could be a silent alarm," I told them."

"I think you're wrong, Lou. There's a siren the size of fire truck's on the corner of the house. We'll hear it."

They were probably right. I finished my wine, and began rocking in my personal rocking chair.

I kept thinking what a difference there is between people. Here's two guys ready to risk their freedom for a few thousand dollars. But, what could you expect, one of them told me a year or so earlier, that for $5,000, he'd roll over 10 people with a steamroller.

Night came, and we ordered Chinese from Luke's. I went home about 1:30 and slept. Nothing happened for about a week. Then Vincent and I were in Sherwood when his brother-in-law Alfred came in. Alfred was a classy man. Small, thin, good looking, always dressed in a nice, conservative suit, and hardly ever spoke above a whisper. He was nervous, but composed. His wife was Vincent's sister. She inherited the same good looks as Vincent, but Vincent always said she was a little slow. I had only met her once or twice, and never noticed anything wrong.

Alfred was a businessman whose success was legendary. He founded Feranti's Sausage Corporation, which became one of the largest suppliers of sausage and other meats to supermarkets throughout New England. Then he started Portion Control Meat Company, and Precise Portion Meats Co. Both companies sold prepared, weighed meats to fast food chains, and his was one of the first companies to sell frozen hamburger patties by weight, quarter pounders, etc., to McDonalds, Burger King and similar type fast food chains.

Everything he touched was successful. Chef-A-Rony, a delicatessen across from Bostich Stapler in East Greenwich, made a fortune. But he was a modest man and never bragged.

This day he had bad news.

"Vincent, they broke into my house. We were in Florida for two weeks, but I had Mike check my house last week, and everything was fine."

Mike was his next door neighbor. So, it had to have been done within the last week. My fucking heart dropped. I planned that score with Ralph and Eddy from my rocking chair at the S&S.

"Did you call the cops, Al?"

"Yes. They said somebody attempted to bypass my alarm, but it never worked anyway, Vincent. The red light came on and I figured that would be enough to stop someone from breaking in. We lost all our jewelry, except what we were wearing. Your sister's furs, diamonds, silver flatware, crystal, china, anything of value, they took. My claim will be more than $60,000."

"It was insured?" Vincent asked.

"Of course", Alfred replied, as if almost insulted. Alfred was not the kind of man who would go without insurance.

"Have you notified your insurance company, Al?"

"No," he replied.

"All right, let me see what I can find out. I will call you later, Vincent."

He said, "See you, Lou," and he left.

"Vincent, I didn't know your sister lives on Oaklawn Avenue. Ralph and Eddy did that job. They wanted me to help with the alarm.

"Those fucking dimwits," Vincent said. "Let's go see if they're around."

We found Ralph in the S&S. He was big and stupid and very easily led. Vincent told him they robbed his sister's house.

"That's your sister's house? We didn't know that, Vincent."

"Where's the stuff?" Vincent demanded.

"We moved two pieces, Vincent, that's all. The rest is in my house in bags."

"How the fuck can you be so stupid?" Vincent seldom used this kind of language. Ralph never even mentioned that I helped plan this fiasco. He may have been a boob, but he was a stand-up guy.

Vincent told him: "Leave the stuff inside the front door at 9 tonight, I'll see nobody's home. There'll be an envelope on the floor. It'll have two grand in it for your night's work."

"Thanks, Vincent, I'm sorry."

Vincent knew that giving them some money was the right thing to do. I knew Alfred was going to freak out.

"Alfred, put $2,000 cash in an envelope on the floor and leave your house at 8:30. Don't come back until 9:30 tonight. Your stuff will be returned then."

"Two thousand dollars?" Alfred screamed, "I don't make two thousand for an hour's work."

Alfred had a reputation for being cheap. Everyone who knew him was aware of it. But, he realized, if he put in a claim, his insurance premiums would either be raised, probably by more than the two thousand, or worst yet, his insurance might be canceled.

Al was not the type to get the stuff back, pay the two grand then file an insurance claim for $60.000. He was probably the only guy in Rhode Island who wouldn't do that. So, reluctantly, he put the two grand in an envelope and left his house with his wife. Everything was returned, and the envelope was taken. Funny, Alfred never mentioned that incident again.

Another frequent visitor to the bar was Anthony Mansolillo, Louie's brother, a gynecologist who, if it were not for his brother Louie, would probably have wound up being a wise guy himself. But Louie pushed his brother to complete school. Louie could be very persuasive when it was required.

Charlie West and Richard Barone were two partners in numerous ventures and were very closely associated with the bar and The Office. The two of them had drawn the attention of Raymond years earlier, when they were very young and just starting out in business. They needed cash so they staged a phony accident, one of them smashing his car into the rear of the other one's car. In those days, this type of accident was paid quickly. They filed an insurance claim and were just waiting for their checks when they were called into the office by Raymond.

The company, based in Massachusetts, was called Resolute Insurance Company. What they didn't know was that Resolute Insurance Company was owned by Raymond. Raymond told them that he heard of a pair of young men from Rhode Island that had an accident and were about to be issued a check.

"Now don't get me wrong," he said. "I like to see young men get ahead in life and I admire you fellows for your cleverness and ambition, but you see I own Resolute."

Nothing more needed to be said. The claims were dropped the next day but both men went on to become very successful when they formed a body shop called Diamond Auto Body. Then in the early 80s, they formed Diamond Associates, a real estate company. With the Family's help, they obtained money and favors that allowed them to build condos around a well-known golf course in North Providence. Originally, they got permission to build 40 units, but when the construction was finally completed, it had some 430 units in total.

Between this and Diamond Auto Body, they made one hell of a start and continued successfully to today, with Richard developing huge projects for companies like Stop and Shop Market, Fidelity Investments and lots of other major Rhode Island construction projects. In the beginning, money was sometimes supplied by City Loan, but later on, they were successful enough to obtain legitimate loans from banks. Both were stand-up guys and I became very close to Charlie West years later when I opened a business called Foreign Car World.

Charlie was a funny guy who came up the hard way and his success never went to his head. He was an orphan who found a family with the wise guys and was a loyal friend for more than 20 years. He and Richard went separate ways a short while back only because Charlie wanted to slow down and Richard continued pushing from project to project. They were different from each other but each a gentleman in his own way.

Then there was Marty Lawrell. Marty was a well-dressed, soft-spoken man who was openly gay long before this was widely accepted. He would bring along his boyfriend Anthony frequently. Marty was the head of the Rhode Island Registry of Motor Vehicles and was constantly doing us favors, mostly obtaining low number license plates, which is a sort of mania in Rhode Island. He also helped us obtain authentic drivers licenses, valid and issued by the Registry of Motor Vehicles but with phony names on them. I used the names of many persons who had died before the license was issued. Marty's job was an important one and it was extremely helpful to the bar.

The S&S bar was a lot of fun but it also had a very serious, darker side. Oh sure, we had Miniestew, always quick with a joke or a neat trick. He might say something like, "Look at my son," referring to how much he weighed. "Look, he's losing five pounds a week, normally he gains 10 pounds a week, now he's only gaining five, so he's losing five pounds."

Sometimes, we started spouting out series of numbers holding a calculator. Say a column of six. Then another six and another four, another five, another six columns to be added. Fuck, we had trouble adding it on a calculator. Miniestew could add it in his head as fast as you could throw numbers out to him. Miniestew could take numbers off the cars of a passing train and add them up in his head as the cars flew by. I couldn't imagine punching them into the calculator as fast as he was able to add them in his head. I never got tired of trying to fool him. He was a character all right, and part of his character was tipping. He would actually tip a doctor or a dentist, and that was considered normal to him.

We had plenty of characters at the S & S bar that could make you laugh, but the S&S was about serious business and serious business on a big scale. I financed George Bashaw, a strong-man for the mob, in a karate business. He was a black belt and was a good instructor. He was the type of character the bar needed, a tough guy, not afraid to do anything and could take orders from the wise guys. People like this were always needed at the bar and The Office. They were necessary to keep business in order. Raymond was always on the lookout for tough guys, and illegal gambling and loan sharking operations need muscle. At first, George was just perfect for this. But, then, things changed.

One afternoon, while I was up in the office above the karate school, I overheard him on the phone with someone getting ready to open his own business. I had just spent more than 15 grand to open his school on Oaklawn Avenue, in Cranston, and he was going to take my customers with him and go in business for himself. I told Andy what I had overheard on the phone and he said that it was no surprise to him at all. To quote Andy, "He's a bad kid," and he told me that he was also stealing from The Office and was an arrogant punk. He was scheduled to be whacked soon.

One night, about 8, most of our crew was in the bar. There was a Lincoln parked in front of the place and George was out there talking with the occupants. There were three of them.

They said, "OK, let's get this over with."

They were supposedly going on a score, that's what they wanted George to believe.

Actually, they were taking George for a ride. He had no idea. The driver and one passenger got in the front seat. Another entered through the left rear and George got in the right rear side. They were all laughing and smiling.

"It'll be a piece of cake," I heard one of them say as they drove off.

But, George was not going to come home from this ride. As I continued to look out the front window, I noticed an FBI car follow them almost immediately. I knew George was going to be whacked and ran over to Andy and told him what I had just seen. We didn't have cell phones in those days, so I offered to jump in my car and alert the guys that they were being followed. Andy looked at me with a little smile and said, "Don't worry Lou, it's OK."

I knew what he was talking about. "Everything is fine," he said. The FBI and the Lincoln both disappeared.

The following day, the newspaper said that the body of a karate school instructor with known ties to the Rhode Island underworld had been found on Croom Street. He had been executed gangland style right under the noses of two FBI agents who were actually following the car. The FBI agents said that they lost sight of the car shortly after it left the S&S. The execution took place as planned and the body was dumped on Shoofly Street. The Lincoln was reported stolen from a Lincoln dealership. It turns out that the dealership was the same one that Charlie West and Richard Barone had obtained cars from in their failed insurance scam years earlier, and was owned by friends of the Family. The FBI was happy to be rid of George Bashaw and so was the S&S crew.

Another hit I remember well and always wondered if I would be connected to was Joe The Baron Barboza. He was a great tough guy to have around the bar. Another example of a necessary character that any illegal activity dealing with lots of money needs. He was a big guy, good looking, Portuguese and from New Bedford with long black sideburns, and dark sunglasses. When he married a Jewish girl, he converted, got circumcised, then changed his name from Barboza to Baron. But his nickname was really Joe The Animal Barboza, and this was much more appropriate.

Nothing changed his personality. He would take care of business that required muscle. But, once again, after a period of time the power went to his head and he got way out of line. He was going to be whacked. The FBI warned him of this and he refused to believe it until one day, using evidence from an illegally planted bug that was placed in Raymond's office a couple of years earlier, they played a portion of it to Joe. Raymond said Joe had gone crazy and would have to be killed. He was way out of hand and no amount of reasoning would work with him. Plans for his execution were being made. The FBI played a tape of a conversation between Henry Tameleo and Raymond, in which they both agreed to whack Joe. Joe was shocked and was offered a deal. He would give up evidence that he knew about the Family in exchange for any pending charges against him being dropped and would be granted immunity from any new testimony he would give. He could say anything he wanted without any fear of prosecution. And he had plenty he could say. Word of his decision to join forces with the FBI spread immediately and was devastating. Barboza testified against Raymond and Henry Tameleo, and using his testimony, they were both convicted and sentenced to seven years in the ACI.

When Raymond's office was broken into a couple of years earlier, I remember Vincent and I going into the office and Vincent asking what was taken. The Old Man answered, "Nothing." Well, if nothing was taken from the office and you had a break-in, what would that mean? You'd have to be an idiot not to know that something was planted and what was planted was a bug.

Raymond never believed this, but the results of that bug were what put several high ranking members of the Family in jail.

After testifying, Joe agreed to enter the FBI Witness Protection Program. He would be given a new identity, complete with a driver's license, a social security number, birth certificate, and all the documents necessary to begin a new life. Joe insisted on moving to California. Joe was a tough character for the FBI to control and before long he left the program. It didn't take long to find out where he was and he was shot dead in a phone booth on a busy Santa Rosa street. Raymond and his Family would soon be off the hook from an appeal, but I wasn't. He was shot while using a device that I had made. How long would it be before they traced its origins back to Rhode Island and then, ultimately, back to me I wondered, "Nothing I can do about it now, so let's see what happens."

What was more upsetting to the wise guys was that Raymond would discuss such important business over the telephone. After all, his office had been broken into and nothing was taken. How could he possibly discuss such important business knowing this? Just using the phone for business wasn't something that somebody of his importance should do under any circumstances. Throughout the years he had always denied that that his office was bugged. But for someone so smart and sharp to refuse to believe, it was a serious mistake on his part.

Meanwhile, on a lighter note, there were other characters that came into the bar. One afternoon, I remember a guy coming in carrying a small briefcase. He was so far out of place there, we wondered what he wanted and asked him immediately. He said he worked for the Patriot Insurance Company and was selling life and disability policies.

Within minutes, a dozen people were surrounding him and everybody was asking about the disability plan that he was selling. He was asked to sit down and explain how it worked.

"Simple," he replied. There would be no physical exam necessary. The company would issue a policy to anyone who requested one. To collect, just a doctor's note indicating the nature of the disability and that the insured couldn't work would be sufficient to file a claim. Previous illnesses meant nothing. But a person could only be issued one policy with benefits of a maximum of $200 a month. We immediately grabbed him and asked who else was selling these policies and where we could find them.

He repeated that it was against the rules of the insurance company to sell anyone more than one policy, then he said, "I guess if it was possible to find another agent or agents, and get them to write you a policy, the company obviously would have to honor that policy."

The whole idea was that each agent was assigned a territory. So the odds of more than one policy per person being issued were slim. The company wished to limit its potential downside to just one policy per person. We shoved him into a car and told him that we wanted to find another agent, and scared shitless after a short drive, he took us to a section of town where there was another agent selling policies for the same company. We all signed up at that location for a policy. The next thing you know, we were back at the S&S where we signed up with our agent for an additional policy. So, now we all had two policies. We asked them when the policies would become effective. He said that the policies were effective almost immediately.

It was 2:25 p.m. He said, by 2:30 the policies would be valid.

About an hour later, we were all putting in claims and getting ready to collect $400 a month for the next two years. Each of us had doctors that would sign a claim form for us. And the beauty of it was that the premiums were even waived during the disability period so the company received approximately $30 or one month's premium from each of us for the policies. Not a bad investment; $30 for $400 a month for the next two years.

Other perks that came from being at the bar were getting tickets to concerts and shows that were very difficult to get, and afterwards meeting the performers in person. One of them, Jimmy Roselli, a well-known singer from Rhode Island was, of course, a regular in the S&S. But anytime someone famous performed in Providence, we would have access to them either after the show or they would actually come to the bar, and we sat down with any number of people, including Tony Bennett, Frank Sinatra, Dean Martin, and many others.

Another person who was at the bar practically every minute of the day was Ronnie Coppolino. Ronnie was a hit man and also a very powerful player in the Patriarca crime family. He was a big man with a deep voice that definitely demanded respect. He had no problem collecting money. He was an intelligent man. He knew when to draw the line, and he was someone to be feared if you got on

his bad side. Ronnie was a good friend of mine, and Ronnie and Eddy Latio were
the closest of friends throughout their entire lives.

Years later, Ronnie would be in a small bar in Cranston. One afternoon, an
aged wise guy who had been a driver for Raymond came into the bar and starting
talking a lot of bullshit.

Ronnie was playing cards and he found the old guy disturbing and obnoxious
and told him to go fuck himself and leave him alone while he's were playing a card
game. The old man's name was Antonio Cuscinata. He left the bar and an hour
later came back with a .38 caliber handgun. He said that he was going kill some
people for having been disrespected. Everybody scrambled from the table. He shot
one of the players in the back, and shot Ronnie in the head. Ronnie died immediately. It was ironic that somebody lived a lifestyle like Ronnie did, and dealt with
so many tough people, was shot by an old man over an insult at a card game.

Chapter 8
Beating Ma Bell

One hundred, two hundred, two hundred and fifty.

"Thanks Lou, I'll need more," he said.

"How many?" I asked. "All you can make," was the answer. "Two, three hundred at least. Probably more."

When I was 12 or 13 years old, I was always an entrant in the Brown University Marvel Gymnasium Science Competition. I remember entering three years in a row, taking second prize twice and third prize once.

One of the projects was building an automobile. Another was a motor made completely from nails.

The third was a very sophisticated project in which mechanical power from a steam engine that I made powered an electrical generator. The generator converted mechanical energy into electrical energy — which then powered a miniature city complete with street lights, traffic signs, and houses. It was extremely detailed. It not only took second prize at the Marvel Gymnasium Science Fair, but along with it came a certificate awarding its originality. My parents were so proud that my mother made a kind of easel to display my awards on.

In the early 60s, black boxes were a common item in any wise guy's house where frequent long distance calls were made. They were not the black boxes as we know them today, used to cheat the cable companies by allowing a customer to get more channels than he is paying for. They were used to cheat the phone company. Bookies used them all the time. They were big, bulky, heavy metal boxes with wire hookups that would challenge even a modern day electrician. Despite their drawbacks, they actually worked. You dialed in the long distance number you wished to call and your phone was charged as a local call. Cool, huh?

I was making a portable black box of sorts, housed in a package of Marlboro cigarettes. It was certainly something no one else was doing. It began as a small project. Every one that I finished gave me a real sense of satisfaction. It took me about a month to perfect the box. I remember every time I tried to use it the anxiety that hit me — the fear and the disappointment if it failed. It did fail several times.

I always used phone booths in other cities or even states wondering if the operator would have notified the police that someone was trying to beat the pay phone and a police car would arrive and promptly arrest me. Finally, after numerous attempts I had it down to a science where each one that I made would work perfectly.

You dropped a dime in a pay phone and dialed a long distance number. Your dime was returned and either a live operator or voice recording asked you to drop in a dollar and 35 cents, for example.

So you put the Marlboro package next to the phone's receiver and press the little red button which indicated it was a quarter — five times for a total of a dollar and 25 cents. Next, press the yellow button which is a code for a dime, once, and your call went through, perfectly, every time.

A dollar and 40-cent call would require all the above plus pressing the green or nickel switch one time.

Calling with the Marlboro package was easy, cheap and entailed no fumbling with change such as slugs. The battery lasted for months; it was inexpensive and quick to replace. The black box gadgets were fun to make at first. They sold and they earned me lots of money.

I couldn't understand why anyone would pay $250 for this toy. You need to make a lot of phone calls to get your $250 back.

One day, I asked Andy why the sales of these units were so strong and why guys would pay so much when they wanted everything else for the bubble. To get a wise guy to put out actual cash for anything was one of the hardest things in the world. They wouldn't spend a nickel for anything. Andy asked me if I knew how much he spent on phone calls in a single day. Of course, I had no idea.

He said, "I spend at least three to four hundred dollars a day for this fucking joint."

I was amazed. No wonder we could sell all these fucking things that we could make and I didn't know what Andy was selling them for. I got $250. Maybe he sold them for twice that. Who knows? The $250 more than made me happy.

Now I knew why the wise guys would pay so much money for some of the things that I made. Not that I ever doubted my workmanship; after all, I'm a perfectionist to the ultimate degree.

Every solder joint had to be bright, shiny, and smooth. Anything I ever made had to look as good as it would function and believe me it had to be perfect. Everything I made functioned perfectly.

The materials — a small amount of wire, solder, a timer chip, three small resistance chips, a chassis circuit, a couple of switches, a battery and the most expensive item, a Zenith hearing-aid speaker — cost approximately $12. Maybe one or two hours of work was needed and the box was finished.

The box was chirping like a bird flawlessly as it fooled one of the largest corporations in the world. As if this wasn't brilliant enough, I decided to make the chassis slide inside an empty Marlboro cigarette box. Flip open the top and you're ready to begin. The Marlboros added about 75 cents to each unit, but at $250 a copy, it didn't make any difference at all to me.

I made these for more than a couple of years and I could easily put four or five together in a very short order once I set up everything I needed. The only tools I required were a screwdriver, small drill, needle-nose pliers, a little bit of wire, some solder, and some thin aluminum for a chassis. The materials were a few micro-switches and some Zenith speakers from their cheapest hearing aid, and of course, a battery. The fact that they fit in a Marlboro box made using them practically undetectable, even if someone was outside the phone booth waiting to make a call.

If you were tracking my purchase of cigarettes you'd have to think that I was a chain smoker, smoking at least three cigarettes at a time to use that many boxes. I thought it was a shame to throw away all those un-smoked cigarettes but it was far too risky to do anything else with them. After all, who gives away loose cigarettes?

I was a smoker all my life but Marlboros, no never. The cigarettes I smoked were Murati Aristons, which my uncle and I would order 10 cases at a time from Nat Sherman's company, a tobacconist in New York who specialized in handmade cigarettes and cigars like Rameses and Gallois and Muratis. Occasionally, we would smoke a twisty, which is a thin, crooked, cognac soaked cigar with a great flavor. I can taste those today, 30 years later. Some of Nat Sherman's customers included Telly Savalas, Dean Martin, Frank Sinatra, the McGuire sisters, and other famous actors and actresses.

Lots of them liked his colored cigarettes. Nat Sherman offered a wide variety of colors from brown which was Kojak's favorite, to bright pink which he sold to the owner of Mary Kay Cosmetics. They matched the color of her yacht. By the end of a relatively short day I had $2,500 to $3,000 in cash and who the hell cared about throwing a few fucking cigarettes away.

They were small, light, clean, and easy to make in small quantities. A very nice combination. But it wasn't long before all of this changed. Suddenly, nine or ten units every couple of days no longer was enough to satisfy a nationwide demand. Soon, soldered wires gave way to a printed circuit board and hand-bent aluminum chassis were now formed on steel dies. The whole process was automated and no longer fun. It was not a hobby, but instead a huge business with no saturation point in sight.

Since the final product was illegal, it was important that no one know what the parts they were making were used for. Some believed they were making cat whiskers radios, another thought he was making a circuit board for a portable radio, and others just didn't care as long as I paid in cash.

I remember one guy, Joe D'Ninno, an engineer. He built a self-powered airplane using only the pilot's leg power to fly approximately one mile at 2 to 10 feet above the ground. It was a standing offer that the first documented flight would bring the successful builder a $100,000 prize put up by a British airline. Although he never actually won the prize he came very close on more than one occasion.

For him, the circuit boards I needed were a simple project and he thought they were being used in a miniature TV set. He made thousands of them and on one occasion said he might like to purchase one of the TVs that his circuit boards powered. I told him that the manufacturer would pull me off the project if I violated my confidentiality agreement. I said it was an American TV manufacturer, Curtis Mathis, which only exited the market a few years ago. Joe understood and never pushed me.

I had made slugs for years, which would fool the phone company and pushed my techniques to the limit by blanking out designs in the center of the slugs, probably more to stick it to the fucking phone company than to sell the valuable copper scrap that this move produced. As the years went by, the phone company made it more and more difficult to produce slugs until it became necessary to keep the center intact and to keep the dimensions and tolerances close and the edges had to have ridges like a genuine quarter.

Still, it was simple work. The money was good. In general, I made at least $800 an hour, not including the scrap, and there was never a point where it looked as if it the deal would ever end. After all, look how many things needed quarters? Laundromats, cigarette machines, bridges and highways, pay phones, car washes, entertainment games and on and on. I never had any questions about the need for this product. It was far too obvious.

Manufacturing slugs was extremely profitable. Generally, I would sell them with 500 slugs to a bag and produced several hundred bags a day.

When Sal needed a shipment, he would usually call me at the S&S Bar and would say, "Louie," in a raspy artificial, mechanical voice. "This is Sal," as if I wouldn't know who it was. Like maybe I got lots of calls from people that were using voice boxes held up against their throat with a battery-operated device. On several occasions he called to Paula's house, and this scared her. I asked him to try to limit his calls to the bar.

"Sal, reach out for me at the S&S," I said.

I could never figure out why he felt it necessary to identify who he was. Still, he was a high-level wise guy and had to be respected. That was Sal and I accepted him that way.

"I could use a couple of hundred bags of those things right away," Al would say. He might as well have given anyone listening my address and social security number. The presses never stopped banging out those slugs.

At the end of the day, I would usually put the bags in the trunk of my car and deliver them to Sal's house in Cranston. I collected my cash and left within minutes. Besides, after my divorce, in 1980, I used a building he supplied to make my slugs, so sometimes they went right in his car's trunk.

Sal had ready buyers with cash and no questions asked, and this was a hard thing to walk away from. Bobby Flowers and Frankie Martino were always at Sal's house to help me unload my car. So was Sal's wife, an aging beauty who was trying desperately to hold onto her youth. I couldn't get out of there fast enough.

Between his blatant use of the phone, our exposure unloading the coins, and his wife coming on to me at every opportunity, and offering me cocktails and the use of the pool at their house, I felt that the FBI was having a party watching what was going on and I just wanted to get my business done and get out. Although I never knew what took place after I left, I imagine the bags were distributed quickly.

Despite my feelings to the contrary, no indications we were ever being watched or followed surfaced during my countless trips to Sal's house.

But, that wasn't the case on Manton Avenue near the corner of Atwells Avenue. So many coins were turning up in Rhode Island, Massachusetts, New York, and New Jersey that the FBI and Secret Service set up a special unit in these states and were determined to put an end to what they said was organized crime activity. Actually, slug surveillance tactics and investigations existed everywhere. On Manton Avenue, the Geneva Watch Company was a major target. Anyone going in and out was photographed and identified to see if he was part of the S&S crew.

Sal was followed until he was eventually eliminated as a suspect or followed even more if he was a suspect. I used Geneva Watch as a legitimate source to buy and sell gold jewelry and as an illegal source to do the same. But, I had access to a private entrance from Manton Avenue through a hidden doorway and kept my visits short and to the point. Still, the FBI knew they were on the right track and when the time was right they would make their move. They hoped ultimately to grab several members of the Patriarca crime family who frequented the S&S Bar.

They came very close to doing just that.

When I was a kid, 13 or 14, I made extra money by alarming peoples' homes. One of them was owned by a family friend, John Mainelli, who owned and operated a very successful family restaurant on Chalkstone Avenue called Mainelli's. Relay switches, motion detectors, magnetic sensors, trip mats, etc., were all new high-tech items at that time and I was familiar with them all. I used this experience to protect my counterfeiting activities on Manton Avenue by a series of alarms which when tripped would sound a warning that someone was on the premises who didn't belong there.

Also, buzzers and lights were located everywhere from the Geneva Watch Company to the Manton Avenue premises. Still, in my pursuit of perfection, I incorporated a few touches that only I knew about. One was kind of like a smart mark in a modern casino token. Months passed and coins and Marlboro boxes were the order of the day.

Then it happened one day. I heard the signal and saw the light blink. But so much time had passed since I installed my security system I really didn't think it could possibly be a raid. I viewed it as just a malfunction of the system or I thought Sal dropped his fucking horn and probably tripped off one of my sensors.

But I was wrong! It was the FBI and the Geneva Watch Company was teaming with federal agents. Everyone was arrested. The door next to where my press was located was battered in and the FBI was shocked to learn that the only thing that they found in the store was liquor. What did they expect? After all, it was a liquor store that they had just broken into. I was standing next to the press in the adjoining building listening to all that was happening. They had fucked up and raided the wrong place!

The FBI was absolutely furious that they found nothing at the Geneva Watch Company or at the liquor store. None of those arrested spent even the night in lockup and no charges were ever filed against any of them. The next day, the newspaper said the FBI was incompetent and that they should have focused their attention on the North End in Boston.

Within a week, the slug operation was dismantled. And, in August 1980, I delivered the last batch of coins that I would be making and wrapped the operation up. This time I did not deliver the coins to Sal's house but instead to a vehicle which was parked on a side street near the S&S Bar the night before. Taking them to Cranston was obviously out of the question. After all, Sal, Bobby Flowers, Frankie Martino, and many of the others were arrested only a few days earlier. Anyways, I transferred the coins to a parked car off Atwells Avenue, as previously agreed to, and now I wanted my money.

I had been recently divorced and was dating Paula, and after a meal at the Old Canteen on Atwells Avenue, I told her that I had to make a quick stop and pick up some money a guy owed me. The guy was one of the top members of the Patriarca family and was responsible for paying me for my last delivery of coins that were finished after the raid.

The problem was that since the raid, the buyers backed out saying there was too much heat and refused to take the coins. I said I didn't give a shit whether they took the coins or they didn't take the coins. I sweated my ass off making and packing this shit and chopping up the scrap as well as cleaning up the place so that if the FBI got a warrant for the right building they'd find nothing. Everything would be in order.

We argued loudly and violently calling each other a motherfucker. Ronnie was a tough guy and he had many hits to his credit and he was a made man in the organization. He had a fist that was so large that if he hit me with it, I'm sure I would be lucky just to wake up a week later in a hospital. Ronnie was a tough guy and I wasn't. He had fists as big as all outdoors, and balls to match.

Because he was a made member of the Family, I used him on many occasions to collect money for my friend, Leo, in New York, who owned International Diamond Distributors. Leo's business was constantly getting beat by people that he sent diamonds to or to whom he extended credit. Just looking at Ronnie was intimidating and the first thought that would come to anyone's mind is that this is one guy you didn't want to fuck with.

And here I was pushing him to the fucking limit. I wanted my money and I inched my car closer to the sidewalk and I told him to get what I wanted inside or I wouldn't leave. It seemed like an hour or so, but a few minutes later he came out the front door of the S&S carrying a small lunch bag.

I studied the bag closely trying to determine if it contained money or something heavy, like a gun. I looked at the bottom of the bag to see if there was any kind of a sharp bulge on the bottom. The visibility wasn't good enough for me to determine this. I didn't think he would shoot me on Atwells Avenue, especially so close to our bar, but then it certainly wouldn't have been anything new. Lots of wise guys were killed on the Avenue, one right across the street from the S&S in front door of a furniture company. I wasn't scared but I reached over to the compartment on my car's door panel and took my Smith and Wesson Chief's Special, loaded with plus P ammo and put it underneath my right leg. If there were going to be shots fired, I was going to shoot back.

Ronnie approached the car on my side and threw the bag in the window. The bag weighed nothing. It landed in Paula's lap. There was no gun in the bag. I breathed a sigh of relief as Ronnie turned around and proceeded back to the S&S calling me a motherfucker.

I asked Paula to count the money.

"Sixty seven hundred dollars," she said.

"OK," I replied and drove the car past the bar and down the Avenue. We went up I-95 North and wound up in her apartment in North Providence. She was turned on by what she had just seen happen and said she knew who Ronnie was from newspaper articles and his picture in the paper. She was a stand up-girl and that turned me on. We spent the night making love and laughing. God, I like this girl I said to myself. We were going to be together continuously for the next eight years. We remain closest friends even to today.

By now, the coin business was over and the Marlboros were finished, too, since the death of Joe Barboza in California the Marlboro box still in his hand which he was using at the time of his assassination. But, life was good. I had Paula, some cash, power, and was being consoled by all who helped me through my divorce. Even my parents, who were devastated when Ann and I finally got divorced, came to my side. In fact, Ann wrote my father a letter, in which she told him that I was a no good son-of-a-bitch, and that I was a wise guy who belonged in jail.

To my amazement, my father wrote her back, "Then you did the right thing by divorcing him."

Ann was tired of all my bullshit, and the divorce was her idea and if she hadn't pushed it, I probably would still be married to her. She did the right thing!! Like my relationship with Paula, Ann and I are still good friends today.

Chapter 9
Dairy Land Insurance

I really wasn't worried because at the time, I still had some cash left from both schemes and there was no problem. My friend Louie, who was very much against the divorce, asked me if I couldn't put things between me and Ann back together. But when he realized that I didn't want the divorce, he kept prompting me all the time to give Ann anything that she wanted. "Sign over the house, give her money. Do whatever she wants, Do the right thing," he would say repeatedly. His rationale was that peace of mind was worth a million dollars, and that I was a good earner, and could always make the money back. Well, my peace of mind came close to costing me the million.

The divorce was starting to eat me up alive. The wise guys at the bar were coaching me in the same way and kept saying that my peace of mind was worth more than a million dollars and that I was a good earner anyway and always could make the money back. The same story Louie was giving me. I signed every fucking paper and document that her lawyer presented me until finally one day my lawyer, who was a friend of ours at the S&S, Bobby Cerelli, a mobbed-up guy, began to question my sanity.

"Do you know what the fuck you're signing? You've signed everything that she put in front of you and you'll be broke in no time."

I said I didn't care, but he was right. It didn't matter. By now I had peace of mind and four dollars in my pocket and an insured Porsche that was about to disappear. What more could I fucking want?

I went through the drive-in window of Dunkin Donuts, and spent $2.85. I left the girl a S1.15 tip. Now I was broke.

I sold a piece of gold jewelry, a chain, for a couple of hundred dollars, found an apartment in a slum area on Rankin Avenue, off Chalkstone Avenue, in Providence. The rent was only $135, so I thought I'd be OK for a least that month. Then the landlord told me he needed one month's deposit. I was short.

We began talking and finally he looked at me and asked, "You're not Dora Colavecchio's son, are you?" When I said I was, he immediately said, "Forget the deposit. You're from great people. I love your mother. And how's your brother Ronnie? Is he still in Brazil?"

Who would have figured he knew my family so well. The apartment was mine. I had three wooden chairs, a TV set, and an old bureau that my mother-in-law gave me. I thought I was a fucking king. I was alone for the first time since I was 21, and I actually loved it.

In June of 1980, my divorce was final. As if this wasn't bad enough, another blow came that took the life out of me. My uncle Vincent died after a short illness. I was with him until a few hours before his death, and he maintained his sharp wit and great sense of humor until the end. We were sitting in the R.I. Hospital's solarium, and Vincent was a shadow of his former self.

The nurse said how he was doing just fine, and Vincent remarked in a split second, "Yeah, that's what they all say three days before you die." He looked at her and continued, "You thought it was more." He died the next afternoon.

In the spring of 1980, I was hanging mostly with Louie Mansolillo, Baby Shack's nephew, little Louie, who was about 15 or 20 years younger than I was. His friend Jimmy Massarone, who was a skilled carpenter, was dealing coke. He was making more money in an hour than he could make as a carpenter in a week. It's funny, because there was probably a 20 or so year difference between our ages, but they thought of me as if I were their age. Kind of how Vincent and I felt about each other some 25 years earlier. They were both dealing and using coke at the time, and wanted an idea of how to smuggle coke into the country.

I didn't know coke from King Arthur flour, but they were making a huge profit with this and needed some help with the project. I told them I didn't want to be a partner in their venture, but I did ask them what they needed. They were looking for a way to smuggle coke across a border.

The first idea that came to my mind was to use some sort of a common container and what I ultimately decided on was using was a shaving cream dispenser. I took the top of the container off carefully and made a machine, a little tool to remove the top then re-form the bezel and put it back on so that it would be unnoticed. The problem was that once you emptied the contents of the can if you were to try to use the can, it wouldn't function properly. For me that was a major drawback because being a perfectionist, I wanted it to appear as if the can were full of shaving cream and not something else.

I found a way around this by purchasing very small shaving cream dispensers that were used only for traveling and would provide enough lather for one shave. They were about an inch in diameter and maybe two inches tall, and I rigged them into the mechanism of the shaving cream can so that when you pressed on the top of the shaving cream, shaving cream lather came out. Perfect. Meanwhile, if you unscrewed the unit it was full of cocaine. Again, I had no idea of exactly what they were doing with this or how they were using it but I made lots of these containers and each one was worth $500 for a can of shaving cream that cost me maybe two bucks.

I remember one beautiful day, Louie and Jimmy came over to the house. They had been driving around rural areas of Rhode Island all day looking for a spot for me to get rid of my bright orange Porsche that we had welded together with another Porsche to get two legitimate VIN numbers on them. We had done this in my garage shortly before I was divorced. Both Louie and Jimmy would be constantly pulling out a vial from their jacket pocket and using the Porsche's key would take a hit of coke and then Louie said that he had found a perfect spot.

"It's deserted and has a very sharp bank with a drop of at least 25 feet straight down into a deep pond. Hell, they'd never find the fucking car in this century."

"Lou, it's perfect," he insisted.

We decided to wait until it got a little darker, then we would take the Porsche, follow with Jimmy's car, and push the Porsche over the cliff, and that fucking pig would be history. Jimmy would help push the car into oblivion. Jimmy and Louie did a few more rails of coke, and each time they did they would talk more and more about the plan and how perfect the spot was.

We laughed a little bit and joked about how funny it would be to watch the Porsche disappear into the pond. We wondered how many other people dropped cars into this same spot. It looked like nature had made this spot just to bury Porches and unwanted insured cars.

Of course, if the Porsche could talk, it could have told the story of how we took a Sawzal, cut it in half, and mated the smashed front part with one from the same model with a good nose on it. The other car had been whacked in the rear where this one had been whacked in the front. Then we did the same thing to the other car, winding up with two cars with different serial numbers, both of them fully insured, registered and ready to go.

Louie had demolished the front end of one of the Porsches while driving in the Silver Lake area of Providence with a girl who was giving him a blow job while he was passing through an intersection on Union Avenue. No one was hurt in the accident, except Louie, who could have lost his dick, which hurt like crazy. To listen to him describe the incident, it was funny as all hell.

I remember welding the two cars together, connecting the brake lines, clutch cables, wires, lights, changing the upholstery, the trunk latches, and anything to make the cars drivable. Perfection was not necessary. The cars had to start, drive, and look reasonably good. They had to pass a vehicle inspection for the VIN number and that was about it. And we knew people who worked in this department of the registry.

They were insurable. The VIN wasn't a problem since both numbers were legal.

To show low mileage, it was necessary for me to open the odometer, reset it, then make a burnishing tool to close it. To put that goddamn speedometer back together was a real project on the Porsche but when finished both cars were in the low 20,000 mile range. The odometer could stand the closest scrutiny. With that kind of mileage on them, the cars were insurable for approximately $15,000 each.

No one looked very closely at anything and the insurance company, Dairyland Mutual was so hungry to penetrate the New England area that they wrote policies on just about anything. They were out to capture the automobile market in Rhode Island and Massachusetts and they certainly did so. Two and a half years later, the president of the company was seen on TV saying that his company would never, ever write another policy on any automobile in New England. They took a beating for hundreds of millions of dollars which almost bankrupted the company.

By now it was dusk. We were driving to our chosen location. The plan was to ditch one of the cars in Rhode Island and in a few weeks the other in Vermont or New Hampshire. Both cars were ready. We drove to our location, wasted no time in putting the orange beauty at the edge of the cliff and then push it into oblivion.

The car rolled easily down the little mound of grass just before the cliff, then sped down the hill, gaining speed with every passing second, finally hitting the water and splashing like an amusement park ride. We watched it go deeper and deeper, the doors were already half buried and disappearing fast. There was less than a foot left to go before it would be completely submerged and buried forever. But the fucking car stopped sinking without completely disappearing. There was about three or four inches of the roof left showing and that fucking top looked like the roof of a Howard Johnsons Restaurant.

I looked at Louie and said, "You fucked this up, didn't you? Did you ever check how deep this fucking shit hole was?"

Louie was my friend's nephew, and his uncle was constantly angry about Louie's cocaine use. To say that I did something like this with Little Louie would be a mortal sin to Louie senior.

"Imagine if he found out about this fuck up." I took both assholes and left quickly.

There wasn't anything that could be done anyway. It was time to get the hell away.

When we left with the second vehicle, I couldn't help but to look at the roof of the fucking car and said, "My God, when you do business with fuck-ups doing coke, this is what you can expect."

I felt glad I had taken the precaution before bringing the car to its final resting place of popping the ignition lock just in the event the car was ever found. Both Louie and Jimmy laughed when I was doing this, as they assured me the car would never be seen again, and it wasn't necessary. I didn't do things that way. I remember telling them that if the car ever was found it would appear that it was stolen.

That could have proven to be a $15,000 decision. I called the car in as having been stolen, and if the car were ever found again, the pop in the lock and the jumping of the ignition would stand up to my story. I wasn't worried about not getting paid. We went back to my house and enjoyed our night's work but this time we were making bets on how long it would take for the cops to find the fucking car. Actually, they never did.

Collecting money on this car was a joke. I filed a claim and within 30 days was paid in full. The second car, which was identical to the first one except for a different VIN number and color, was a little more difficult to collect on. The program was about the same except that it was ditched in another state and two claims for

Porches stolen from Providence people alerted the insurance company. The company said it was conducting an investigation and it held up payment for about 60 days.

One day, Louie and I were sitting in the house and Louie said, "You know what, I'm going to call the fucking insurance company."

When he dialed the company, I said, "It's a waste of time. We might need our lawyer to collect." He dialed the company anyway, got right through to the president's office, told him who he was, that he had filed a claim and that he wanted to get paid. The president of the company actually apologized, said that the investigation was complete, that it was somewhat suspicious that two Porsches would disappear from people in Rhode Island within a short period of time, but that a check would be issued soon. We thought it was a joke but within a couple of days, another check for $15,000 came in the mail.

The company that had been so anxious a year earlier to get our business got the business from us, then decided to pull out of our market. Go figure.

Later that year, Jimmy was complaining of having pain in his testicles. We told him to stop fucking those whores he was always with and find better class of girls. I urged him to see a doctor, as I knew it could be serious. One afternoon, I took him to see a urologist who insisted that it was nothing more than Jimmy's poor choice of women, and he had a urinary tract infection. The doctor gave Jimmy an antibiotic. When the pain didn't go away a week later, I took him to another doctor who immediately diagnosed Jimmy with testicular cancer, which had spread to his lungs. Jimmy would need immediate surgery to remove his testicles, followed by chemotherapy for at least a year after that, and gave him about a 50-50 chance of survival. Jimmy refused the operation, but did take one or two chemotherapy treatments, before telling the doctor he no longer wanted to be treated. If he was going to die, he would die complete with his balls and all. The cancer went into remission on its own and 30 years later, Jimmy is still going strong.

Chapter 10
Foreign Car World

In 1972, I was working from the garage in my house repairing, painting, and selling exotic cars. Ferraris were my favorites, but Lamborghini, Maserati, and DeTomasso were also great. I hung around in a garage on Phoenix Avenue in Cranston which was a repair center for exotic cars. It was run by Lee Gianelli and his son Reno, with Lee's nephew, Mario Gianelli.

Lee Gianelli was a Ferrari trained mechanic and a close friend of Enzo Ferrari, founder of the famous Ferrari race cars. Ferruccio Lamborghini, the tractor manufacturer who was once snubbed by Enzo Ferrari, began manufacturing his own sports cars which competed directly with his rivals Enzo and Mario Agnelli, the owners of Fiat Motor Company in Italy.

Lee was also a very close friend of Marcello Gallo, one of the owners of the famous Gallo wine company. Marcello Gallo was the director of sports car racing for all of Italy. In short, Lee knew anyone and everyone who was of any importance in the automobile industry in Italy.

Lee was trying to make automobiles. He would take a Pontiac, cannibalize it, removing its body and then replacing it with a body made by Ghia, one of Italy's famous sports car body manufacturers or carrozzerias as they are known in Italy. He took an Italian body and put it on the Pontiac's chassis. Some fine tuning was done to the stock Pontiac engine to improve the car's performance. The car was called a Stutz Blackhawk.

Lee was an absolute genius as a mechanic but had no business sense at all and no marketing strategy whatsoever. He had an automobile dealer in California selling about 12 of his cars per year. He had sunk his entire life savings in this project and there was no way it could ever become profitable.

I was interested in having Lee work for me. If he did, I would build a large garage and a showroom. With Lee's reputation and contacts, I was sure we could make some money, so I made Lee an offer to buy him out.

Lee was agreeable but insisted that I take Reno, his son, who was a total incompetent and leave Mario his nephew, who was almost as skilled as Lee himself. I said no, but offered a compromise. I would take Lee who I wanted, Reno who I didn't, and Mario who I also wanted. They would come as a package. Lee agreed. We settled on a price of $100,000, approximately all of the money that Lee had invested in this business. I would run the business for a while. We had several car bodies finished and ready to be transplanted to the Pontiac chassis.

I immediately flew to California to talk to our sales rep and find out if it was possible to increase sales a little bit so that at least we could break even until I could liquidate the business.

One suggestion that he made was to raise the selling price. We were retailing our cars for approximately $18,000, which was too close to other cars like Ferrari and Lamborghini. He suggested we raise the price to the mid 20s and add something to the inside of the car to justify the higher price. This was considered a marketing strategy that would add more prestige to the car and hopefully make it more desirable. I raised the price by $7,000 to bring the retail to more than $25,000 and added a nice burl wood rear bar which cost us about $2,000 in total.

Sales rose from 12 units per year to almost 20. We sold cars to Eva Gabor, Elvis Presley, Dean Martin Jr., and several other celebrities at the higher price.

Higher pricing put the cars in a more prestigious position and the buyers of the cars were more than happy to pay the extra money. But, 20 cars per year still couldn't make the company break even.

By now I had purchased a huge tract of land on Atwood Avenue, near Hartford Avenue, in Johnston. I paid $80,000 for the land. Half of it was in cash and the other half with a phony mortgage which I obtained from City Loan Company, our Piggy Bank. I simply gave them $40,000 in cash and they gave me paperwork and a check for $40,000. I wanted to get out of the car manufacturing business and begin buying, selling, and repairing exotic automobiles. I eventually sold the business to our distributor in California for a fraction of what I had paid for it and opened the new business which was now called Foreign Car World, on Atwood Avenue in Johnston. The building was 5,000 square feet. The building was completed in just a couple of months and we moved there in the spring of 1973.

The business was an immediate success, with customers coming from as far away as Maryland. With Lee's connections in Italy, we were making trips every few weeks or so to buy cars and also to go to the Ferrari and Lamborghini factories and various other manufacturers to get parts for cars that we were repairing. There were so many cars in our shop at any one time that it was necessary to build a fenced in area behind the building to park the overflow of cars at night.

While all this was going on, I continued buying swag diamonds from some wise guys and sold the smaller ones to Leo in New York. The larger ones I brought with me to Italy, especially the very high quality pieces as they sold for far more money in Italy. Europeans have a different mentality than the Americans. The American buyer wants a big stone of lower quality, but cheap. In Italy, they bought the best quality stone, even if it was a lot smaller and the cost was higher.

A very unusual incident happened on one of my trips. I had a stop to make, using Carlo as my driver, and it turned out to be in a very dangerous area of Rome. No problem, Carlo said, except when I told him the appointment was for 11 at night. He was uneasy about this stop for sure.

At 11 p.m. we pulled up to a building with a small showroom. It had a little sign in front indicating that it had some affiliation with the Lamborghini Motor Company. A tough looking Neanderthal of a man let me in without so much as nodding hello. Carlo waited in the car. I also told Carlo that if I were in trouble I would try to throw something out of a window. This would warn him to take off, that the deal had gone bad. He didn't like the idea, but business was business. I had a supply of top quality, 1-carat- and-over diamonds and a buyer was waiting in his office.

The owner of the business was a tall, well-dressed man in his mid 50s and was extremely polite. He ushered me into his office and told both my buyer and me to help ourselves to anything that he had on a beautiful small bar, on which was located a cappuccino and an espresso machine. He asked if I knew how to use them. He would show me if I didn't. I told him I would help myself to a glass of wine. He closed the door leaving me and a stout, shabbily dressed man to conduct our business.

The man spoke English beautifully and we had absolutely no problem striking up a mutually acceptable and profitable deal. No more than an hour was necessary for him to examine each and every stone. They were all to his liking and the final figure was $110,000, which he promptly paid in cash.

I was tired and ready to go back to my hotel. Carlo had been waiting for me more than an hour and a half and I wondered if he thought something had gone wrong. The owner of the small business knocked on the door and we told him that our business was concluded and we thanked him for the use of his office and the buyer left. The owner of the place asked if everything was satisfactory and I responded absolutely. Everything went just fine.

He wanted to show me the whole place, and asked me to follow him to the back of the building where he had a repair shop and a small storage area with some cars for sale. I was carrying over $110,000 and was a little nervous, but still I never had a problem with anybody I dealt with who had connections to my friends and my family in the United States. Entering the back room, two other goons showed up making me nervous. I remained cool as I continued even deeper into the back room. There were four of us now in this dark room and he immediately flicked on a light, revealing several cars in various stages of repairs and several cars that were ready for sale.

Before I was able to say a word, he glanced at my left wrist and spotted my watch. It was a very special watch which I had custom-made by the Bueche-Girord factory in Switzerland several months earlier. The watch was a square shape, which could slide onto an 18-carat yellow gold, hand-made watch band. It could also be removed and slid onto a necklace if so desired. The movement in the watch was referred to as a 9 Dusselier movement, 23 jewels and had chronometer accuracy. The 9 Dusselier designation referred to the fact that it was the thinnest movement made in the world at that time. The length of the bracelet was custom made to fit my wrist.

The man remarked on how beautiful it was and asked if he could hold it. I slipped it off my wrist reluctantly, figuring my business was finished and I wanted to get the hell out of there. What could he possibly want? The clasp on the watch was unique, one of a kind, and was designed to blend in perfectly with the bracelet. It took a minute or so just to find and undo it. I handed him the watch. He placed it on his wrist and he seemed to have no problem in locking and securing the clasp. It fit him as if it was made for his wrist. I had paid $6,000 and waited close to a year to have this watch made. Looking at it on his wrist, I felt I got a bargain.

The watch stayed on his wrist too long — it felt to me like shaking someone's hand and he won't let go. I finally asked him to return the watch as it was very late and I wanted to get back to my hotel. At this point, he actually refused to return it.

I was thinking, "What the hell am I going to do next?" I told him to stop clowning around and if he really wanted the watch, I would be glad to order one for him. I told him I paid $6,000 and that I waited almost a year for it so I had to have the watch back.

Again he said no. The watch was his now. What a fucking problem this was. Me alone with three fucking wise guys who I felt may have wanted to rob me. I had no idea where this was going to lead. He pointed to several of the cars he had for sale. One of them was a beautiful white Lamborghini Miura P400SV. He said, "Anything you want, you can have, but the watch stays on my wrist." I looked to the white Lamborghini and in Italian said, "Io voglio quella macchina," which translates to, "I want that car."

I expected to be laughed at or more likely be beaten up or maybe even worse. He told one of the goons to have the car removed from the storage area the following day and that I should return the next afternoon at around 3 p.m. to complete the paperwork. I didn't know if I'd get out of there alive or not, so I followed one of them to the front door.

So far, so good. Then one of them came running after us. I figured this was it for sure, but remember, "That which you think is going to happen, inevitably never does."

The guy just wanted to ask if 4 p.m. tomorrow was OK instead of 3 p.m. because they still might be closed for lunch. I said 4 p.m. was fine and he unlocked and opened the door and I exited immediately. I opened the door to Carlo's car and we sped out of there. Then I broke the news to him. We had to return tomorrow afternoon. This, he said, didn't bother him as at least it was going to be during the day and wasn't anywhere as risky as tonight's visit.

We had a short night's sleep, and the following day Carlo took me to look at several other cars. At 4 p.m. sharp we arrived at the Lamborghini showroom and to my absolute amazement all the paperwork, bill of sale, title, and even insurance papers were prepared and ready for my signature. Even Carlo was impressed. I bought, or rather traded, a $6,000 watch for an $11,000 Lamborghini. I took the car back to the hotel and the following day drove it on the Autostrada where I cruised for about 100 miles at more than 160 miles an hour. What a fucking thrill that was.

Over the next couple of years I was a frequent visitor to this place and bought cars and sold diamonds there and we made lots of money together.

I knew Al "Albo" Vitullo because I had taken junkets to Vegas with him, for the bubble, of course. Albo was a character, and anything he did, he either made money with, or totally fucked up. He owned Action Rocket Tours and was running junkets to Italy. He knew I made frequent trips to Italy and asked me to give his Action some business. He had a tour leaving in a couple of weeks, and there was room for several more people. I decided to use his Action to go to Italy.

We were supposed to go to Rome and stay in the Grand Excelsior on the Via Veneto. The Grand Excelsior was a very exclusive hotel, located almost at the beginning of the Via Veneto, next to the Café de Paris and down the street from Harry's Bar. It was a happening area.

Somehow, I just couldn't see Albo fitting in this scenario, because Albo was a real street hustler. Anywhere he went he always took cheap jewelry and trinkets and tried to swindle everyone in the hotel. But, the ticket did say the Grand Excelsior and Al Italia Airlines. I spent ten days instead of my usual twenty one, for about the same price of $650, with room and airfare included. I gave him a shot. I had plenty of business in Italy on this trip, and had lots going on in Rhode Island, so 10 days was perfect.

We arrived at the Excelsior around 1 p.m. I thought they were going to shoot us. When Albo walked in, he had on a cap with black stripes on it and was arguing with the manager of the hotel. Albo had swindled a lot of people in the hotel on his last visit, and as if that wasn't enough, he hadn't paid for his last stay there. They wanted us out, and all Albo's bullshit would not work this time.

So, there we were. Maybe 35 or 40 of us, with our luggage sitting on the Via Veneto, stuck without a hotel reservation. Albo was trying to calm us all down, but he was desperately looking for a hotel that did not know him and that he had not fucked yet. He got lucky, and so did I.

Adrianna Bertani met us at the front desk. Albo was trying to con her to give us all rooms, and Adrianna called the manager and Albo and him worked some deal and we were going to stay at the new Holiday Inn, not the Excelsior. Hell, after the long plane ride, all the hassle of moving luggage, then getting back in the bus at the height of the traffic hour, I was fucking glad to sleep anywhere.

But, this was not anywhere. It was only the second day the Holiday Inn was open in Rome, and it was brand new. Adrianna Bertani, Assistant Manager, is what the badge read. She was, without any doubt, the most beautiful girl I ever saw in my life. Maybe she was 22 years old, and she was just too beautiful to take in at one glance.

"Hi, I am Louis," I said. "I'm sorry, I forgot my last name, because your beauty makes me dizzy."

She smiled, "Your Italian isn't bad, but I think you wanted to say that my beauty makes you forget your last name."

I smiled. "I am sorry. I hope I didn't offend you with my poor Italian, my crude remark, or by thinking you didn't speak English. You've got me going again. I am sorry."

She started to laugh.

We both said simultaneously, "Let's try it over again." Now we were both hysterical. I thought she was as attracted to me as I was to her, if that's possible.

I didn't give her any stupid line. Well, maybe I did, but it was sincere.

"I like you, Adrianna" I asked, "What are you doing tonight?"

"I am working late," she replied. "I am sorry."

"I'm not sorry," is said. "I want to take you out."

She replied quickly, "Then meet me after work, and we will go for few drinks."

I called Carlo and asked him to meet me at the hotel at 1 a.m.

I just arrived in Italy, was thrown out of the Excelsior, moved to the other side of Rome in the busy traffic time in a shitty bus, and checked into the Holiday Inn. I was tired. But, I felt like a 15-year-old and I couldn't sleep, waiting for 1 a.m. to arrive.

We met in the downstairs guest room, and she said, "I have a Fiat Cinquecento. We'll, go to a place I know that's open all night."

I said, "No, I have a Mercedes and a driver waiting. His name is Carlo Panzironi. He drives me around when I'm in Italy."

I could have knocked her over with a feather. I wasn't kidding and she knew it.

"Carlo, this is Adrianna, Adrianna, meet Carlo." I felt 10-feet tall. I loved this girl. Soon, she loved me.

We saw each other frequently, and I'll never forget the song playing on the radio in her apartment the first time we made love: "I beg your pardon, I never promised you a rose garden."

We were together every day she wasn't working, and every night when she was. I wound up staying in Italy more than a month.

That song always brings me back to Adrianna. I used this song to break up with her a year later. I did not want to fuck up her life. I told her this was the most difficult time I ever faced in my life. I didn't have to say anymore. I never saw her after that. But I have beautiful memories burned in my mind. I still think of her after 30 years. I hope she still remembers me. Now, I'm no singer, but I know what I like and Sinatra's song said it perfectly. "Once in a while, along the way, love's been good to me."

Lots of women passed through the doors at Foreign Car World, but I was to meet one who became a long time part of my life, and who eventually became a co-defendant in a major casino counterfeiting crime that ended up with both of us serving time. Her name is Donna Ulrich.

I've said on numerous occasions that criminals have a secret code when it comes to women, and that, especially in jail, the letters LLO run rampant through any jail. It means "ladies love outlaws," but Donna's case was much more complicated than ladies love outlaws would imply. Outlaws are generally more colorful characters than the average working Joe who puts in a 40 hour week where he hates not only his work but his boss as well. Outlaws live by a different set of rules, and I can think of many reasons women might be attracted to them, even if out of sheer curiosity for some other style of life.

This was not the case with Donna. She was an intelligent girl, with below average looks. She was married several times, but always to some average slob, and she found an attraction to me immediately at Foreign Car World. She took an uncanny interest in my whereabouts and actions. She pursued me throughout the years at Foreign Car World, and followed my movements for the next 30 years, once renting an apartment no more than a couple of blocks from my house in North Providence, where I lived with my wife and children. Without sounding pretentious, she made a pattern of popping in and out of my life, even though I had no contact with her, sometimes for years on end. It seemed she knew my every movement at any one time.

When Ann and I were divorced in 1980, I rented a third-floor apartment on Rankin Avenue, in Providence, and wasn't there more than a few days when Donna rode a bicycle to visit me. I have no idea how she knew where I was; no one except for my immediate family knew my whereabouts. I told her I was seeing other women, but she still came by frequently. I never felt threatened by her presence, physically at least, but her inopportune visits aggravated me at times, to say the least.

Years later, when I bought a townhouse in the Louisquissett Condo Complex, in North Providence, Donna also purchased one in the same complex, and monitored my movements so closely. Once, when she didn't see my girlfriend's car parked in my driveway over a Labor Day weekend, she realized that we may have broken up, and popped into my life once again. Looking back, I realize that she had an obsessive compulsive personality, but never hid it. I just never saw it.

It's ironic that I made hundreds of thousands of casino tokens and never really got excited about playing them in a casino. I loved making them. Donna played until her fingers bled, and could easily spend hours sitting in front of a stupid slot machine. Perhaps it was in her genes: her brother did exactly the same thing all his life.

Spending time in prison gave me an opportunity to think about my life, successes, and failures. I realized that Donna had convinced me for so many years that she was someone she was not. I now began to see her as she really was: an unstable woman who was a compulsive gambler. She loved the wise-guy lifestyle so much that the day before our last trip to Atlantic City, we had broken up and she was now living back in her unit in the complex. She called me, and when I wasn't home, immediately ran to a friend's house to beg to come to Atlantic City with me the next day. She packed the coins that night and the rest is history.

This was weighing on me, that's why I digressed just a bit from my foreign car adventure stories.

"Well, it's got a nice paint job, I'll give you that much," a man said about the bright red Ferrari Boano Coupe. The car was ugly despite its paint job and was going to be a difficult car to sell, that's for sure. I realized that, but I owned it for practically nothing and it was necessary for me to purchase this car when I bought Lee out. Part of our deal was that I purchase all of his inventory.

One day, a buyer from Specialty Motor Cars, a small business located on Jerome Avenue in the Bronx — the heart of the wholesale car business in New York — came by the shop.

Jerome Avenue was a real scummy area in the Bronx, filled with fat, cigar-smoking, used car dealers who would sell their mothers for a profit. The man he worked for was Bill Blywise, who made a high-living buying exotic automobiles.

He had a deal for me. He said he'd trade me an Alfa Romeo and $3,500 for the Ferrari. I decided to take the Alfa, clean it up, and sell it real cheap. Anything over zero was, I reasoned, a profit attributable to the Ferrari. I gave him the Ferrari and took the Alfa and the check for $3,500.

The lesson here is not all Ferraris are desirable and this certainly was one that wasn't.

About a week later, the $3,500 check was returned, marked insufficient funds.

"Insufficient funds," I screamed. "That's a fucking lousy $3,500. This guy runs a business buying all kinds of exotic cars. How could a lousy $3,500 check bounce. The bank must have made a mistake."

I put the check through again for deposit a second time and the second time it came back marked insufficient funds. I called Bill at Specialty Motor Company and the cocky motherfucker told me, "Shove it up your ass."

I asked for the Ferrari back and he told me it was sold: "You'll get paid when I've got some money, asshole. Meanwhile, stop calling here."

I asked around to a few dealers on Jerome Avenue and found out that he was getting ready to go bankrupt. I then called Paddy. We decided to drive to New York immediately and get my money for the bad check before any more time went by. It didn't matter what was involved. Oh sure, I could've sent someone to collect it for me but this one was personal. He not only fucked me and my money, but he was making a fucking fool out of me at the same time when I asked to get the Ferrari back.

Paddy was a smart choice for this project. He had been a professional boxer since he was a teenager and had many situations that required using restraint or he would have beaten his opponent to death. In *Ring* magazine he was named as one of the toughest opponents anyone could fight in spite of the fact that he was a super lightweight. He had a great combination of speed, agility, and intelligence, a nice combination for a boxer.

Besides, at about 5-feet, 8-inches, and 135 pounds or so, he wasn't about to intimidate anybody at first sight like some of the other collectors I had used from the bar. The mere sight of some of them would have been enough to scare the shit out of the fat car dealer before we got in the place and especially before we got our money.

I went along on this collection because I wanted to see the motherfucker's face when I showed up at his place.

When we got there, it was late in the morning. Paddy drove his new Cadillac convertible right up to the front door of the joint. The lot was capable of displaying at least 30 or 40 cars, but he only had 10 or 12 that were really shabby. The two best cars were two Triumph TR 6's, which were in decent condition, and there was an MGB which wasn't too bad. The rest looked like they might not even start.

I stepped out of the car with Paddy and we looked for the Ferrari. It was nowhere to be found. Bill Blywise spotted us and, at first, didn't recognize me. He came towards us and when he glimpsed at Paddy's Rhode Island license plate, the fat fuck ran and made it all the way into his office before Paddy caught up with him. He was almost behind his desk and Paddy leaped over the old wooden relic.

I said, "That's the motherfucker right there, Paddy."

Paddy hit this guy so many times and so fast, the guy's nose was spitting blood like Old Faithful. He was close to being unconscious but he was still screaming for help. Paddy was like a bulldog and the guy was silent in a matter of a few seconds.

"Don't kill the asshole," I told Paddy. "I want my fucking money."

Paddy said not to worry: "The only thing that will kill this fat fuck will be a heart attack."

He stayed right beside him even though he had stopped beating him. I casually walked over to the safe which was unlocked and swung the door open. A small money box within the large safe was locked. I told the bloody asshole to open it and he refused. Paddy began to pound his fat face a couple of times but not hard enough to render him unconscious. You could hear the guy's fucking nose breaking in couple of places and the familiar sound of a broken jaw.

"Enough, Paddy," I said, "or he won't be able to see the numbers on the small safe."

Paddy said, "I'll shove a pen in his fucking eye and with his other eye he'll open the fucking safe."

Bill was trying to catch his breath by this time and stay conscious. He wanted the safe open as badly as we did. He fumbled with the combination at least half a dozen times before he finally got the fucking door open.

One, two, three, four hundred. Four hundred and twenty six fucking dollars.

"Where's the rest of my fucking money?" I shouted.

Bill cried, "That's all I have."

"Paddy."

That's all I had to say. Paddy gave him a shove in the back of his head that sent the guy's face into the dirty cement floor. The guy was unconscious and we waited for him to come back to fucking earth. I asked him to give me the rest of my fucking money or I would leave him there alone with Paddy and he wouldn't like the way Paddy left him.

He cried like a baby.

"I don't have any cash, I swear, I don't have any cash," he insisted.

I said, "Where's the paperwork for the cars that are on the lot?"

He said, "I have some paperwork but I don't know if I have it all."

I said, "You better hope, for your sake, that you can find the paperwork for every one of those fucking pigs."

Boom. Paddy hit him again. Another fall to the floor.

"OK, OK, please no more. Pull out the small wooden box."

It was a little hidden wooden box with a drawer behind the safe.

"It contains everything that I've got," he said.

In the drawer was a stack of papers, some returned checks and other worthless bullshit. I sat at his desk and sorted out the paperwork. The keys to the cars were all hanging from a makeshift coat hanger wire strung across the inside of the safe's larger door. I told him to get the fuck up and sign all the paperwork over to Foreign Car World. We wanted every car on the lot. He refused only once and then couldn't sign fast enough.

Now I had this fat fuck's cars that were in the lot.

Paddy said, "I can get a few guys here right away, Lou."

"OK, Paddy."

Then, I called my friend in Rhode Island who did a lot of odds and ends jobs for me, Frank Martucci, a gopher, more or less, but a reliable driver. I told him what had happened and that I needed him to put together a few drivers and that we'd meet him on Mamaroneck Avenue, in Connecticut, which was about 25 miles away from Jerome Avenue. We'd make three or four trips to get the dozen or so cars from Specialty's lot to the commuter train's parking lot at the bottom of Mamaroneck Avenue. Frank said to get started moving the cars there and he'd put together a crew, which would take maybe two and a half or three hours at least. I paid three professional drivers from the avenue to move the cars to Mamaroneck Avenue. The drive from Jerome Avenue to Mamaroneck Avenue wasn't much of a deal for us and it didn't take us long, not more than two or three hours to get all the cars there. Now the cars were all parked in the commuter train's parking lot and everything was safe and secure.

Bill Blywise was on his way to the hospital to get his nose and jaw put back in place, and Paddy and I were on Mamaroneck Avenue babysitting about a dozen cars.

"Nice job, Paddy," I said as I handed him four hundred bucks. In Connecticut there were five drivers and Frank. They were just getting ready to take half of the cars to my lot in Rhode Island. Several of the cars had difficulty starting but we were prepared for that by taking jumper cables with us. The whole process took more than eight or nine hours but every one of the cars we took from Specialty was now mine.

A couple of weeks later, Specialty closed up for good after declaring bankruptcy. No mention of what we had done or consequences were ever brought up, and Paddy and I actually felt we helped him a lot. After all he was going bad anyway and we just cut his torture a little shorter. Each of the drivers that helped us was happy to get a hundred dollars and the whole episode cost me approximately twelve to thirteen hundred dollars. I sold one of the TR6's for almost twice that amount and had another 10 cars that were still sellable left over. Not too bad for a day's work.

Ann had always suspected that I was having an affair while at Foreign Car World, so one day, she decided to hire a private detective to follow me.

"The guy's nuts," the private detective told her. "He pulls out of the shop and before you know it, he's doing 140 miles an hour and I can't keep up with him. He's driving a silver Lamborghini and heads north all the time. There's no way that we'll be able to follow this nut. The only thing that I can suggest is that you rent a helicopter and we could follow him that way but know exactly when he's going to be leaving the shop because this is an expensive proposition."

Ann said that it would be on a Friday night, always on a Friday night, and decided that she would go for renting the helicopter. The cost was $60 per hour and a minimum of two hours was required. So, when I left the shop the next Friday night and the helicopter was following me, I assumed that the helicopter had something to do with Foreign Car World business, that it was either an FBI agent or a DEA agent, or some other fucking initials and that they were interested in seeing where I was heading. I never thought it would be Ann having me followed.

I was heading towards a girl that I was seeing. Her name was Jackie Skipper, and she was half Indian, a beautiful petite girl that I liked an awful lot and was a lot of fun to be with. She worked at one of the local nightclubs in Pawtucket, and we would get together as frequently as possible, but for sure every Friday night.

When we met at the airport, I was shocked to see Jackie's mother. She was a thin, petite, nice-looking woman in her mid- to-late 40s. Her husband, Jackie's father was as full-blooded American Indian. Jackie was a lot younger than me, maybe 21 years old, and I was 33. We met in a busy Pawtucket nightclub, called Downtown's, where she was tending bar. She was witty, bright, smart, beautiful, and in love with a married man- me.

"Don't let anyone know about what you're doing," her mother told her in the airport. Her mother didn't approve, but she knew she couldn't stop Jackie either.

She said, "I love you, mom," then Jackie and I boarded our plane for our flight to Rome.

We stayed in a small hotel near the Coliseum. A friend of mine owned the place and I had stayed there many times before. I always got the best room available. I had business to conduct so Jackie walked to the Coliseum and spent the day alone. Later, Carlo met us and took us to pick up my yellow Ferrari Dino.

Jackie loved my lifestyle and I envied her naivete. She would look out the window of the hotel room and fantasize about the people living in all the little houses below, wondering what kind of cars they had, what they did for a living, and all kinds of little details that I would probably never have given a thought to. She was so bubbly she found excitement in the smallest detail. We made love while she was looking out the window and I was behind her. But I wasn't looking out the fucking window.

"Oh my God, this is unbelievable," she said with tears streaming down her face. It was Venice in all its splendor.

I said Jackie, "See, I told you I had lots of friends in Italy."

Thousands of people were everywhere, and the canals were roped off with the same kind of colorful restraints found sometimes in a bank. A purple rope with a beautiful, brass hook on the ends was strung from one side of the canal to the other. It was controlling the traffic in Venice.

It was Il Giorno Della Regatta: The day of the Regatta. All of Venice was celebrating, with elaborately decorated gondolas, private boats and taxis or as they are called in Venice, motoscafi, parading through the canals of Venice. It was an awesome sight indeed.

"Thousands of people came out to see us, Jackie," I said with a huge smile.

I felt like some kind of royalty. While we waited at a liquid street corner, we weren't far from the Excelsior and I began wondering if we shouldn't get out and try walking. If Luigi wasn't there we wouldn't even have a room, because only he knew I was arriving that day.

The moment was too romantic and I knew it wouldn't ever happen again. This was a once-in-a-lifetime experience and I wanted to absorb it. Whatever happened at the Excelsior, well, I couldn't change that. Anyone having any appointments in that city, on that day, would be very late indeed. As it turns out, Luigi was waiting for us and stayed an hour and a half beyond his shift to set us up in our room, and what a room it was. Our room was right on the Grand Canal and we could see St. Peter's Basilica clearly across the other side of the Canal. The view was magnificent.

Downstairs, the hotel had a writing room with a number of desks, chairs and hotel stationery, envelopes and pens, and it was only a few feet away from the canal itself. Everywhere you looked, there was marble. This was the most elaborate room in the hotel, and our room paled in comparison. But, again, the view was breathtaking.

That night, we walked around Venice, and Jackie was like a kid in a candy store. Small, little, narrow alleys, then St. Mark's Square. Shops all around the square. Ann didn't miss a shop in all of Italy. But Jackie didn't have any interest at all in shopping. She was fascinated by every piece of stone, brick, mortar, and marble that made the shops, and had no interest in what they were selling, except for the little gelati shop that sold the richest ice cream in the world.

The small band was playing music in front of a bar, and we went in for a couple of cappuccinos, then took our drinks to the tables outside. It was romantic. I was seeing Italy at a slower pace than I usually did for so many years and this was nice. When the woman came by our table, I bought Jackie a rose. You might think I bought her a Rolls. That night neither of us could wait to get in bed, and we didn't' make it that far into the room. We undressed each other, and I made love to her holding her in my hands, my body in hers and looking out at the lights in the canal. Then we made love again in bed, my arms were getting tired.

I took Jackie to Murano by motoscafi. Murano is famous for its glass and ceramic products, and we watched masters working at their skills, melting glass, turning it into colorful, hand-made works of art, right before your eyes. Sure, it's a tourist attraction, but I only knew another side of Italy up until now, and this was a welcome change. Besides, I still did some business on the trip, and had fun at the same time.

Ann not only found out about this trip, she had my friend, Luigi Tolin fooled into making up an invoice for the room we stayed in. A few months after this episode, Ann wrote to him in Italy, and said that she was my accountant, and needed a copy of my bill from the hotel, for a tax investigation I was undergoing with the IRS. Luigi made up a bill and sent her a copy which stated Due Persone, or two persons, had occupied the room. Ann was very clever at gathering information. But she also knew that I was breaking the relationship off.

I remember one night I was at Jackie's apartment on Cherry Street in Pawtucket, not far from where I live now. We had made love and fallen asleep, and in the middle of the night, I heard sirens. I thought I was dreaming and Jackie was sound asleep beside me, neither one of us had any clothes on.

I said, "Jackie, I think I smell smoke," and she woke up and said, "I hear a siren," and looked out the window. Outside the front door were two fire trucks. The building was on fire! And, I'm in there and I'm trying to keep a low profile but here is the fucking building burning down. Jackie immediately threw on a robe and as soon as she got in the hallway there was a fireman there.

He said, "Is there anybody else inside?"

She said, "No."

Meanwhile, I'm standing on the other side of the door with nothing on, and so I tried to put a pair of pants and a shirt on quickly.

This was the dead of the winter and it was very, very cold out that night, and another fireman turned around and hollered to the fireman upstairs, "Break the door down."

Every door had to be broken down. This building had to be checked to make sure that it was empty.

Meanwhile, I'm still standing on the other side of the door, half dressed. I opened the door very casually. I had on a pair of pants, a jacket but no shirt underneath it and I walked down the stairs as if nothing were wrong and that I belonged there. By now there were a lot of news media outside and I just kept walking and had several firemen ask me if I needed oxygen and I said no.

Several TV reporters asked what had happened, but I continued past them as if they didn't exist. I couldn't find my fucking car. My car was missing. I knew immediately that Ann had taken the car, and that it wasn't stolen. This was the kind of thing that Ann was capable of doing.

So, I walked around for a couple of blocks in the freezing cold, and guess what, there's Ann and my sister-in-law, Terry, sitting there laughing their balls off. When I went up to the car, I said, "This isn't fucking funny. Will you give me the fucking keys, please, take me to my car."

Ann had known that I had been seeing Jackie and had actually caught me with her in both in Italy and then in New York a month or two later. I promised Ann I would end the affair and managed to survive this disaster in our marriage. I was also able to get my car back. I drove home and we spent the night together.

When Bearcat police scanners were such a fad, my son was listening to police news and one of the broadcasters announced that an as yet unidentified man had been caught in a roadblock on Atwood Avenue. He was clocked at over 140 miles per hour driving some sort of a rare sports car. He was being handcuffed and brought to the Johnston police headquarters.

My son overheard this conversation and said to his mother, "Do you think it's dad, ma?" Ann replied, "Who the hell do you think it is? Of course it's him."

They both arrived at the police station about the same time that I did. When I entered, two cops, one of them Tony Rossolino, nicknamed MooMoo, greeted me immediately and removed the cuffs.

He asked the two rookies who arrested me, "Don't you know who this is? It's my cousin from Foreign Car World."

Actually, MooMoo was Ann's cousin. MooMoo was a sort of a zany cop who was always causing trouble for the chief of police, my friend, Bill Tarro, by wearing long ponytails, dark sunglasses and constantly beating up somebody in a bar brawl. The chief had tried to fire him on several occasions, but MooMoo always got his job back. This night he got me out of there.

The next morning, Bill Tarro walked in my showroom and apologized for the misunderstanding the night before.

"Just a couple of rookies doing their job," he said. "Lou, I'll need the Rolls Royce for the weekend. I got a party to go to."

I handed him the keys and said, "Have a great time."

"I'll bring it back Monday or Tuesday," the chief said.

"That's fine," I replied, "Say hello to everyone for me."

The car I had been driving at 140 mph was a DeTomasso Pantera. I had race prepared it for the Mille Miglia, a thousand mile race, to be held in Italy the following month. It was owned by Marcello Gallo himself, who until recently was head of all motor car racing in Italy.

This car left my shop a few days later to be brought back to Italy via Al Italia Airlines and featured in a news story. The syndicated article was called Auto Whirl and was written by Ken Parker who was a contributing editor to the *Providence Journal*. It went on to say that of local interest was a Johnston company, Foreign Car World, and described how we had raced prepared a car owned by Marcello Gallo, then sent it back to Italy to race in the famed Mille Miglia.

Ken wrote of us up frequently, but those days would be ending soon. The government went after Foreign Car World with a vengeance. I couldn't chance bringing in any more cars. The FBI and Customs were watching me far too closely and as if that wasn't fucking bad enough, the IRS was doing an audit on me and kept asking me so many fucking bullshit questions, I actually set up an office for the agent across from my office where he spent more than six weeks poring through my records. He actually found nothing, but I agreed to pay the made up fine of $9,000 just so he could justify his lengthy investigation to his bosses. All the time the IRS guy was there I was pulling deals all over the place.

One bright, sunny day a girl came into the shop wearing a skimpy tennis outfit. She was a blonde with blue eyes, tall, good looking, and extremely bubbly and smart. A minute or two later her husband came in. Turns out that her husband was Dr. Thomas, a dentist who had his practice just a block or so up the avenue. His wife's name was Linda Thomas.

They were interested in a yellow Fiat X19 that was in the showroom and she kept asking me all kinds of questions about it, as did her husband. I had several photos hanging in the showroom of me racing the car. It was a small, two-seat sports car. The car had been only partially race-prepared and I took him for a ride. Afterwards, she insisted on going for a ride as well.

In the car she made a pass at me and told me that she would come back tomorrow afternoon. She asked me if I liked boats.

I said, "Of course, I like boats."

That afternoon, they bought the car.

The next day she returned to the shop. This time she was dressed with very short shorts and underneath was a bikini bathing suit. She had on a tiny halter top. She was a very sexy, attractive woman. She insisted on showing me her boat and I agreed to go look at it.

The boat was a 26-foot sailboat. The minute we entered the boat she laid out a blanket, grabbed a bottle of wine and proceeded to undress me and herself and we fucked around for a couple of hours. We saw each other almost a year. One day, my very close friend — a surgeon named Al Carlino who referred the Thomas's to me in the first place — asked me how they liked the new Fiat X19 they had purchased from me.

I told Al, "Thanks a lot for sending these people over to me, oh, and by the way, I've been fucking Linda for the last few months."

He laughed, then said, "Oh my God, no kidding. Don't let the doctor find out, he's my friend."

Linda left her husband a couple of months after we first met, and several times, after we had left a motel, she would follow me almost to my front door. One night, she came so close to my driveway, that I stepped out of my car, and asked her if she would like to visit with my wife. She was beautiful, but I began realizing that she had some very serious problems. I didn't know how serious until a few months later.

Paddy Rease was my friend for many years as well as my bodyguard for a good length of time. Now he was going bad and wanted to do a bust out with his American Express card. He said that he needed immediate cash and asked if there was something that I needed and I told him that I'd go on a shopping spree with him in New York, and take Ann and that I'd give him 50 percent of the cost of everything that we bought. He was thrilled with that.

Ann kept telling me that she wanted to get a divorce and this was something that for some reason I didn't believe and I thought maybe the trip would help our marriage. So, we set out for New York and I decided that since I had been banging Linda all of this time, it might be a nice idea if we combined a little pleasure with this trip and that I would have Linda meet us in New York. The first two days in New York would be with Ann.

Ann wanted a fur coat, so we went to a very exclusive furrier and Ann picked out a $15,000 coat. She wouldn't buy the coat unless she could get a hat that matched it and the hat was an extra $1,200.

When the merchant called it in on Paddy's American Express card, he said, "There's a telephone call for you, they'd like to talk to you" and Paddy picked up the phone. The call was from American Express verifying that it was Paddy that was using the card and Paddy said, "I'll be doing a great deal of shopping in New York for the next couple of days," The company was quite happy with that. They only wanted to verify that the card wasn't stolen. Ann had a $15,000 fur coat and a $1,200 hat.

The thing that impressed me most that day was that when the coat was monogrammed Ann did not have it monogrammed ADC but ANN, just her first name. That was the first time I actually believed she was going to go through with the divorce. She took a train and returned home to Rhode Island. Now I believed her.

The next day, Linda arrived in New York and met us in the Penn Garden Hotel. We had a friend there that was a security guard and we could always stay there for nothing. There was always a room available for any of us guys from Providence. We decided we wanted to go out that night and we had a contact with Rodney Dangerfield. He owned a place on First Avenue which appropriately enough he called Dangerfield's.

When we tried to make reservations the place was packed and they would not accept any more reservations over the phone, so we decided to go there in person. When we did we recognized several people in the place and a table was setup immediately in the best location in the restaurant, only a few feet from the stage.

The show began first with a warm-up comedian. We were partying and drinking and enjoying ourselves when Rodney Dangerfield comes on. He's as funny as all hell in person and probably funnier in person than he is on TV.

Anyway, during the middle of his telling a story Linda, all of the sudden, stood up turned around and looked right at him and shouted, "You fucking Jew." He was lightning fast in replying: "Oh, thank you so much, usually they call me a fucking Jew bastard." Both Paddy and I were mortified. This fucking girl had embarrassed the daylights out of us.

I couldn't get out of there fast enough and said, "Paddy, get this piece of shit out of here, will you."

We grabbed a cab, and went back to the hotel room and Paddy and me had to hold her up walking to the elevator because she was so fucked up. I honestly thought she was going to die on us, right there in the lobby. I put her in bed and then decided to go through her purse. When I did I found a needle and syringe and a bottle marked injectable Valium. She was a fucking drug addict who was doing heavy doses of liquid Valium. Since her husband was a dentist, she had access to all kinds of drugs. But she also had a medical background and worked in a nursing home from time to time, so drugs were easy for her to obtain.

I called Paddy over to my room and I said, "Paddy, we got a big problem here. She's a drug addict. I hope she doesn't fucking die tonight."

He said, "Just keep an eye on her, I'm sure everything will be all right and don't worry too much."

It looked as if it was going to be a long night, but it was soon cut very short by another incident.

Paddy comes running up about four thirty, quarter to five in the morning and says, "Lou, we got to get the fuck out of here, really quick, right now."

I said, "What's the problem?"

He said "Lou, they're doing an investigation on our friend that got us this room and they know we're in the fucking hotel right now, and they're looking for us … They'll be up in a couple of minutes, I'm sure."

I tried to wake Linda up and she woke up instantly, just like nothing had happened. It was only five or six hours earlier that she was so fucked up I thought she was going to die. Within 10 minutes we were out of the place and in Paddy's car on the way back to Rhode Island like nothing had happened.

On the way back, I said to Paddy, "Let's change positions, I'll sit in the back and you ride with Linda."

Paddy and Linda began talking and it actually seemed like they had a lot in common. This girl could talk with anybody. She was very intelligent, beautiful, a nymphomaniac, and a drug addict. I could see that Paddy was absolutely flabbergasted by her and that he liked her and I said to myself, "This is terrific. Paddy will wind up with Linda and I'll be off the hook."

Paddy began dating her and every time I would see him, he'd say, "Lou, you're absolutely wrong, this girl is great. She's great with my kids, she's great in bed. She's great when you take her out."

I said, "Paddy, do you remember what happened at Dangerfield's?"

He said, "Yeah, but I think that was an isolated incident."

I said, "Well, you do what you want but be very careful Paddy, she's a drug addict and a nymphomaniac. She's a very sharp girl. Watch yourself."

Some time passed.

"Lou, I guess I didn't tell you, did I?"

"What is it Paddy? I haven't seen you in a while, where've you been?" I asked.

He said, "Linda and I got married."

I was flabbergasted.

"Yeah, we got married by a judge about four or five weeks ago."

I said, "Good luck to you," Paddy. "You're going to have your hands full from now on."

He said, "Well, maybe she'll be all right, although she has had a couple of episodes."

The marriage lasted four or five months before Paddy said he was either going to kill her or she would have to move to Florida. She moved to Florida and we never heard of her again.

Meanwhile, the business was in its heyday at this time. There were so many cars parked all over the place and always something was happening.

Lee was constantly swearing up and down. With his strong Italian accent he'd scream, "How are we gonna get this car out in time and how are we gonna get this job done?"

But somehow, all these jobs did get done perfectly and on time, despite Reno. Reno was still the biggest liability that the shop had. I could never get it through his head that you don't open a can of oil by putting it on top of a Ferrari fender and punching a screwdriver through the top of the can.

His father actually came over one time and threw him a shot in the face and told him, "If you do that again, I'm going to fucking shoot you."

But it was that he just had no talent at all and that's the way it was going to be.

On the other hand, I had Mario and he was a young Lee Gianelli, with almost as much talent as Lee had.

Lee was beginning to show his age but was still active. He had developed a very big chest and I asked my friend Al what that meant. He told me Lee had a certain type of a disease in which the lungs became enlarged and his chest cavity was also becoming enlarged. He told me to expect this to get much worse and that his knowledge of this disease was that people who had it usually didn't live more than three or four years. Well, I felt bad for Lee. Lee not only worked for me but we were close friends. Lee would go out of his way anytime at all to do something for me and he did so on many occasions. I can still see him today working on the cars and it's just as if time had not passed. His memory remains very vivid in my mind.

Life with Lee in Italy was always exciting. He knew anybody and everybody who was connected to sport cars, including race drivers, engineers like Dallata who designed the Ferrari motor, Enzo Ferrari, Ferruccio Lamborghini, Marcello Gallo, and so many more it's impossible to remember them all. When we went anywhere he knew just who to ask for and everywhere we went we got the red carpet treatment.

He introduced me to Pierro Drogo in Modena, who was the distributor for De Tomaso Automobiles — both the Mangusta and its successor, the Pantera. DeTomaso, was a joint venture between Ford's Mercury division and DeTomaso as the body was Italian, and the engine was a 351 cubic inch Ford Cleveland. I always thought the Mangusta was one of the most beautiful cars I have even seen in my life, but wasn't very dependable. Its replacement, the Pantera, was a little more reliable. It was sold through Lincoln-Mercury dealers in the United States. New, the car retailed for about $11,000. I race-prepared these cars with some degree of success for the Mille Miglia race in Italy.

"Let's go watch some racing, Lou," Lee said. "Vallelunga is opening for the season tomorrow, and all the top drivers from around the world will be there."

The next day, we had box seats at the Vallelunga race track, located in the small town of Vallelunga, some 100 kilometers southeast of Rome.

The cars were moving at speeds in excess of 180 mph, and our seats were right at the point where each driver shifted gears, from third to fourth. Their precision in shifting was perfect, every shift was made about two feet to the right of where I was sitting, lap after lap, without a foot of variation, and this at over 180 plus mph. The Ferrari engines had a deep roar, almost like a barking sound, and they shifted at about the nine thousand rpm mark. I got so that I could close my eyes and tell you what car was passing just by the sound its exhaust made.

Lee was the real master though at diagnosing an engine's condition just by its sounds. In fact, in one race where I had prepared a car at Foreign Car World, and shipped it to Italy, the motor was misbehaving. I was in the pits at the Modena Areo / AutoDromo. This is a great racetrack in the city of Modena where so many exotic cars are manufactured. The race car track has a small airplane landing field in the center.

One pilot, Luigi Il Patza, or Luigi The Nut, flew inverted only a few feet above the cars which were racing around the outside of the track. Lee was at the shop in the U.S., and

Back to the pits. Lee had us put the phone receiver on the motor and led us through the fine tuning just by the sound alone. He tuned the car from thousands of miles away, and it went on take third place in its class. I was used to this kind of thing from Lee. In the shop, he used a stethoscope to fine tune engines all the time, and he could tell you the condition of an engine just by pulling out the dipstick, and feeling and smelling the oil.

After the race, Marcello Gallo took us for a meal and a couple of drinks. When we left him that evening, we took my silver Lamborghini and drove home. I forget the name of the hotel we were staying at, but the owner was Lee's friend.

The women in the restaurant were drinking Cokes and, for me, that's a dead giveaway. So, I changed my table, and moved closer to them. It was a small restaurant located on the hotel's first floor, but the food was good and we got a little extra attention because of Lee. He wasn't hungry, so I was alone. I was right. The three gorgeous girls were speaking English. They were Americans. I moved right next to them and started up a conversation.

The three had just left Greece and this was their first night in Rome. At Cheryl's invitation, I moved to their table. "I'm Louie," I said. They were Linda,

Cheryl, and Dawn. They were taking a couple of months from work in New York to travel Europe. Cheryl worked as a secretary and was the most aggressive and beautiful of the three. I don't remember what Linda did, but she was petite and pretty. Dawn was a junior high school teacher, who had big hazel colored eyes and a very pretty smile, innocent looking with a beautiful shape and quick wit. Beauty and brains in all three.

I offered to show them Rome in a Lamborghini. The Islero was a 2x2 model, is very small, but is capable of carrying four passengers, at least for a short period of time. I wouldn't take a 1,000 mile trip with four people, but the back seats are handy for groceries and luggage, and in this case, the girls. The girls had never even seen a Lamborghini, let alone ridden in one. But Dawn was tired, so it would be just the three of us. Cheryl and Linda could not finish their meals fast enough.

After dinner, we walked across the street to the underground garage where my car was parked. Parking on the street was dangerous. Dawn went to her room, which was just a few doors from my room: the three women were sharing the same room.

I did say I was going to show them Rome. So first we went to the Coliseum, where I drove around it once at about 80 miles an hour. So much for the sights in Rome.

Next we headed to the Café de Paris on the Via Veneto. It was a lovely night, and we sat at an outdoor table. We ordered drinks, and watched as lovers rode in horse-drawn carriages up and down the avenue, then we headed up the street to Harry's Bar. The girls knew of this place and were excited to be there in person. They were doing their trip on a low budget and Harry's Bar is not a place one goes to on a low budget.

We stayed there, drinking, laughing, talking, and looking for famous people who frequented this place. An early evening soon became 2 a.m.

We were all feeling good and decided to head back to our hotel, which was not more than a few minutes ride away. I parked the Lamborghini in the underground garage. Walking up the twisty underground ramp was scary; there was no area on the side for walking, and a couple of cars came by us that were traveling too fast for that twisty, narrow driveway. I told the girls to stay close to the inside wall. It was safer. Soon, we were across the street from our hotel and the car was parked, safe and sound.

Inside the hotel lobby we began talking and hugging and the next thing I knew, I was in my room making love to Cheryl. Linda left us, after first coming to my room. She went down the corridor. Cheryl was young and beautiful, may be 20 or 21 years old and was exciting. Youth is so fascinating, I remember thinking to myself.

The next day, Lee knocked on my door. Cheryl was in the shower, and Lee saw the empty bottles of Chianti and heard Cheryl whistle while the water was running.

"Get a good night's sleep?" he asked.

"Not really," I said.

Lee laughed when I told him what we did the night before. He reminded me that we had to go pick up some parts at a small Ferrari dealership in Rome. We spent most of the afternoon getting the hard-to-find parts we needed.

The girls knocked on my door only minutes after I entered my room

"It's us," Cheryl said.

"Come in. Want to go somewhere tonight?" I asked.

"You bet," Linda replied.

"I just need to shave, shower and get dressed, and we can take off in an hour."

"Can we stay in the room while you get ready?" Cheryl asked.

I was trying to stay cool, but my heart was pounding. "Of course," I said so matter of fact-like. "Put the TV on; it gets three channels."

It was going to be another great night.

After my shower, while I was shaving, totally nude, Cheryl and Linda came into the bathroom. They wanted to watch me shave. It was around 5:30 — 6 p.m., and the two bottles of wine on the bureau were staring at us. I finished drying myself off and wrapped a towel around my waist.

"Want a drink?" I asked.

"Yes," all three answered almost simultaneously. The first bottle was empty in less than 15 minutes. So we opened the second one and before long, that was gone, too. We decided to go downstairs, grab a bite to eat, then go buy more wine. Nobody wanted to eat but me. So I gobbled down a fast antipasto and we walked around the corner where I bought six bottles of wine: two chiantis, which I was not crazy about, and four merlots, which weren't bad.

We were back in my room an hour after we left it. The three girls came in, but Dawn left for her room. It was only 7 or 7:30, but she knew what we were going to do and she wasn't ready for it just yet.

Actually, the quality of the wine didn't matter because most of it was spilled on the sheets and into the mattress anyway. Linda and Cheryl poured it on my body, then on their nipples, their belly buttons, and between their legs and we were all licking it off each other. That was only the second or third time Linda had been with a girl and wasn't sure if she liked it or not, but wanted to try it enough to be sure. Cheryl had been a switch hitter for six months and even though she said she liked men more, she was equally comfortable with Linda. Actually, we were all very comfortable and within a few days Dawn would join us also.

I really liked these girls. They we honest about their sexuality and none of us ever felt sorry or regretted anything we did — with one exception. The next morning, I was lying between Cheryl and Linda. I was like a fucking target in a shooting gallery, going back and forth every time it's hit by a bullet. It ended with me and Cheryl, and Linda was upset, but she was sweet. I liked them both.

Then there was a knock on the door. It was 11 a.m. and Lee was asking to see me. He said room service was complaining because they wanted to clean the room and they left at noon. It looked like a bomb hit it. Wine stains were everywhere. We all took a shower together, three of us in a small tub with a shower and a weak stream of water. I ran down the corridor. The cleaning woman had a mad look on her face. I was embarrassed at the condition she would find the room in. I gave her a $20 bill and told her I would see her every morning, or to look on the bureau when she cleaned. I left her $20 every day. Her anger turned to a nice smile. She got $20 dollars for the next three weeks. From that day on, my blankets were always fresh and clean, at least until the girls and I got in bed.

One night, in the middle of partying, around 2 a.m. Lee called my room. Dawn had joined us by now.

"Come down right away, Lou," Lee said.

"I'm with the girls," I replied.

"Well, throw on a pajama bottom, there's no one here but me and the night manager."

I went downstairs to the check-in desk which was located near the window. Both Lee and the manager yelled, Guardi, Guardi. Look, Look. There were a string of cars parked along the street, the first one parked almost directly across from the hotel's window. Thieves were systematically breaking the windows of each car and removing the radios. Crash, then a radio was removed. Crash, another radio was gone. It took 30 seconds to smash and grab the radios. I watched seven or eight cars get victimized, then went back to the girls upstairs.

Everywhere Lee and I went, we took at least two of the girls. When Lee wasn't around, the four of us went sightseeing. The three girls were the epitome of the saying, "Everybody's different." They were nice girls and when I left for home, we felt sorrow. Even though we exchanged phone numbers, we knew we wouldn't ever see each other again.

On the flight back home, I was quiet for hours. Lee tried to cheer me up and said it was like watching a great movie, and when it was over you wanted it to continue.

I smiled: "It was three beautiful weeks, Lee. You thought it was more."

During this period of time, Charlie West was a frequent visitor to Foreign Car World. Charlie owned Diamond Auto Body along with Richard Barone. Diamond Auto Body was their starting ground but they later went on to build Louisquisett Condominiums and became very big in the real estate business.

Charlie and I always got along well. Charlie was an easy going kind of a guy, a down to earth person.

I had another person working for me whose name was Jack Elliott. Jack was capable of selling a refrigerator to an Eskimo. He was a great salesman, but in reality he was a real piece of shit. I kept him around because he was good for business but outside of that I never trusted him and I never let him know any of our secrets.

Charlie and Jack never hit it off and lots of times Charlie would say, "Be careful of him."

I'd say, "I know, I know, I'm well aware of the fact that he's just a piece of shit."

Jack had kids all over the place. He was married four or five times and I don't think he could remember the names of the women he had been married to. He brought people into the shop and he made sales and the women loved him, so he had a good combination. I kept him around, but I always kept him at a distance from any of the business that was going on at Foreign Car World.

With all of that, it was still a small place. He was there every day and there were conversations that took place. Although we tried to exclude him from knowing anything that was going on, I'm sure he heard a lot of things. He was a meek type of a guy and nobody worried too much about him. We knew he wasn't a stand-up guy, but we wouldn't have a problem if he went out of line. He never did.

***

It wasn't supposed to happen that way. It was supposed to be nothing more than a simple insurance fire.

Andrew needed some cash. His house was in western Cranston and he needed a fire so he could collect 10 or 15 thousand dollars from the insurance company. That was all it was supposed to be.

In reality, there was nothing left of the house but a hole in the ground. Not even the foundation remained. There wasn't a piece of wood or a piece of anything that was larger than six inches to be found. The house just seemed to vanish. It was the talk of all of Rhode Island for months and months.

The house was owned by Andrew Mansolillo. Andrew ran the S&S Bar and the arsonist that made this thing happen was Andrew Marino. Muzzy, as we called him, was a real whack-job but very talented with fires. He did some of the biggest arson jobs around the country.

I was the liaison between Andrew and Muzzy at the time and all of these conversations that took place were in the front showroom in Foreign Car World. Andy had asked me what I thought of this guy and I told him immediately that I was leery of him because while he might have been very good in his field, he seemed like a whacko to me. Andy decided to use him anyway.

I had the key to Andy's house so Muzzy and I went there in his Lincoln. We entered the house and Muzzy looked around.

Muzzy said, "OK, this is what I'm going to do."

He gave me the lowdown and it was all kind of a technical thing. Muzzy was an expert at what he did. At that time, his fires could withstand any kind of an investigation by the fire marshals, the FBI, or any other government agency. Muzzy was a super professional.

Muzzy was supposed to receive $5,000 and the house was to catch on fire, period. No mention of an explosion was ever made.

I had met him through somebody else in Rhode Island whose restaurant he set on fire several times. The only thing that he was concerned about was that there were no animals in the place when he torched it. When the fire marshals investigated Andy's house, the job was so professionally done that there were no signs of any kind of explosives or accelerants. It was known that there were only a few people that were capable of doing this, one of them being Muzzy.

A year or so prior to the explosion, I had Chief Tarro fix a speeding ticket for Muzzy so now there was a whole lot of heat on Foreign Car World to see what I knew about this house explosion.

Bill Tarro came in from time to time and I'd let him borrow a car for the weekend, usually a Rolls Royce. He was always a pleasure to see. He liked to hang around Foreign Car World. He did me lots of favors with speeding tickets and other things. This was not a social visit.

He pulled me aside and said to me, "Lou, word is out that Muzzy was in your shop a lot of times before Andrew's house blew up. What can you tell me about this?"

I said, "Bill, believe me, the one thing I can tell you is that I'm sure Andy would never allow Muzzy to blow his place up. If Muzzy did this kind of a thing, to me it would not be something that would be sanctioned by Andrew or his brother Louie. I would say he would probably be killed for doing something like this."

Muzzy had done it, and I was going to take lots of heat for this.

Muzzy was a weird guy. He was a good looking, very sharp man. He traveled all around the world. He did jobs and he vacationed in places that are only becoming popular today. He had a strange sense of reasoning. He loved dogs but he hated people.

If you asked Muzzy to do something for you, the first thing he would ask, "Is the fucking guy going to be in the place?"

No matter what it was, Muzzy would continue: "Is he going to be in there? I'd like to set the place on fire while he's in it."

And I'd have to tell him, "Who do you think is fucking paying your fucking bill to do this? You're going to kill the guy that's paying you? Are you fucking nuts?"

He'd understand that, but he'd always say: "If there's any dogs in there, make sure the dogs are out, I love dogs. People are no fucking good, but I love dogs."

Muzzy might have been a paranoid schizophrenic character, but he was the best arsonist in the business.

While Muzzy was doing his thing with the house, Andy, Big Al, and I were at Andy's Bonnet Shores beach house with our wives having a barbecue. The police came by that afternoon and said they wanted to talk to Andy, and he followed them to the station in Cranston. He never returned that day, and we all left.

The next day, Andrew came over to Foreign Car World and pulled me aside and said, "Lou, what the fuck did you tell this guy do?"

I said, "Andrew, I passed your message along exactly the way you told me to."

Turns out Muzzy parked his Lincoln right in front of the house, did what he wanted to do, and left the house as slow as can be with the house blowing up while he could watch it. He was not only putting his own life at risk, but the lives of anybody that could've been outside the house because there were pieces of that house that were embedded in the house next door. It was amazing to see. It was a like spears thrown right through a door.

Also amazing was the fact that none of the houses around Andy's, including the house that had this piece of wood in it, were badly damaged. It was a job that brought a lot of heat and a lot of attention on everybody, especially me. Louie was furious when he heard of this and how the fuck Muzzy stayed alive, I will never know.

The problem was that Jack Elliott had been in the shop on all the occasions when Muzzy came in and Jack Elliott could pose a problem for Muzzy. Muzzy wasn't about to let anybody pose a problem for him.

Muzzy was actually surprised when I told him that Andrew was mad at what he did. He thought he had done a great job.

"The house is gone, isn't it. So what's the big fucking deal?" he asked me.

Muzzy was supposed to collect $5,000 for doing this job and Andrew told me to tell him that, "Instead of collecting five grand, he's going to get six fucking feet of dirt thrown on top of him."

So Muzzy not only didn't get paid for the job but was catching heat all around on top of it.

When he spotted Jack Elliott, he viewed Jack as a possible weak link. I'll never forget when he went up to Jack and grabbed him, pushed him backwards and Jack's head smashed up against the paneled wall in the showroom.

Muzzy said, "Do you know who I am?"

Jack said, "No, I don't."

He said, "Good, you keep it that way, you motherfucker, or I'll fucking blow you up, too. There won't be a part big enough for you to be identified."

Jack Elliott was scared shitless. I'm sure he was afraid that he was going to be whacked sometime soon.

***

Importing cars from Italy was getting more and more difficult with each trip. The government had passed a lot of regulations in 1967, some of them regarding seatbelts which had to have their date of manufacture marked on the belt's label. Then they required AS-1 safety glass for the windshield and AS-2 safety glass for the side windows, then they wanted each tire marked Department of Transportation, plus a whole lot more bullshit.

At first they exempted small car manufacturers who imported 500 cars or less per year to the United States. Within a year or so, they amended that regulation. All cars that were manufactured after December 1967 needed to conform to the United States regulations. As if that weren't bad enough, they also had to conform to the Environmental Protection Agency regulations, which dictated the amount of carbon monoxide per million parts that would be allowed to enter the atmosphere. In other words, they wanted the exhaust pipe of a car to smell like it was fucking designer perfume.

All cars had to pass both the emission control and DOT regulations before they could be certified to be sold in the United States.

Soon after, they also had to pass crash control tests in which the passenger compartment would remain intact in a 35 mph head-on collision. After that, bumpers were regulated so they all had to be the same height and had to survive, intact, a five mph impact. Hell, none of these fucking cars that I imported even had bumpers, never mind the capacity to survive any kind of an impact. Most of the engines were 12 cylinders with six or more carburetors and they were considered monsters by the government. They were very dirty engines, of course. There were so few of the cars that I couldn't see any logic whatsoever in regulating them. Just drive behind a bus, or a truck, and you'll see what I'm talking about.

Many features that found their way to private, mass-produced cars were derived from these limited production sports cars. But they kept coming up with more regulations. Next, the steering column had to be offset, so that in a collision it would not act like as a spear aimed at the driver's chest. Some of the laws were possible to meet and many of the larger companies began bringing their cars up to code. It was an expensive proposition and the performance of the cars was almost certainly adversely affected.

The government wanted Foreign Car World out of business. They thought it was a haven for all sorts of illegal activities but weren't exactly sure what these activities were. So this was a way to bust our balls. Letters from the Department of Transportation were coming in on a weekly basis. They would inspect a car, then send a letter saying the car didn't conform to government standards for one bullshit reason or another. I have a folder full of this shit.

A letter from November 1974, District Case # 74-1303-10619, from the Department of the Treasury, U.S. Customs Service, states that, "On June 10, 1974, you notified the [agency] that three automobiles, a Lamborghini chassis # 3336, and two Ferraris chassis numbers # 3838 and 6102, were fully in compliance with the Federal Motor Vehicles Safety Standards. That statement was false. On June 10, 1974 the [agency] found that one of the automobiles tires had not been marked DOT and, therefore, did not conform to their regulations. Since the statement was false, penalty in the amount of $16,630.00 has been assessed under the authority of section 172.22 of Customs Regulations. Penalty must be paid within 60 days from the date of this letter. Sincerely, Fletcher F. Potter, Jr, District Director of Customs."

A car had one tire that didn't have the letters DOT stamped on it. The other cars and the other three tires on this one car all were in conformity. I overlooked one fucking tire. The fine was $16,630.00. Can you imagine, for one fucking tire, $16,630 dollars? And they said I was a thief.

Lee had lots of strong contacts in Italy. We were able to duck many of these fines or pay just a small fraction of them by obtaining letters written by the manufacturers of the vehicles that the chassis of the automobiles that we imported — if not the whole car itself — was manufactured on or before 1967, before the laws were instituted. But it wasn't difficult to see the end was definitely near.

I had five cars on the water which had left from the port of Livorno and were destined for a port in Boston. I was alerted that the cars would be impounded on the dock upon their arrival. I was able to divert the cars to Port Elizabeth, in New Jersey, but any more cars coming in would be grabbed no matter what I did.

Even with this maneuver of bringing the cars into Port Elizabeth, the government found one of the cars in my garage with me working on an electric fuel pump. They were thinking that I was smuggling something in the electric pump. Two federal agents informed me that the car was going to be impounded. They took it apart with what looked like a fucking can opener. I got a judge to return the car to me as quickly as possible. Nothing was found in the car, of course, but the car was ripped apart.

One of the "initials" said he knew I was smuggling diamonds into the country. What a fucking moron. I told him that a five-year-old kid could figure out that wasn't the case. A perfect one carat blue West, D color diamond cost about $9,000 in the United States and they were easy to buy at that price. Smuggled into Europe, that same diamond would sell for 15 to 17 thousand dollars and have a line of buyers lined up to purchase it. What fucking goof would take something from a lucrative market like Italy and smuggle into a weaker market like the United States, losing money and risking a jail sentence at the same time.

I called the agent a stupid moron and he threw me a slap that knocked the wind out of me. It was time to end the importation of European cars. To make matters worse, Lee had developed a very fast spreading cancer and died within six months

Chapter 11
'The Bust Out'

The final blow to Foreign Car World came from my right fist, which I placed squarely in the face of a bank officer in a Woonsocket nightclub.

Despite all the adversity that Foreign Car World was facing — the loss of Lee, the government heat via the DOT and the EP, and the importation of cars from Italy almost finished — there was an opportunity that opened up. I was in a perfect position to take advantage of it.

I still had Mario, Lee's nephew, and by this time he was as skilled as Lee had been in his younger years. I had made new contacts for cars, especially Volkswagens, Fiats and, more importantly Porsches. This was through my friend Rick Moretta and a renegade, but beautiful aging daredevil, Chandler Lawrence whom Rick worked for and who owned Lawrence Volkswagen.

Chandler was a pilot, crazy as can be, and we became good friends. I bought the newest models from him at his cost. It was even better than owning a dealership. I didn't have the expenses associated with being a franchised dealer. I still had strong racing contacts and was preparing cars for Tommy Gallino and his brother Mike, who owned Gallino Construction Company, a major road builder; Russel Bovin, who owned Cross Pen Company; Tommy Cicchetti, who was a race car driver sponsored by Datsun and whose partner was Paul Newman, the actor from Connecticut. So, bad as things were, I could still keep the place together.

The opportunity I refer to was bringing exotic sports cars up to conformance with the government's new, stringent specifications, then receiving certification from the government that these cars then were legal for the United States market. Several new companies that specialized in this field sprang up with Amerispecs, Inc. being the largest. Hell, we had more experience than all of these companies put together.

I had been doing all my business with the Woonsocket Institution for Savings, a bank that Donna worked for and had contacts in. Specifically, I dealt with the commercial loan officer, Bob Collins, who was a small, meek, soft-spoken, and polite. He was a typical bank officer, and we were never very friendly. I was the only car dealership the bank had, and I had what amounted to a floor plan with their bank. Any checks written for the purchase of an automobile were automatically paid, and then they became a loan. Kind of like a home equity line of credit is today, only my loan was secured by the cars I purchased.

This was, and is still today, the financial structure of an automobile dealership. Every once in a while a surprise audit would be conducted by the bank, just to verify that the dealership still owned and possessed the vehicles that were securing its loans. No one at the bank had any knowledge of cars, especially foreign or exotic cars, or this style of financing. A five-year old Ferrari was still worth several thousand dollars wholesale, while a brand new car like a Ford, Buick, or most others, were less than that. Hell, Volkswagen was advertising, "Still under $2,000." A new VW cost $1,995. To make matters even more confusing, the older the Ferrari, Lamborghini, or other exotic car was, the more collectible it became, and the more it was worth.

Every time I sold a car I would send the bank a check indicating what car the check was paying off. The loan would drop by that amount, until I repurchased another car. I had a line of credit for purchases up to $100,000. If I had sold a car, and hadn't yet paid it off, I would either send a check immediately, or I asked the people to bring it back for a free service. In reality, of course, I just wanted it on my lot for the upcoming inspection. I may have played a few games with the line of credit, but for the most part, I was pretty honest.

Bob Collins came in one day, and I figured he was snooping around to see what Foreign Car World was all about. I played such a conservative phony with him, it made me sick. But, that's what I thought he wanted to see, and that's what I showed him. He asked me if it would be possible for him to borrow a sports car for the weekend. When I heard that, I was relieved. Maybe this was my opportunity to warm up to this asshole and possibly get a higher credit line, or at least, not be under such close scrutiny as I currently was.

"Of course you can have a sports car, Mr. Collins," I said.

"Call me Bob, not Mr. Collins, Lou."

"Of course, Bob, what did you have in mind?"

"Well, I love the new Porsche 914. Is that possible?"

"When do you want it, I'll have it ready and deliver it to you if you need me to."

"No, I can pick it up this Friday afternoon, around four would be great."

"You got it," I told him as he walked out.

Then, 4 p.m. Friday came and went without any Bob Collins. I decided to wait another hour or so, and somewhere around 5:30 he picked up the new, yellow 914 Porsche.

"I filled the tank, Bob, have a great weekend," I shouted as he drove off the lot. I never asked him when he intended to return the car, I was just glad he took it. This would give me some leverage, I was sure.

The following week, on Tuesday morning, I received a call from a Bentley Tolin, an attorney who represented the Woonsocket Institution for Savings. He asked me if I had loaned a car, a yellow Porsche, to Bob Collins. I said, of course, that I thought he was a great guy, and was so pleased to have met him.

Tolin informed me that Bob Collins was in the hospital after a bad car accident, in which he was charged with driving under the influence of alcohol and vehicular assault, as he plowed the Porsche into the rear of a car being driven by two elderly women. Both women were in the hospital in serious condition. Bob he was traveling at an estimated speed exceeding 100 mph.

Bob Collins was, of course, terminated immediately from the bank's employ. Then it got much worse.

The bank was doing an audit on loans Bob had made to the bank's customers, and I was one of his biggest clients. He had been taking kickbacks, using his position as chief loan officer and was about to be charged with all kinds of fraudulent behavior. The bank was investigating everyone associated with Bob, and I was at the top of their list.

Shit, if I ever knew this asshole was stealing, I would have been first in line to grab money and not just a lousy hundred grand. I had no idea he was robbing from the bank. I felt like a moron, and a moron with real bad timing. And this was only the beginning.

The new head of the loan committee was Paul Fowler, owner of a large Pontiac dealership, in Woonsocket. He knew how floor plans worked, and he was envious of the deal I had with Woonsocket. I was floor planning my cars at 100 percent of their purchase price. Not only that, but they were old cars, and some of them makes he never heard of.

"Hell, that's a better fucking deal than I got," he told the loan committee. "I want to meet this guy right away."

Max Winston and I were old friends, and had gone to court together. When I explained everything that had happened to Max, he suggested that we three — Fowler, Max, and me — go out for a drink that Friday night. Max would try to mediate some solution to keep my loan in position, even if only temporarily.

We met at Foreign Car World, but this arrogant asshole Fowler never even went inside my building. He wanted to go to a strip joint around the corner called The El Morocco.

He had been drinking most of the afternoon and already was on his way to having a major buzz going. We stayed in the El Morocco until midnight, when Max suggested we go to Woonsocket to a bar called The Bull's Head. It was loud and packed, and I had trouble hearing our conversation from my side of the table. Fowler had been making remarks about a used car dealer being loaned more money for a 10-year-old car than he got for a new Pontiac. He made so many obnoxious remarks, I really couldn't stand him. But, I knew his position at the bank, and I kept my mouth shut as long as I could.

Every time he asked me something, I had to lean over the table and ask him to repeat it. With all the noise in that place, and with his slurred speech, I couldn't understand a thing he was saying. Max suggested we change places, because Max was sitting right next to this asshole, but Fowler wouldn't move. Then he asked me another question and when I leaned over the table to ask him to repeat it, he said, "What are you, fucking deaf?"

That was the straw that broke this camel's back. I hit him with my right fist right in the fucking asshole's face as hard as I could and heard the familiar sound of a fighter getting a broken nose, and the blood began flowing. He fell to the floor immediately. That fucking piece of shit didn't get up for 10 minutes.

Max was able to persuade the police not to arrest me that night. We decided to go to his house, which wasn't far away and try to figure out what comes next. I had a real problem, and we both knew it.

The bank sent me a registered letter saying that I could no longer purchase any cars on the line of credit, and they demanded all monies owed on this line be paid within the next 10 days. I still wasn't out of business yet. I had a friend in the S&S

who was in charge of distributing small business loans for Rhode Island who could set me up with a similar type loan; in fact, an even better one than I had with Woonsocket. But, he needed about two months to put it all together.

Max advised the bank that they were on shaky ground calling my loan in on such short notice, and that I had a signed agreement which went from year to year and had at least four months remaining. They were violating their part of the agreement, and, should I declare bankruptcy, close my doors, and sue the bank, they would be forced to defend their action. I had a very good chance of prevailing. Their damages would far exceed any money I owed them on the floor plan.

The new agreement reached was simple.

Whatever the line was at this particular time, it would not be increased. I had 60 days to pay it off, and then we would sever any further business agreements. So, I could still buy and sell cars, but I had only about $60,000 on the floor plan at the time. I was capped at that amount. Still, it wasn't a total disaster and it would only be for a short period of time.

I sold a car and paid the loan on it immediately. No problem.

Then, I purchased another car for a much smaller amount. A week later, the check was returned unpaid and stamped account closed.

I went wild. I called Max and he called the bank. They said that we had misunderstood them. They wanted the loan paid in full in 60 days at the latest, but sooner was more like what they really wanted. No new loans would be made against my purchases, and only pay downs from cars I sold would be acceptable. The lying, fucking pricks had put me out of business.

The end of Foreign Car World was here. A bust out was going to be an absolute necessity.

"Lou, this guy's our friend," he says.

OK. That meant I couldn't do anything to hurt him. This is our friend also. But, that left 20 or 30 others that weren't associated with any of the Families in New York. They were car wholesalers on Jerome Avenue, they were and the scum of the earth. But, like my friend was pointing out, some were connected to our people and had to be left alone.

Now, my friend would lend me his right-hand man who could act as a trusted gofer for me. His name was Bob Miller and I had known him for several years. My friend was Kenny Guccione, a member of the Profacci Crime Family in New York. He pointed out all the places to leave alone and would help me grab the others.

"Give Bob five dimes for his help," he said.

I had done Kenny so many favors throughout the years, he was now repaying some of his debt.

On one occasion while alone, I was in the middle of replacing a clutch on a Lamborghini, and was dirty and greasy. Tom DeFusco, Kenny's attorney, called me and said he needed me immediately. They were in the middle of a trial in which Kenny was being charged with possession of a machine gun and illegally filling out the documents to obtain it.

I was with Kenny when he bought it. When he picked it up, we were taking pictures of each other sitting on an old, black Rolls Royce, which I was restoring. We were holding the machine gun in the photos. At issue was the question of whether the charges were federal or even valid. They needed me to testify that the gun dealer who sold Kenny the gun had asked him if he had ever been convicted of a Rhode Island felony, to which he answered no. The government's version was that the question he was asked was if he had ever been convicted of any felony crime. The answer to that question would have been yes.

I had to practically fly home, wash up, change clothes, and be in the courtroom by the time the trial resumed at 1 p.m. The federal prosecutor had no idea who I was. He objected to my being called as a last-minute witness for the defense, but the judge allowed it.

I was a great witness. I even had pictures of the two of us sitting on the old Rolls, jokingly holding the gun as if we were gangsters. If only they really knew, I thought. But I was introduced as a respectable businessman, the owner of an automobile dealership without any police record.

"Yes," I replied when Tom asked if I knew Kenny, and again "yes" when asked if I was with him when he purchased the gun.

"And what questions, if any, did the gun dealer ask Mr. Guccione?"

I said he asked several questions, his name, address, phone number, and so forth.

"And did he make any reference to the defendant's having a criminal record?" Tom asked.

"Yes, he did," I replied.

"What was the question, Mr. Colavecchio?"

"He asked Kenny if he had ever been convicted of a crime in Rhode Island," I answered.

At this point the prosecutors went furious. They stood a good chance of losing the case and they knew it. Even if Kenny had no police record of any kind, the greedy gun dealer should have had a special ATF form filled out, merely because the gun was a fully-automatic machine gun.

Not guilty, your honor, the jury foreman announced after deliberating less than an hour. I had saved Kenny from an almost certain jail sentence.

Back to business. It lasted about two weeks, selling cars at auction and not paying Woonsocket Institution, then buying cars on the avenue with checks that the bank wouldn't pay before word spread that it looked as if Foreign Car World was doing a bust out. Then, at the last auction, which was a small auction house that I hardly ever used before, I heard two enforcers were looking for me.

I left both cars there and took Bob Miller back to Rhode Island with me. The next day at Foreign Car World the two enforcers showed up in the shop. They were looking for a brown XKE Jaguar and another car. While I was talking to them, I was leaning on a brown XKE Jaguar, the car that they were asking about. I told them to get the fuck out of my shop and go back to New York.

They said they had a shooter outside the shop and that I was trapped inside. I was armed with a 9 mm automatic and had my gun in my hand underneath a light jacket. It was obvious to these assholes that I was pointing a gun right at them. They left the garage and sat in their car outside of the two large overhead doors. The front showroom was all glass and there wasn't any security there, but my office was located down the corridor. We moved there to ponder what we were going to do for the next few hours. We finally decided to take a chance, open the door, and speed out in the car. We did and nothing happened.

We were expecting gunfire, and maybe a car chase, and we were able to get out of the shop without any problem. We hid most of that night at my house, until we saw some guys going from door to door. The numbers on Hawkins Boulevard were mixed up with no logical sequence. They were actually a few houses away, having trouble finding number 31 Hawkins. I unscrewed the light bulb in my garage, kissed my family goodbye, and opened the electric garage door quickly and sped away.

The following day we had to decide what we were going to do.

It still makes me laugh today because I was told that there was a wise guy from New York — one of the enforcers whose name was Harry the Cut — and he was going from apartment to apartment in Bob's complex on Hartford Avenue in Johnston, asking everyone if they knew where Bob Miller was. Meanwhile, Bob was insisting that it was mandatory he go back to his apartment because he had bills on the counter which needed to be paid.

I looked at him and I said, "Are you fucking kidding me. You want to go pay your electric bill? These fucking guys are out to kill us."

He still insisted that I go there and I said, "You know what, if you're that fucking crazy, let's go."

The apartment complex had a traffic control arm, and to enter, it was necessary to put in a pass card. The arm moved up to allow a car to enter. After entering, I felt trapped in this place, so I waited outside in the car with the motor running.

Bob went inside and got his electric bill and other bills that he said he had to pay. Meanwhile, I spotted this guy who had been going from door to door and knew right away that this was going to be a close one. Bob was just leaving his apartment when the two men saw each other at the same instant. Bob ran toward my car, with Harry chasing after him.

When Bob got in my car, Harry had just reached the door. I sped out, and went through the traffic arm, which was down. It flew onto Hartford Avenue, breaking into several pieces. We were barely able to get away from this asshole who was looking to fucking cut us up.

But, crazy Bob had his bills, and he was happy. I could feel that the next few months were certainly going to be rough ones.

Chapter 12
On The Run

There I was, on the run.

Not only from the cops, but also from the wise guys. I had gone to see Raymond that morning and asked if he had a beef with me. He said no. He wouldn't cause me any trouble, but that I had my hands full with the New York families. He said I disturbed a hornet's nest and his best advice to me would be to let things cool down then try and straighten this out.

Then he said, "Now take off Lou and be smart."

If he ever knew Kenny was involved in this thing, I think he would have killed both of us.

I decided to stay a few nights at Kenny's house. After four or five nights there, I could see he was getting a little nervous.

One day he said to me, "You know I'm living with my girlfriend Paula and someday somebody could come in here and just shoot this whole place up. What the fuck do I do if they do that, sue them?"

I knew what he was talking about and I knew it was time for me to move on. It was more difficult because Kenny was associated with the Profacci Family, but took money from the Nick DiGiusto, Nicky the Butcher, to start his pornography business. Nicky was tied to Raymond's family in Rhode Island, so Kenny couldn't get afford to involved in any kind of a dispute. He was part of the setting up of the car bust-out scheme including lending me Bob Miller to help me pull it off. If word of this ever got out, he would be in real big trouble because he'd have a beef with both New York and Raymond.

Kenny was getting away without paying Raymond any percentage of his action. I don't think Raymond ever knew the amount of money Kenny was making in the pornography business. In reality, he was the head of a multi-million pornography empire, and even went public selling shares of his business on the stock exchange.

During these years, Kenny and I were friends and we had made many trips to New York to pick up porno plates. Kenny was able to do his own printing and ultimately wound up having the largest porno operation in the United States. Usually, I would try to combine some of my business on these trips, and when I was done, I'd meet with Kenny. We used to go to a massage parlor where we'd get a bath, a massage, get laid, or a blow job and then we'd wind up in SoHo. He had a cousin who owned a restaurant and would open it for us at any hour of the night. By this time, it might be 4 a.m. and he would cook us whatever we wanted. We'd enjoy a couple of hours of talking, eating, and drinking then we'd head back to Providence.

After leaving Kenny's house, I stayed at Joe Capone's house in Jamestown, RI. It was a summer house, but it had been completely winterized. Joe and his family were back at their winter home in Providence so I had the entire house to myself. Joe brought me food once a week. He was a doctor, a gynecologist, but it turns out that he was a real stand-up guy. Some wise guys wouldn't have taken the risks that Joe took for me.

After leaving Joe's house, maybe two or three weeks later, I went to a small cottage in Bonnet Shores, an upscale part of the Rhode Island shoreline. The cottage was owned by Andrew and his brother Louie. It was off-season and the place was deserted.

Andy would have food delivered to me every few days, but there wasn't a fucking thing to do at that house. There was no TV hooked up, no radio. I got a newspaper once in a while. The only thing that was in the house was an old copy of War and Peace by Leo Tolstoy. If I was a weight lifter I probably would use this book as a barbell. To this day I hate the goddamned book.

I had a routine to contact Andy and his brother Louie at predetermined times. But, Louie was on the run from a murder charge and it was difficult for him to do much for me. Andy was a huge help. He found me a safe house in Miami, a place called Sneaky Pete's.

I was given a car to drive to Florida. Of course, my uncle Vincent was keeping in touch with Andy and was aware of everything that was going on with me and with my problems.

Sneaky Pete's was a lively spot, lots of action and lots of girls. It had a beautiful bar, and one night I met two girls there who were spending some time in Florida.

One of them, Marion Forden, was going to stay almost six months, and her girl-friend, Chris Condrey, just a few days. I dated Chris at first and when she returned to City Island, in New York, I began dating her girlfriend, Marion.

Soon, we moved to a safe location, in Fort Lauderdale. It was like a six-month vacation. She was gorgeous and we spent most of our time on the beach where guys would actually whistle when we went by. The guys sure loved her in her bathing suit. I would have preferred if she had smaller breasts, but she was sensual, and we fucked and had a lot of fun.

What I didn't know was that she was writing to her father and mother fre-quently and telling them what a wonderful man she had met, good looking, a business man, and she was beginning to fall in love with him. Her father wrote her back and he said that he thought that possibly I was the guy that was wanted by the FBI, and that I might be a wise guy. She probably knew that he was right, but she denied it to her father repeatedly. I didn't know her father was a captain on the New York City Police Department.

During the next few months, I would call my lawyer, Eugene Truro, one of the top criminal attorneys in the country.

The conversations were always the same, "We're doing fine here Lou. I'll have you home soon. Just don't get caught right now. Oh yeah, and send me another $3,500." I could have easily taped my part of the conversation because his answers were always the same.

One day he finally said something different: "I've just about got your legal problems solved, and soon you'll be able to put your key in the front door and walk in your own house."

I answered, "Eugene, if it takes much longer, I won't have any house to put this key in."

One day, I had some business in Miami and spent the night in a motel there. I glanced out my window and saw three police cars parked in the parking lot. The cops were just getting out of their cars, and I was completely unpacked and wearing only pajama bottoms. I knew they were on their way up to my room, so I slipped on a shirt and pants, and went down the corridor. They were on the elevator and on their way up to my room while I was walking down the corridor. I ran down the stairs and managed to get away.

It was not only a very close call, but I also had to leave all my clothes behind. I would need to shop for new clothes soon, but thought they had alerted stores to be on the lookout for me. I would be caught for sure.

I returned to Fort Lauderdale, to my safe house and Marion. There were cop cars everywhere. I had nowhere to turn. About a million thoughts a second were going through my mind. I was definitely going to get caught, I figured, but first let me call Marion who was probably being questioned and let me tell her that I'm safe but that I might have to head back to Sneaky Pete's. But, what if the phone was tapped — I couldn't tell Marion I was going to Sneaky Pete's.

I decided to call and let her know I was all right and I cared for her very much, and that I might not see her again for a long time.

I picked out the pay phone carefully. I could see for blocks up and down the street. My car was parked in the direction of a small alley that I might be able to hide in when the cops traced the call. I dialed Marion's number, then I hung up before it rang. What if a cop answers? He'll know it's me. I wasn't afraid to be caught and spend a few nights in jail until I made bail. But, I knew I'd be killed if I was caught and sent to jail. That was the problem.

Still, there was no choice. I liked Marion and she loved me. I was going to do the right thing and take the chance.

"Where the hell have you been?" she asked. "I was so worried about you."

She said the parking lot was filled with cops and DEA agents. The unit next to ours was being used by a major Miami drug dealer, and cops were digging up the floor looking for cocaine that one of the drug dealers said was buried there. She said it was major news on radio and all of the TV channels.

I hadn't heard any of this, so naturally I thought they were looking for me. I almost burst out laughing, I was so happy with relief. I told her I'd hide the car and walk back to the house.

"Expect me in about 20 minutes," I said. "Don't worry, I'll be careful."

I had built this big scenario in my head about how they were looking for me, probably questioning Marion and waiting for me to return. By the time I got there, the cops had found a huge stash of cocaine buried under the floor. They were getting ready to leave. I remembered Vincent's words, "That which you think is going to happen inevitably never does."

I did something I hadn't done since running from Rhode Island. I called Vincent at his home.

Vincent and I had been working with Andy on a regular basis to try and straighten things out, and I knew he was up to date on everything I was doing. I kept the conversation short.

"Vincent," I told him, "I'm safe. I love you, Vincent, you know that."

He said, "I love you too, Lou, be careful."

Marion and I made love all night, hour after hour. She used to call me superman. It felt so good when she told me she was falling in love with me. I told her that I was falling in love with her but neither one of us could afford to do that. She knew I'd have to leave whenever I got a phone call to go back to Rhode Island or at least nearer to Rhode Island. She said that she knew that I was right but that she'd love me anyway. That was one of the greatest nights in my life.

But, the following day was very close to being disastrous.

The cops had found lots of evidence already, but the suspects they had in custody told them the unit they found the coke in was rented at least a couple of times after they had occupied it and anyone could have put those drugs there. The cops were going door to door questioning everybody. They were carrying photographs, hoping to find witnesses who could identify both their suspects and a few of their suspects' friends.

Marion talked to the cops and told them that she had never really paid much attention to her neighbors and didn't recognize any of the photos. The cops asked her a number of questions regarding noises, smells, strange sounds like digging, and all sorts of things trying to get an idea of what took place next door. But, Marion was a stand-up girl and handled all the questions in stride.

One day I called Andy and he told me to get ready to move in closer. I would be leaving Florida any day now. I told Marion I didn't know how much longer I would be able to stay in Florida.

Things were settling down in Rhode Island and New York, and my friends were talking to the New York families. A meeting was going to be set up with representatives from the New York families — my friend Nicky Bruno, me, and an arbitrator from Florida. Nicky Bruno was a top Patriarca family member, equal in status to Louie, and who was so loved by the New York wise guys that he stayed in New York most of the time. He was a liaison agent who negotiated beefs between the New York families, as well as others. Nicky was someone that absolutely everybody loved. For now, in the meeting with the New York Family's representatives, he was a Patriarca Family representative. It wouldn't be long now. A week and a half later, I was told to return to Rhode Island and would be staying at Bonnet Shores again.

The same Bonnet Shores cottage, and that fucking book was still there. I don't know what bothered me more, that book or my anxiety over my soon-to-be meeting.

The details of the meeting were worked out and the meeting place would be in the parking lot of Valley's Steakhouse, near the airport in Warwick. I would drive my car alone to the rear of the parking lot and step into a waiting limousine. In the limousine would be two members of New York's five families, my friend who had helped set up the bust out, Kenny Guccione, Nicky Bruno and a mobster from Florida that I didn't know and never would.

I was guaranteed only one thing: I would leave the limousine alive whether or not we were able to come to an agreement.

For some reason Kenny was acting as the representative for the Patriarca Family and not Nicky. If I had ever said that Kenny was a part of this bust out he would be in at least as much trouble as I was, or probably a whole lot more. I took a couple of precautions by situating two of my trusted friends just outside the parking lot in their cars. They were armed with high powered, long range rifles and were supposed to protect me. In reality, they couldn't even see inside the limo through its tinted windows.

The meeting got started on a bad note immediately.

The two New York assholes were real punks. They were screaming that I had fucked everyone and was a stupid disrespectful motherfucker who should have known better than to do what I did. The Florida mobster was supposed to be a moderating influence, but he didn't possess the skills to mediate any kind of beef. Kenny remained silent for the most part, hoping that I wasn't going to say too much and hoping that his name would never come up in my conversations. If I ever mentioned his name, I think he would have shot me himself.

"Here's the deal asshole, we want three times the score's money back."

They didn't want just the money back. They wanted it back with 300 percent juice. I freaked out.

"This meeting is fucking over," I said, "you assholes. Who do you think I am, some sucker from the street. Here's my deal. Not one fucking cent. Do what you fucking have to do. I'm no asshole."

I opened the door on the limo and stepped onto the parking lot. As I walked towards my car with my back to the limo, I remember wondering to myself if I was shot, would I hear the sound of the gun or would I be dead first?

I walked at a normal pace expecting a bullet any second, but as I was opening the door to my car, I thought, "I'm going to actually leave this place alive."

The time to have shot me was in the limousine, or in the parking lot as soon as I left the limousine. Not now that I was in my car. I was right. I left the meeting alive.

The next day, I saw Vincent. He didn't know what they were planning. A hit was a very real possibility at this point.

Vincent said Minniestew was in Raymond's office right now asking Raymond to grant me some kind of protection. Mini thought he was very close to Raymond. When he returned to the S&S Bar, he had tears in his eyes. Raymond told him to go home and mind his own business. Mini was crushed. I decided to continue as if nothing had happened. If I was going to get whacked, there wasn't much I could do about it.

I had done lots of favors for the Rhode Island wise guys, earning them fortunes. I made portable black boxes hidden in Marlboro cigarette packages, I made slugs for years, then the silencer for a Ruger Bulldog automatic pistol, and disguised the piece so that it could be screwed onto a contemporary lamp and you could actually be searching for it and it'd look like part of the lamp's decorations. Then I made shaving cream containers that actually dispensed shaving cream but in reality contained cocaine, and several times a year, I would pick up Louie's mother while Louie was away and take her to meet with him.

You know, if Louie is one of the smartest men I've ever met, then his mother, who was almost 90 years old at the time, was one of the smartest women I had ever met. She used to call me and tell me if her son didn't meet her on certain holidays, she would call the FBI and tell them exactly where he was hiding.

When I was making counterfeit Gucci belts and buckles, I would deliver them to a New York handbag manufacturer, Sam Latt. Sure, the wise guys owned Sam, as he was a degenerate gambler. I ran errands back and forth leaving money there for Louie to pick up and selling Sam counterfeit Gucci belts with Andy as my partner. Christ! We made more Gucci belts and buckles than Gucci ever did.

There were so many favors and so many things that I did, but I figured I was still going to be hit.

While I was never a member of the Patriarca crime family, I was a very important gear in their mechanism. I didn't realize it. I was a very talented mechanic and aided in the construction of many scores. Soon I was to learn a big lesson. I might not have been an insider in the Family but I still had lots of power. Like Vincent said, "You're an earner and nobody demands more respect than somebody that earns money for the family."

Raymond used all his power to keep me alive. I was a good earner who manufactured things that earned money for wise guys, and I helped plan scores that also earned them money. Within two or three months, the entire situation was history. I was safe!

Louie wound up coming back to Rhode Island at almost the same time I did. He was furious with his brother, Andy. When Louie was around they had a huge gambling business, two houses, a summer cottage in Bonnet Shores, and were in a real strong financial condition. He came back to find out one of the houses was fucking blown up, the other cottage in Bonnet Shores was mortgaged to the gills and business profits were marginal. Andy, he thought, had fucked up business while he was away. But, Andy had a point. Louie lived like a king when he was away. Skiing in Vail, traveling to Pebble Beach, spending months at a time in New York City and Europe.

"Where the fuck do you think this money came from?" Andy asked his brother.

I could understand Andy's point of view. I had been on the run myself for only seven or eight months and I already had spent more than $150,000 between my expenses and my lawyer, not to mention that I had to send Ann money every week to keep the house running. I knew what it would be like to be away for 10½ years. When you're on the run, your expenses increase enormously and your income drops to nothing. And, because of my trips to Sam Latt's New York office, I could see how much being away was costing Louie because I would leave money there for him.

My trips to Sam's place were always a pleasure. The elevator would stop on the fifth floor and lead into a marble corridor. The floor, walls, and ceiling were done in a Breccia Damascata Italian marble. A large glass and black, anodized, aluminum double door led into another marble waiting room with a marble bar and tables for buyers to enjoy themselves while waiting for Sam. At least two gorgeous girls would ask if there was anything they could get for me while I was waiting. All of the girls working there were model material and wore see through tops without any bra, or if they did have on a bra, the area of the nipples was cut out.

Louie is the ultimate example of a soft spoken, intelligent, modest gentleman and one day he asked me if he could take my son, Louis, for a ride; that he had something that he wanted him to see. When they returned several hours later they had a beautiful Airedale Terrier pup in the car that looked more like a stuffed toy than a real dog. Louie was quick to point out that when the dog got a little older he would give up his life to defend my family. He said this is the smartest, most loyal dog in the world, and he was certainly right.

He said, "You know they've been actually known to take down bears. Most loyal dog in the world."

He had given one to his brother Andy, one to Andy's son-in-law, one to his mother, another three to his brother Anthony, and the last one to me. It was always funny to drive by Anthony's house on Pleasant Valley Parkway and see the three Airedales lined up sitting on an embankment, watching every car and person that went by.

"They're the most intelligent dogs in the world," Louie added. "Smarter than a lot of fucking people I know. He was right. We quickly named our dog Otto, and he brought 14 years of happiness into our lives. When Otto died I swore I wouldn't get another one, ever. I was so devastated and heartbroken. But, I bought one about a year ago from a breeder in Ludlow, Vermont. His name is also Otto.

Chapter 13
Trop Jewelry Company

The bright orange hood was glittering in the sunlight in that pond, but nobody ever spotted it — at least to my knowledge. I needed a rental car now that the Porsche was gone, so I went to a place called Action Auto Rental, AAR for short. They owned a string of rental companies and used the ARR logo to identify all of them.

There was one girl working in the whole place in Johnston and the phones were ringing off the hook that day. I sat down and waited a few minutes, then our eyes really met. I fell in love with her immediately. She was petite with a beautiful figure and the largest hazel eyes I ever saw and I knew I wanted her.

I picked up one of the ringing phones, just as if I worked there and said, "Action Auto Rental, may I put you on hold for a second, ma'am?"

Her name was Paula, or at least that's what the sign on the desk said. I asked her to hand me a rental form and returned to the caller.

"Okay, ma'am, can I have your name, address, how long you will need the car, what type of a car did you want, did you want to take out the extra insurance coverage," and any questions that were on the form which needed to be answered.

Paula hollered, "Tell her that a car won't be back for a couple of hours."

"Ma'am, your car will be ready by two o'clock," I told her.

"OK," she said.

I had rented a car to a customer and I was proud of myself. Paula pointed to another ringing phone for me to pick it up.

"Hello, Action Auto, may I help you?"

Shit, I could have gotten a job there in a flash. I was just trying to impress Paula and she knew it. I helped out for a while until things quieted down and then I told her I needed a car until my Porsche was either found or the insurance company paid me.

"I may need it for up to 30 days," I said.

Maybe I was paranoid because I thought I detected a little smirk from her when I told her my Porsche had been stolen. Maybe I was wrong, I don't know, but I knew immediately we were going to be together a long time. I asked her out that night and we were together every night for the next eight years.

I believe that everyone makes some major mistake in his life that he never fully recovers from. Letting Paula slip away from me was mine.

"So, how's the car business going?"

As if I gave a damn. Paula was far smarter than me and so quick-witted with a great sense of humor that we never stopped laughing. Somehow, we began talking about animals. She said she was in Australia for two and a half years, and that the kangaroo was a marsupial, because they held their young in a pouch. We had some kind of disagreement. I don't remember exactly what it was.

When I left the rental place, I called the library in downtown Providence and began asking questions about kangaroos. I wanted to know what requirements an animal needed to be called a marsupial.

The woman went nuts.

She said, "What's this, marsupial day? You're the second person to call today and ask that same question."

Paula had already called. I couldn't fucking believe it. When we got together that night, we realized that we had great chemistry. When we finally made love, it drove me crazy. But then we made love thousands of times over the next eight years and I never tired of her. She was my soulmate. Better, she was my best friend, and she still is today.

I spent most nights at Paula's house and soon I moved in with her. I knew nothing about the car rental business but I sure knew lots about the car business. I asked her how many cars she rented. She said maybe 150 cars a week and that at all times there were at least 125 cars on the road.

"How many accidents do they get in, Paula?"

Paula said that they had at least five or six accidents each week and that each car cost about $5,500 to $7,000 to repair.

"Where do you send the cars to be repaired?" I asked.

She replied, "Universal Auto Body."

Now, I knew Universal Auto Body and its owner, Billy Ricciardi, very well. He was a small time wise guy but with many of the very same connections that I had. I knew he was making a fortune on these repairs and I wanted a piece of that action.

Paula went on to tell me that only that morning she had sent a car there, so I knew that it certainly hadn't been touched as of yet. She was waiting for another six or seven cars to be finished. She said the damage to the car was estimated at $6,500.

"Tomorrow, I'll talk to Billy. Maybe we can make some money."

The next day I was at Universal Auto Body looking for the car that they picked up the day before. I wanted to see how badly it was hit to cost $6,500 dollars to repair.

What I saw didn't shock me. The bumper, grill and the hood were slightly damaged. Only the bumper and the grill needed to be replaced at a cost of $500-$600 in parts at the most.

Billy and I shook hands and exchanged pleasantries, but I'm sure he knew why I was there. By now, everybody knew that I was living with Paula, and Paula was sending cars to Billy. Why else would I be there?

I got down to business very quickly.

"Billy, I want a piece of this action. Sixty-five hundred dollars for that fucking scratch. Come on Billy. Take care of this girl for, me will you?"

Billy went furious. Nicky, a big, tough guy who took care of problems at the Foxy Lady next door came over quickly, as did Beans, a small time wise guy who beat a murder charge on a technicality. We called him Beans because he did every type of pill invented.

I knew this wasn't going to be easy.

I told Billy, "Keep all the money for the six or seven cars that you're working on, but bring the last one back to Action."

It hadn't been touched yet. I wanted that one. Billy told me to get the fuck out of his shop. Nick and Beans looked like they wanted to kill me, but they knew better. I was very connected and Billy was also all mobbed up with the same people. It was going to be a war between Billy and me.

Billy wasn't giving up any of his action to anyone — no one but a shit-ass adjuster who was happy with a couple of hundred dollars per car. On the other hand, I always earned for the family and that actually had been one reason I was still alive. So, I approached Louie and told him what was happening.

"He's our friend, Lou, but I'll see what I can do."

It turns out that one of Louie's crew needed my help in a hurry. That was my leverage.

"Get me the Action account, and I'll get you what you need immediately."

A couple of days later the last car was delivered back to Action from Universal Auto Body, and any repairs that took place after that were mine. So, now I already had one car.

A second car was involved in a small fender bender the very next day. I had two cars and nowhere to take them.

I knew lots of body shops, but I needed to choose wisely. I needed someone who did only commercially acceptable work and would do it cheaply. It would have to pass a quick inspection by an Action representative and a check would be issued on the spot.

The first few jobs had to be real good work, I reasoned, as they would be writing the checks to another body shop and I didn't want to arouse any curiosity or suspicion as to why Paula was using another repair shop. Of course, Paula had a ready answer.

"General was too slow to repair the vehicles and every day that went by without the car on the road was a day's revenue lost." It reflected on her performance, she would say, and she didn't want any more down time than necessary. Anyone, including me, would see that as sensible.

I finally decided on C&J Auto Body, which was owned by two brothers I knew, Jimmy and Dominic Colardo. Jimmy was a small man, very nervous, stuttered and had timid, little-boy manners. Dominic had some kind of a disorder that required him to take Klonopin and other very powerful drugs just to function. He was never more than half conscious as far as I could see.

But, they had a legitimate auto body shop with a real license and they were capable of doing passable work. The biggest asset of all was that they would be easy for me to control. So, we made a deal.

Twenty five percent of the gross repair bill was mine. I told them to keep the bills to less than $7,000, and $6,500 was even better. Seven thousand dollars bordered too closely on the company declaring the car a total loss and not repairing it. That would defeat our entire purpose. I said if they decided to take the car off the road and call it a total we'd all lose.

"OK, OK, Lou, sixty-five hundred dollars, that'll be the maximum, OK?" Jimmy said repeatedly. Dominic was still at the stage of our introduction when Jimmy and I finished our business.

The first car was delivered to Action about a week and a half later.

Paula told Jimmy that he'd have to go to my shop to pick up the check for $6,300 from me. I was at Trop Jewelry Company, 131 Washington St., downtown Providence.

She said, "Louis will handle all the money from now on."

Paula called me and said Jimmy was on his way up to collect the check.

I said, "Thanks, I'll see you tonight. I love you, Paula."

Jimmy arrived at the shop around 11:30 a.m. He said Paula told him to pick up the check here.

I said, "That's right, Jimmy, give me your $1,575, and take the check."

He was expecting me to give him the check, deposit it, wait for it to clear, and then pay me my 25 percent.

"No fucking way," I said. "I want the $1,575 when I hand you the check, not two weeks later, Jimmy. This is the way it's going work. You pay me first, all the time. I don't care what bills you have. I don't care if you have a mortgage to pay, if your kids are starving. I get paid first."

Jimmy was easy to control. He left and returned that afternoon with an envelope with $1,575 in cash in it.

Half of the $1,575 was almost $800 for Paula. She didn't make that much money in three weeks and we now had a backup of cars coming in that needed repairs. Paula was turned on by this whole incident, not for the money, but for the way I handled the situation. I was a survivor, she realized, and so was she. It's too bad that I didn't allow our relationship to survive also.

Paula refused any money and was happy just to have the cars properly repaired and back on the road and not to have to deal with "body shop" mentality, as she called it. Action was being run by a bunch of coke heads who would rather spend their profits snorting it up their noses rather than treat their employees better.

Within two months, I was seeing Jimmy and his brother Dominic four or five times a week. The average visit brought between $1,400 - $1,500 — sometimes even more. I was back on my feet in no time earning around $8,000 in cash every week. This wasn't big money to me but it sure beat the four dollars that I had to my name only a few weeks before.

Trop Jewelry Company was an old custom jewelry manufacturer owned by my father's best friend, Frank Troppoli. Since Frank was old, in his early 80s, I asked my father if Frank might be interested in selling the business to me. He had a daughter but she was a teacher and had absolutely no interest in the business. He also had a brother, John, who was old and he had extremely limited skills in the business. All he ever did was polish items when they were finished. He was not interested in the business. He was not capable of running it, but he was with the business from 1919 when it was originally started.

The business had been at the same location at 131 Washington St. In its heyday, it employed eight or nine jewelers and had an enviable carriage trade which included some of Rhode Island's richest residents. But, Frank never stayed current with the business and it was dying a very slow death.

I was the perfect person to buy it. Frank was an honest, hard-working man who liked my father so much he said he wouldn't sell me the business because it was losing money. He was sending most of his customers to his competitors, two of whom were located in the same building. He said that the only reason that he kept it open was because his brother John and his friend Anthony Capazolli, another old jeweler, worked there. They had both been with him from the beginning, and he felt obligated to them.

Can you imagine anyone in today's business world doing something like that? He said he could pay his bills only because he had purchased gold so many years ago when it cost $20 an ounce and then later $35 an ounce. Now, gold was around $350 an ounce, so whenever he had to pay bills he would sell a little bit of gold.

Frank told my father that I would be buying gold at $350 and the business would never be able to survive.

When my father told me this, I was disappointed. I decided to go see Frank myself. He explained the whole scenario again to me and said that he didn't want to see me lose money. I told Frank that at the worst, I could run the business as a jewelry repair center and pay the bills based on the revenues from repairs, which is mostly labor. Frank was skeptical. He still insisted it was a bad idea.

So, we made a bargain. I would work there for no salary for several months. If Frank didn't think that I could repair jewelry and that I had the skills to run the business, I would forget the idea and move on.

About a month and a half later, I was purchasing the shop.

Frank remarked to my father that I was not only the best workman that he had ever seen, I was also the fastest. He told my father he thought I was a genius. If only he knew the truth.

It was about 95 degrees that day and I was about to pass out. I was splashing cold water on my face to keep myself awake. Frank was putting the contents of a two-inch by three-inch box — which he was using as a separator for gold jewelry parts — on an old fashioned scale.

Each drawer in the safe contained about 100 of these little boxes without their covers. Whenever you opened a drawer, you could see the contents of the box immediately. He would take parts from those boxes to make jewelry.

One box might contain shanks needed for rings and another the tops that hold the stones in a ring, each with various sizes and shapes in different boxes. The boxes contained all the parts that were needed to assemble jewelry and to make custom-gold jewelry. In each box were only about four or five small gold findings and he put these on the scale.

This was an old-fashioned brass and wood scale and it required putting a weight on one end and the parts on the other end. It was as slow as all hell. Frank never invested in a digital scale and weighed everything by hand.

There were four, two-door safes, approximately six and a half feet tall and five feet wide with hundreds of these boxes in each safe. The average contents of each of the boxes, probably weighed about 10 penny weights, which is about a half an ounce of gold. With all of those boxes, this was going to be an enormous task.

Frank was very slow and meticulous to a ridiculous degree. He weighed each package precisely to the last goddamn grain. At this rate, it would take about six months to a year to finish and establish the price I was going to have pay for the business.

I suggested that we weigh a few of the boxes, take an average, then just eyeball the rest of them and add 10 or 20 percent to whatever figure we came up with. This would speed up the process. Frank refused to do that. He said I would be overpaying for everything and surviving would be difficult enough without any extra expenses.

After about six weeks, I just couldn't continue. I saw no end in sight. If we finished the gold weighing, we still had to evaluate the contents of the stone safe. That safe contained approximately 4,000 stones: garnets, onyx, tourmalines, emeralds, sapphires, aquamarines, jade, pearl, amber, moonstones, cameos, and many one-of-a-kind German porcelain pieces and other items that would be almost impossible to place a value on. I didn't think Frank would live long enough to finish this monstrous task. I certainly knew I wouldn't.

Frank and I struck up another compromise. We would weigh the gold on a modern digital scale. I purchased the scale. Since all the gold findings were in approximately the same size cardboard box, I took the scale, put an empty box on it and moved the scale back to zero. We would put the box and its contents on the scale and this would give us an accurate reading of the weight of the contents.

This speeded up the process, but it was still so painfully slow. I would rather have been incarcerated than do this work. Frank would ask me to double-check every figure he wrote down. I really wanted to scream, but I respected his honesty and sincerity and I verified his figures, or so he thought.

It was so fucking hot in that shop that all I ever did was just write down whatever he wrote down and told him that I was verifying it. I was always on the verge of fainting. I just wanted to get this thing finished, to get it over with. Eventually, we did finish the gold.

Now came the stone safe.

I told Frank we couldn't possibly open several thousand envelopes and count the contents of each one, piece by piece. I told him to think about a price for the entire safe and its contents and I would agree to whatever amount he thought was fair.

Before he gave me the figure several days later, he said, "Louis, you won't get your money back for years with this safe. You'll use one piece every once in a while but it would take a long time before you would be ahead of what you paid for it."

I said, "OK, I understand," but at least I wouldn't have to buy stones for years and would have everything right there and would be able to run the business quicker.

Everything was so logically arranged that I wondered who had done that because it just didn't look like Frank's style. For instance, black onyx was arranged by shape. The first envelopes contained round stones, then it went to square, then to cushion shape, then to kite shape, then diamond shape, then to pillow shape and so on. Then it was arranged by cabochon, which is a rounded-style top, then it graduated from small to large in millimeters. It was just mind-boggling at how much stock was in that safe and how easy it was to understand because it was so logically organized. It was too logically organized to have been done by Frank.

So I asked him, "When was this done? It's so easy to find something in here."

Frank told me that in 1930, he hired an out-of-work gemologist to put everything in order. It took the gemologist four years of working every day to get organized. In my opinion, the safe's contents were worth at least a couple of hundred thousand dollars at a minimum and that would have been a bargain.

Frank said, "Supposing, Lou, I say two thousand dollars. Now, remember you won't get your money back anytime soon, so think about it."

I said, "OK, Frank. Now let's move on to the machinery, tools, furniture and all the rest of the shop."

Frank said the machinery had a negative value as it was old, at least 60 years old, and in many cases even more than that because he had bought most of it used in 1919. He said the furniture was the same. The price of the gold findings was determined not by their value, which means that they weren't treated as a jewelry part — but only by their actual gold weight. I was paying only for gold which if I had just liquidated it at any time I would have probably got my money back as long as the price of gold didn't drop.

There was $30,000 worth of gold in all of the findings in total and $2,000 for the stone safe. The total came to $32,000.

"I don't know how you'll get your money back," Frank said when I paid him.

When I finally began operating the business, Frank, his brother John, and Anthony Capazolli continued to work for me. My father also began working there. It was a real joy to hear all four of these old men sitting at the bench in the rear of the shop talking about trips that they had taken in the '30s and '40s and calling Anthony Capazolli a baby because he was only 78 years old. They talked about girls that they had met along the way and it was kind of a different twist that I had never seen in my father before. It was very nice.

These were probably some of my father's happiest years of his life. Throughout the decades Frank had bought out many companies that went bankrupt. He bought all their molds and models and we had probably seven thousand of them when I purchased the shop. It was amazing because there was no order to any of these molds or models. When Frank needed something like a shank of a ring or a head of a ring, or anything else he knew his inventory so well that he was able to find anything at all.

That would not be the case with me because I had no idea where stuff was and there were just too many molds to go looking through. So, I decided to put everything in order. It took me probably about a year before I got everything numbered and each piece was put on top of its corresponding mold.

The original models were made out of silver and there was no need for this. I replaced the silver models with brass castings and sold the silver as scrap. The mounds of dust that I talked about that Frank pushed aside to clean an area, I vacuumed with a large shop vac. The old, used polishing wheels were thrown in 30 and 50 gallon barrels that Frank used to store them in. I sent them to a precious metal refiner. Then I would go on the floor and tap on the floor and suck up the dust with the vacuum cleaner.

About 30 days later, after taking all of this gold laden dirt to the refiner, I received a check for $7,200 from the gold that was recovered from this scrap rubble. I now had $7,200 of my $32,000 back in only a matter of a few weeks.

Then I had a carpenter start removing the floor to replace it with new wood. Another $15,000 came in from the gold that had dropped in the floor — plus more than a dozen one-half carat or so diamonds and hundreds of small little diamonds which we call "melee." In his older years, if he dropped a small diamond, Frank couldn't, and didn't even try to find it. Their value was at least $10,000. Now, I had probably most of my $32,000 back in four or five months.

And, there was more, much more, to come.

The four safes in Trop Jewelry really ate up a lot of space, so I decided to get rid of one. I called a couple of safe movers and they quoted me prices anywhere between $2,000 and $4,000 just to move one safe out of the shop.

I then looked in the phone book and found a rubbish removal company. It said AAA Rubbish Removal, so I gave them a call. Later on I got to know the owner who turned out to be a real character and a very nice person. Eventually they moved a great deal of machinery from my shop.

The safes were very big and heavy, but they were on wheels. We decided to move the safe the only way that we could, which was to roll it out the hallway, toward the service elevator. The safe was so damn heavy that I was afraid that it was going to make track marks all the way to the back of the building, so I placed two sheets of one-half-inch plywood in front of the safe. The AAA owner Bill — along with his son — moved the safe by pushing it on the plywood. When it was on the front piece of plywood, I would take the plywood from the rear and put it forward of the safe again and he would push it onto that piece. We continued this until we got it to the elevator in the back.

The plaque on the elevator read that it had a capacity of 2,000 pounds. The safe weighed more than 4,000 pounds. By now the safe was right in front of the open door to the elevator and all it needed was a push to get it on to the antique lift, as the elevator was called.

We all looked at each other and Bill said, "I don't know if it will hold." The elevator was probably 75 or 80 years old and was being held up by a single cable.

We didn't know what was going to happen if we rolled the safe onto the elevator.

I finally told Bill, "Well, we can't leave the safe here anymore. Let's move the safe slowly and inch it onto the elevator a little at a time and see how the elevator reacts."

When Bill and his son gave the safe a push, the safe practically flew onto the elevator, because it was about an inch lower than the corridor floor. The elevator dropped down the shaft about a foot almost instantly. But, it stopped and it appeared to have just stretched the cable. It didn't snap.

Nobody would get in the elevator and ride it down to the first floor so I got in it, held my breath, and pushed the button. The elevator began to moan and groan but it made it down to the first floor.

Now we had the safe on the ground floor. The next step was to move it out of the building, which was easy enough to do. When we went to lift it and put it on Bill's truck, the whole front of the truck lifted because the truck wasn't heavy enough.

The safe stayed exactly where it was. Now we were in real trouble because the safe was sitting outside of the building in a parking lot and was in plain view of anybody driving by.

We decided to remove the doors from the safe, hook it up to the winch, and drag it on its wheels to Beverly Street just around the corner.

I told Bill, "Take the safe and put it on its side, that way somebody can put a number on it and use it as their house. It was bigger than some of the cardboard cartons I've seen used by some homeless people. And certainly a lot better constructed. We had a hell of a laugh out of it and I made sure that any identifying marks that indicated it belonged to Trop Jewelry Company were removed. The doors were then lifted easily onto Bill's truck, and he took them away. I never did find out what became of that safe but I know it had to be one hell of a mansion for someone.

***

Gloria Leavitt was a friend who worked at Newberry Auction House on Newbury Street in Boston. She was fascinated with my shop. She went through old, hand-drawn sketches for jewelry that resembled Rembrandts, the quality was so fine. She went crazy over these items and over all the old furniture in Trop Jewelry.

The desk Frank used was an original oak roll-top desk with dozens of little pigeon-hole compartments. We put it in Newberry's furniture auction. It brought $3,000. The hand-drawn sketches of jewelry brought another couple of thousand dollars. There was an oak blueprint cabinet which I almost cut in half just to get it out of the shop. It brought in another $1,600. There was a wooden cash register from the era when William Harding was the President. That brought in another $600.

Every item in the place was a treasure. The German porcelain cameos were so valuable we sold them a few at a time, so we wouldn't saturate the market. The same with the cameos, jade, pearls, and on and on. Before the year was over, I had at least another $50,000 in cash from the sale of items that I would never have used anyway.

The molds and models alone numbered approximately 7,000. The shelves I built to hold them were approximately six feet high and 18 or 20 feet long. We used to refer to it as "the million dollar wall." Even the ceiling, which was made from tin square panels, I sold.

The place turned from a museum to a modern jewelry shop. No one had the selection that I had, and every time I made something original, I made a mold of it. The first customer to buy something that was hand-made would have to pay for the design, the fabricating labor, the gold, the model, the mold, everything If I made a second piece, it came out of the mold in one shot. About a dollar's worth of wax , some gold and a little labor and for about a $150 or less I could duplicate a piece that I had sold for maybe $3,000 or more.

This was not my original idea. I was just doing what Frank had done for all those years and I continued it. It was a formula that was so successful I wound up being a supplier to just about all the jewelers in Rhode Island. The saying was that if you needed something and you couldn't find it anywhere, go to Trop Jewelry, they'll have it.

On Sundays, when the building was vacant, my son and I would go what we referred to as quahogging. We would pound the showroom floor and suck up its bounty, which included all sorts of small diamonds, rubies, sapphires, emeralds, and some gold. It wasn't as rich as the back shop area, of course, but still lucrative.

After a couple of hours I would say, "Well Lou, I think we have a 928 red Porsche with a tan interior. What do you want to do? Do you want to quit or do you want to go for a 328 GTS Ferrari?" Everything I touched there made money.

Paula was absolutely flabbergasted at the money that was coming in. Shit, eight or nine thousand dollars a week was nothing, more, much more, was usually the average. Of course, I was divorced at least a couple of years by now and was supporting Ann, Louis, my daughter Susan, and myself, and the reality of it was that I never valued the money that I was making.

***

"They're gone, Lou, you can come by now."

They were three demented, sick motherfuckers who would enter a jewelry store with their machine guns begin shooting up the place. They would rob from the safes, showcases, employees, and customers. They stood for everything my family hated but they robbed so much jewelry I just couldn't pass it up.

Jerry Riendeau was a small time real estate agent and gold buyer. He had a licenses to sell firearms and put on fireworks displays, even though he was arrested every single year around the Fourth of July for selling illegal fireworks to undercover government agents.

It was Jerry who dealt with the machine-gunners because I never wanted them to know who I was. Between those guys and Jerry, hundreds of diamonds passed from his hands to mine until the madmen were finally caught one day during one of their violent robberies.

All three were sentenced to life in prison without the chance of parole. It was almost a welcome relief, because it was just a matter of time before they killed someone in one of their wild escapades. No more hectic trips to New York City to dump the stones to Leo, taking the flights once or twice a week at 10 a.m. and returning back that afternoon. It was extremely tiring and for what? I had so much money coming in I didn't need anything that risky. I wanted to settle down and earn my money at Trop Jewelry. Diamonds that came from machine-gun robberies were crazy. It just wasn't worth that much risk, I mean, how much money did I want or need?

But, eventually, everything changes. Vincent was dying and I watched him slip day by day. He had all his sharpness and sense of humor right until the last minute.

If the nurse said, "Oh, you're fine, Mr. Miele ," he would make a like, "Yeah, that's what everybody is a few minutes before they die, real fine."

I was having problems dealing with this. Then, the next big blow!

Anthony Capazolli was taken to the hospital with a kidney stone. It was in November just before the busy season. Frank told me not to worry about it. He was always going into the hospital for a kidney stone, but he would always be back within a short period of time. Frank assured me that this would be the case this time, too. Unfortunately, this was not the case. Anthony died a few days later. Believe it or not, on his way to the hospital, he actually apologized to me for leaving me and the company during the busy season. What a man he was, a real gentleman.

Then, the worst of all possible things. My father was diagnosed with incurable pancreatic cancer. He would live about a year and a half if he had surgery.

My father hated doctors, hospitals, and medicine. Hell, I don't think my father was ever in a hospital except to visit somebody. He wasn't even born in a hospital, but now he was dying and I had to play actor and tell him one fucking stupid thing after another. Either he was run down or his blood sugar level was too high or he had a gall stone. I couldn't come up with enough things to tell him. He wasn't stupid, but I think that I was convincing enough for him to believe he was not dying.

Then one day he turned completely yellow. I told him that his bile duct, whatever the hell that is, was blocked and a minor operation would be necessary. It took several days to convince him to have the operation in which they would bypass some organ or another and he actually improved for the first several months. But he was dying and he was getting worse and worse and I was having trouble dealing with it. I was never one who could admit to weakness and crying was for me always out of the question. Still, I was up all night rocking in my chair crying and asking God to take me instead of my father.

I needed to do this my way and I told Paula that I had to be alone. She understood and we separated. I let everything go while my father was dying. It was one doctor's visit after another. One story after another.

One time towards the end, my father was in great pain and he wouldn't take any kind of a pill to ease it. I pulled the druggist aside and I told him that I would smash his windows if he ever wrote on my father's prescriptions again that they were to be taken for pain. My father used to cut an aspirin in half all his life.

I used to smile because my father would be high, but not know it, and he'd say to Paula, thinking she was my mother, "Dora, you're working so hard, please, sit down and relax."

He was so sweet it was funny. Sweet talk was not one of my father's normal qualities.

During this time I was neglecting Paula and she needed my love, but I was not capable of understanding what was happening. When she told me she was going to get married, everyone expected that I would run to the church and stop the wedding at the altar. I didn't. I regretted that decision the rest of my life.

In Rhode Island Hospital, there was myself, my father, my mother and my brother, Ronnie, my sister, Angela, and her husband, Fred. I told my father that I was so sorry for the grief I caused him all his life.

He whispered, "I love you, now go tell your brother and the rest of them to get in here quickly." He knew the end was near and he wanted everybody to come in before he died. Now everyone was in the room together and my brother Ronnie, a Jesuit priest, said what is called a prayer for the dying. My father asked everyone to leave the room but me.

He looked me in the eyes.

I said, "Dad, I love you very much, close your eyes and go to sleep." A big smile came over his face. He died. A large part of me died at the same time.

About a year and a half later my mother died. Nothing had any value to her anymore after my father's death. My mother's death was quick. She was being placed in an ambulance when I arrived at her house. I went to see her every morning after my father's death, had breakfast and left for work. She died an hour later at the Lady of Fatima Hospital.

I had given up the car income, and was spending very little time at Trop Jewelry Company. Before long, I was almost broke. I needed to make money fast. My whole financial life was like a yo-yo, up down, up down, up down. Now I was on my way down.

I called my friend Leo in New York. Together we planned was what to be my final bust out, but this time I didn't want anyone to get hurt financially.

Leo gave me a number of ideas. He told me there were certain diamonds that he needed and we had set prices that he would pay. It was just a matter of me ordering these particular stones. When the stones came in a day or two later, I had a robbery in the store which was considered one of the largest diamond robberies in Rhode Island at the time.

The diamonds that were stolen were at least two to three carats in size, extremely high quality diamonds. They were shipped on memo and this is how the plan would work so that no one got hurt except the insurance company.

The newspaper read: "Thief assaults and robs a jeweler," and went on to say that, "the owner of a downtown jewelry store told police he was knocked out, bound and gagged early yesterday by a robber who made off with an undetermined amount of cash and jewelry. Louis Colavecchio, owner of Trop Jewelry Company, suffered cuts and bruises in the attack, police said. Detective Lieutenant Terrence Crowley said Colavecchio had accidentally set off his hold-up alarm about 7:30 a.m. shortly before the robbery occurred. Police went to the shop and verified that the alarm had been accidentally set off and left, Crowley said. About five minutes later, Colavecchio said there was a knock on the door and then all the lights went out and someone hit him on the head, knocking him unconscious. While he was out, his hands and feet were bound and his mouth was covered with duct tape. His son found him about 20 minutes later."

When my son came into the store I was all bound and gagged with duct tape, I was trying to tell him to take the duct tape off slowly. I was mumbling because obviously I couldn't talk with the tape on. Leo grabbed one corner of the tape and pulled it off with all his strength. He almost pulled my fucking lips off with it.

I turned around and I said, "I was trying to tell you to remove the tape slowly."

The robbery was over and it was time to notify all of the dealers that had sent me diamonds to file an insurance claim with their memo company that the stones had been stolen.

***

Paula was gone, and Maureen came into my life. She was beautiful and not too bright, which was exactly what I needed at the time. I was feeling depressed with no place to go because I had closed Trop Jewelry. I felt I had no purpose in life.

Next thing I know, Maureen and I decided to open a place called Diamonds in Design. Basically it was just something to keep me active and to give me a place to go in the morning.

Diamonds in Design was located on Mineral Spring Avenue on the second floor. At that time, there was a product called Friendly Plastic. It was a material made of multiple colors and when you boiled it, it could be formed into jewelry. Maureen was very talented at this. She could take strips of this material and make an attractive pair of earrings, a pin, a necklace or something else out of this colorful plastic.

Maureen's mother owned 10 acres of waterfront property on Waterman Lake on the Gloucester-Harmony line. Her father was dead. She had an aunt, Mary Tortelli who was the wife of a very famous mobster, Louie the Fox Tortelli. The Family had killed The Fox some two decades earlier.

Mo, as I used to call her, and I lived together for eight years during the summer on Waterman Lake. God didn't make a more beautiful place than this. We put on a deck, which went around the entire house. Then we winterized it, added a boat dock, fireplace, deep water well, and so many other things I can't even remember. I kept spending money. This was not my house. This was not even Maureen's house. It belonged to her mother and any money that I put in there was obviously money that I would never get back. Maureen kept hounding me all the time about getting married. She wanted to get married so badly that after a few years, I agreed. The minute I did, she left me for some fat slob mechanic. Go figure.

Chapter 14
The Counterfeit King

Larry Sargenta came by one day. He wanted me to take a ride with him to Foxwoods Casino. So we did. It was a small casino with mostly table games as its main attraction. There were very few slot machines.

Foxwoods was still under construction at the time but they were running it around the clock. Larry was playing blackjack and when he picked up a couple of the chips, I glanced at them and I said, "Let's take these home with us."

On our way back home, he asked, "What are you thinking?"

I said, "The same thing you're thinking."

"You think we can actually make them?"

I said, "I think maybe we can. Let's study them closer."

We took the chips to my place and that night and examined them. One was black, a $100 denomination, the other a green, a $25 chip. We looked at the labels and I carefully removed them from both chips.

There was no microchip under the label of the green chip, but there was one under the black, $100 chip. That was the first big break. I knew I could make the green. It was a beautiful-looking token. I studied it for hours, until around 2:30 in the morning when I decided that I was going to counterfeit it.

The black token had the labels off, and I placed the microchip in a little plastic bag. I wanted to study that one further. I needed to know what difficulties I would have reading the information on the microchip. It was round, very thin, and smaller in diameter than a dime. It was hidden right under the label, with no recess in the chip itself to accept it. That's how thin it was. When passed over a detection plate, it would release information to the casino's cashier that indicated whether the chip was genuine or a counterfeit.

In the casino industry they're known as cheques. We call them chips. I began with the green chip. The black one with the microchip would be a long, drawn-out deal. I wanted to educate myself more on the functions of the microchip, before making that token.

I started sawing the green one apart and thinking about the different ways to make it. Before long, I was totally involved in the new project of making casino chips.

The project of making the casino chips was going to turn out to be a very difficult one, even without attempting the black one. The dealers who handled these chips could spot a counterfeit a mile away.

Genuine chips at Foxwoods are very heavy, approximately 11 grams, and nothing could duplicate their feel. If you took a stack of 15 or 20 pieces and let them fall in your hand, nice and flat downward, they actually fell on top of each other slowly with a cushion of air that would break their fall. They fell one upon the other, indicating they were genuine.

Players as well as dealers love to run these chips through their fingers and let them drop in the palm of their hand or on the felt covered tables.

Years ago, professional quality chips like these were called clay chips. In reality, they are a blended type of plastic. This is or was a closely held-secret in the casino industry. No other type of material feels like this.

Then there was the color. Each casino used its own specially-formulated color. They all had parameters to follow, which included color and size. The West chip represents $1, a red chip represents $5, a green chip is $25, a black chip is $100, and a purple chip is $500. Some casinos have even higher denominations, but these were too limited to be of interest to me.

Each of these colors, like the green, could be any number of several thousand different shades of green. They could run from a dark green to a very light sherbet color green to what's called a Munzle green, and it was a similar range with all the other colors. Some were very black, some were black with little silver pieces in them, some had little gold pieces. At any rate, it was going to be the colors and feel that were difficult to duplicate.

Even with the latest and most comprehensive Pantone color chart it wasn't possible to find a chip's exact color. And if I did, the chip had various surfaces, and they would reflect color differently.

I could see two problems with this project.

One was going to be with the material, duplicating its weight and feel. The second was going to be with color, and that seemed to me like it was almost going to be an almost impossible task.

The best place to look when you're doing something of this nature is to look within the casino itself. All casinos, and actually all businesses, have their security weaknesses. You just have to know where to look for them and to recognize a weakness when you find one. I am good at doing that. I would later scout various casinos to find anything that could speed up or make my project easier.

I seemed to look at a task with one overwhelming question in mind: Is there something in this project that I can't overcome. In this particular project, the answer was both yes and no. The green chip would be difficult, but definitely possible. The black chip would be difficult, and maybe, impossible without drawing attention to my actions due to the microchip.

I decided to dive right in.

My first objective was to physically duplicate the chip with perfect dimensions so that my later experiments with color and weight would resemble the finished product. This is critical because I may have a perfect color, for example, on a sheet of material — but when it is formed into the finished shape of the chip, it may throw shadows that reflect light in a different manner than the original, rendering it easily detectible.

The dies had to be perfect. Some areas were polished. Other areas had to be sandblasted and required various finishes and textures. There was a great deal of work to do to duplicate them, but this is work I understand very well. It had to be exactly as the original and the reality is this was no problem at all for me.

Foxwoods used a series of top hats and canes, a very nice design that went around the outside diameter of the chip about one eighth of an inch from the outside edge.

The casino had been counterfeited when they first opened for business by some clever but not very skilled people. They took advantage of the fact that the place was new and the employees were not too experienced. They got away with their scheme for a short time until they were finally caught by a very simple check that the cashiers were taught.

Each cashier was trained to stack the real chips, then stack the chips the players were cashing in. Using the same quantity for both stacks, the cashier would then slide the two stacks together. The counterfeits were slightly thicker. When stacked up against 10 or more in a column, they were very easy to detect. The counterfeits column was higher.

Also, the colors and feel were not exactly perfect and the cashiers were trained to feel the difference between the real chips and the counterfeits. The counterfeits were not good enough to bring to a table, where some sharp dealer would have recognized them immediately as being phonies.

This altered my plans because the casino was now aware that they were the target of counterfeiters and would become increasingly cautious. They made a smart mark on the design of the chips which was a big help in their detecting future counterfeits, and which rendered any existing counterfeit dies that had been made useless. They made the canes, which went through the top hats, a little longer and it became easier for employees to see the difference quickly. This was a clever move on their part, but I picked up on it instantly.

Before long, I could produce a perfect replica of a Foxwood chip. It was in one solid color, of course, but the dimensions and finish were flawless.

The next step would be to make the center of the dies removable so that the die used to make a $5 chip could also make a $25 or $100 denomination without making a new set of dies. I could then develop the green chips immediately, and when I overcame the microchip obstacle, use the same dies to counterfeit the $100s. The shape of the various denominations' centers were different, but the rest of the chip's design was the same.

Now to deal with the material. I could have put a brass insert inside the chip, thereby getting the necessary weight. This was risky as the counterfeit chips could then be easily identified by x-ray. I experimented with all types of plastics, but none were heavy enough.

Finally, I located a plastics manufacturer based in New Jersey who had a small plant for specialty mixtures near me in Wyoming, Rhode Island.

They produced a material that was heavy enough to give me the 11 grams for the chips that I was going to need, but the color was never even close to what I needed. Color and feel were my next challenges.

I found, in one form or another, all the colors I needed to counterfeit almost any casino from within the casinos themselves. My research found that certain casinos use pink tokens for a game or promotion. The tokens didn't have to match the size requirements because they were not officially chips — rather, they were but symbolic tokens, sometimes sold in the casino's gift shops. Unfortunately for the casino, they often used the same company that made their chips to make their commemorative tokens. Many times, the manufacturer used colors that matched the casino's chips.

This was a major breach in their security that I slid right into.

I had a very heavy plastic material from my supplier in Rhode Island, so if I wanted to make a $5 chip, I would have the heavy plastic material made in a shade of red. It didn't have to match exactly the color of the chip because it wasn't going to be seen. It was only going to be used as a core to add weight to the finished product.

A $25 chip would begin with a green plastic filler. Again, filler was only used for weight. If you sawed or broke a piece in half, it would appear to be the same color all the way through and would look like it had been made from one piece. It could also be x-rayed and show no brass inserts used to add weight. In every way, the chip would appear normal.

The heavy plastic material that I had made was used as a base and was green. Then it was placed in a set of round dies which contained two electric cartridge-type heaters, with a temperature adjustment, and which were the diameter of the finished chip. When pressed together, the heated dies produced a round, plain, green flat blank that would become the core for completing the chip.

Now, I took a chip from the casino I was attempting to counterfeit, and put it into another set of round, heated dies, like the blank dies. These dies were much larger in diameter than the finished chips. When the press exerted pressure on them, they would flatten the token to almost paper thin and excess material would flow out the edges of the dies, and produce a round, large, flat thin piece, about three thousandths of an inch thick and several times larger than the chips diameter. Then I would place them in a trimming die, and blank them out to the exact diameter of the chip. The average chip is approximately 250 thousandths of an inch thick. When flattened to three thousandths, it would yield one large piece more than 12 inches in diameter. From that I could blank out about 40 pieces of the chips at their original diameter. This was enough to make 20 new chips. One original chip would eventually yield about 20 new pieces.

Next, these two flat thin pieces would be cemented to the heavy blank I made earlier, and placed back in the round heated dies. When pressed under heat and pressure, they would adhere to the core.

I now had a blank that was the perfect size of a chip, with the exact color and feel on the top and bottom. It had an edge, though, that might show a slightly different color. Think of looking at a new quarter, which is a clad material but whose edges give away the fact that the quarter is not made from one solid material. My edges were not that far off color. Still, they weren't perfect, and I would deal with that next.

I took a piece of the green token, or even the scrap that had been trimmed from the flattening process, and placed it in the round, heated dies. The pressure from the press formed a blank that was the exact size of the chip I was counterfeiting, but much lighter. Next, I made a trimming tool which was a round punch that pierced a hole in the blank, leaving only about an eighth-of-an-inch rim. It was this rim, or edge that I wanted.

Next, I took the blank, with the correct top and bottom, and placed it in the same blanking tool I had just used to make the edge. Only this time, I only wanted the inside, smaller piece. I already had the edge. That piece, with the outside piece, the edge, that I had previously blanked out, formed a round, perfect color blank with the exact weight and feel of a genuine casino chip. It had an inside round core of my material, two thin clad pieces, one on top and one on the bottom, from a casino token, and an edge, from a casino token. It was as strong as if it were one piece. It was a perfect blank.

Next, I took a chip to be used as the insert in the previously formed blank. I had no trouble finding all the materials I needed from one source or another. In one case, I actually went to a store that sold flooring. This place had a designer vinyl tile manufactured by Armstrong that was exactly what I needed for some inserts. I purchased a case of that material. Then, I blanked it out, placed it in the dies, and made it round, the proper diameter of the chips.

I made a tool that blanked out the four inserts. This tool blanked out the inserts from the main core piece, which was green, and from the insert piece, which was pink. I took the pink square inserts that fell from the blanking tool, and placed them in the four holes left in the green blank. Before doing that, I took an ordinary Dremel tool and made a notch in the green pieces blanked out areas. These were retaining notches. Then I put the assembled pieces in the dies that had the chip's design, and under a little heat, and pressure, had the exact chip, with the proper weight, feel look and dimensions, as the original. It also had a recess for the label.

If you ever look at a chip's edge, you will see that where the inserts are located, there is kind of a diamond pointed piece of the insert in the green body. That was the purpose of the Dremel tool. The piece was lacking only the center label now.

The label is made by taking two original labels off a genuine chip, gluing them to a piece of paper, and photocopying them. Filling an 8½ inch by 11 inch piece of paper with labels allows you to get lots of labels from a single sheet. I made a tracing of the label, so I could locate the cutting tool quicker over each label. If the casino was using an ink that glowed under ultraviolet light, it was necessary to spray the labels with a chemical which glowed bright orange, or red, or whatever color was needed to match the casino's ink.

Then, the entire paper was laminated. After that, the back of the was charged with heat- activated glue. With a cutting punch the shape of the label, I cut the laminated labels with heat-activated cement on their backs out of the 8½ inch by 11 inch paper.

The labels were placed in the recess in the chip on both sides. The final step was to apply dies that form the lines that are usually found on casino chips under slight heat and pressure. The heat allows the labels to adhere to the body of the piece, and the pressure puts the necessary lines on the chips.

The tools needed to create these lines were extremely difficult to make. It was a security precaution that Foxwoods implemented. The lines were so close together, and so very fine, that it took several attempts to get them correct. I kept at it until they were perfect.

This wasn't too unlike the process I used years earlier of taking two parts of cars and putting them together to come up with a single, perfect car. Only this time I was using parts from casino chips and putting them together to form a perfect casino chip.

Now I had a brand new chip with the proper weight, color and feel as the one purchased by the casino. Of course, to age the pieces to the proper look of those that are used at the casino, I'd have to place 100 or 200 of these chips in a tumbler and tumble them until they receive the desired finish required. They would get scratched up a little bit and that's exactly what I was looking to do.

All of this sounds very complicated. The truth is that if you ever saw the process done, it is so simple that it's hard to believe. Hundreds of pieces a day could be produced very easily by one person and could be made for less than a dollar each.

The look, weight, feel and sound would be so perfect you couldn't possibly tell a counterfeit from the real one.

This preparation process, though, was expensive and time consuming. I was using up all of my cash to keep it going.

I was actually working out of the garage at my house. I used to spend hours and hours there and I think I fell in love with every piece that I made. Believe me, I made a lot of pieces.

As soon as possible, I began taking chips to casinos everywhere and started getting some of my investment money back. I loved sitting at the blackjack table, which was the only game that I really understood and played for an hour or two before cashing out.

It was a thrilling life.

I finally overcame the obstacle of the microchip in the $100 cheque, but I needed equipment from the 3-M Corporation to duplicate it. This was far too risky. I wasn't sorry. I put their microchip back, glued the labels on and cashed it in.

Lots of casinos today are playing with chips I made in my garage!

Making counterfeit items must have appealed to me in some way that I didn't understand.

Between the Gucci line of belts, the Charles Garnier jewelry, the Barry Cord Kieselstein silver alligator belt buckle made famous by the tragic death of Nicole Simpson, the slugs, the casino chips, and my last project, the casino slot machine tokens, I must have counterfeited more items than anyone alive. Everything I made attracted me one way or another. Most of them, with the exception of the last two, were relatively simple to duplicate.

The chips were harder because they involved materials that weren't easily available. Sure they still required a press, but it was a low tonnage press, one that I could move around alone. All I needed to operate it was an ordinary air compressor. Chip colors that needed to be ridiculously exact, along with weight and feel that an experienced dealer could detect in a second, well, these were difficult qualities to duplicate.

Although the slot machine tokens should have been more difficult, they were actually easier for me, if that makes any sense. This is because they drew on all my experiences, and I saw nothing, from the first minute, that could stop me from being successful.

All the necessary skills from model making, to plating, understanding metals, tool and die making, matching finishes, working with close tolerances, I had done at some point in my past. It was like I had reached the mountain top.

Funny thing, though, that in retrospect, I never appreciated or recognized the multiplicity of talents and skills I possessed until I began reading about them in my pre-sentence investigation and other legal documents the government presented after my arrest. The slot tokens were a challenge that probably would have defeated most people, even those with comparable skills.

There were so many obstacles to overcome it seemed to never end. At one point, I laughed at Vinny, and said, "These fucking things are going to cost a hundred thousand dollars each by the time we're through." In the end, the actual figure was closer to 50 or 60 cents.

I often wonder why I'd chosen the most difficult token, rather than the easiest, to begin my slot counterfeiting project. The more difficult the coins were to make the more interested I was in making them. Given two coins of the same denomination, I would always do the more difficult of the two first.

I had a $100 token from the Foxwoods Casino. It's not only two different metals, but two different parts, with some plating in the lettering, making it rank right up top with the difficult tokens to duplicate. By contrast, the Mohegan Sun Casino's $100 token was one piece made of .999 silver, and for me, a very fast, simple token to counterfeit. Oh, I did counterfeit them, but only after the more difficult one.

First, I had to determine what materials I needed. The $100 coin made this easy. The edges on these coins were marked .999 fine silver.

I overcame that obstacle quickly. The center looked to be brass. I tested it and it was low brass, which is a common team for brass which contains copper and is a fairly soft, malleable material to work with. It is easy to squeeze the design with approximately 170-ton pressure. This is a reasonably low tonnage and close to the same pressure needed to form the silver edge.

I made two blanking-out tools. One tool blanked out the outside diameter of the coin from a strip of pure silver material approximately one and a half inches wide by six feet long. The material was 90 thousandths of an inch thick. This is less than one tenth of an inch.

Next, I took the round blanked-out piece, put it into another blanking tool, and blanked out the center hole. This was about seven eighths of an inch in diameter. All that remained of the first strip of silver was a round rim about 90 thousandths of an inch thick and approximately one quarter inch wide. Picture a washer for a bolt with a large hole in it. This was part one. It weighed 11 grams.

The second part was to blank out a piece of brass using the same blanking tool that made the seven eighths of an inch hole in the silver, about 90 thousandths thick. This was the same thickness as the silver edge. Since this was the same tool that cut the hole out of the round silver piece, the two pieces — the silver rim and the brass insert — fit together perfectly.

I then made a tool that cut a small groove around the outside diameter's edge of the brass insert. This groove — when the two parts were placed together as the dies squeezed the design on the faces — forced some of the silver rim into that groove, thereby locking the two pieces together. So that none of the material would just ooze off the round edges of the dies, I made what is referred to as a containment ring.

OK, let's go over this one more time. You have two dies which have the casino's design on them. One die is attached to the top of the press, while the second half is fastened to the table of the press. The bottom die rises to meet the top die and continues to rise until a pressure regulator reaches the preset pressure needed to force the material into the nooks and crannies of the designs on both dies. Then it releases the pressure and allows the press table to drop back down to its resting position. Now, in order for the round token not to move sideways when the pressure is applied, a containment ring fits over the two dies exactly, and absorbing the side pressure which the tokens' metals exerted on it.

I sometimes characterize 170 tons not much pressure. This is because the press had a capacity of double that amount. Still, 170 tons is 340,000 pounds. That's a lot of pounds. These numbers became second nature to me after a short while.

The use of the containment ring was not only ingenious, but necessary, to guarantee consistent results. Most items that are formed using hydraulic pressure do not use this system. The metal is allowed to flow both in the dies' designs and out the edges. This is simply because the dimensions, especially the thickness, are not that critical.

Just as a comparison, the average thickness of a human hair is two thousandths of an inch. What difference could it possibly make if a buckle, for example, was one or two thousandths of an inch thicker or thinner; you would never see that small a variation. The excess that flowed sideways from the dies would usually be cut with a trimming tool. You would simply put the piece over the trimming tool and the outline of the piece would be finished. While not simple, it was a lot easier than using a containment ring.

My project could not afford any variations in the thickness or any of the dimensions, for that matter, so the containment ring was a necessity. The problem was the pieces, when subjected to such extreme pressures, would tend to bulge out sideways, and would put tons of pressure on the containment ring. The token would form, with a beautiful top, bottom and sides, but would not release from the containment ring without damaging itself.

Sometimes, it took a heavy hammer to get them out of the ring, and, of course, they would then be useless being all marked up and bent. This was a major problem to overcome.

I finally tried putting a two-degree angle on the inside walls of the containment ring, then polished the surface with a variety of diamond compounds. I began with a purple, or coarse, grit then yellow and finally a West diamond compound, which made the hard steel look and feel like a mirror.

This time, the token dropped right off the dies after being squeezed with 170 tons of hydraulic pressure.

Coins requiring ridges also could be done by the containment ring method. By putting the ridges in the containment ring, the coins would drop out complete with the necessary ridge design.

Usually, an indexer is a tool used to put ridges, or divisions, in something. A circle contains 360 degrees. If you wanted, for example, 180 graduations, I simply set the indexer to divide by two degrees at a time, thereby dividing 360 by two, for a total of 180 evenly-placed serrations.

Casinos, however, used uneven amounts of ridges, making the use of an indexer impossible. I found that I could use the same electrode I used to make my coins to put in the proper number of edges on the coin, just by reducing the electrode's diameter by a few thousandths of an inch.

The vast majority of casino tokens are made from what is called 18 percent nickel silver. This is kind of a misnomer, because, in reality, the metal contains no silver. It's a very difficult material to squeeze a design into because it hardens as it is compressed.

Legal operations would allow the parts being formed to be removed from the press after one squeezing. Then they could be sent out to be annealed, which is heating the material until it's red hot, then allowing it to cool on its own. The material then becomes as soft as the first time it was pressed. Next, the item can be put back in the die and squeezed once again. This time, the impression in the dies would be full and deep.

Of course, in my case I couldn't send these coins out to be annealed. I found ways of getting the design to come up on the first press. This usually involved increasing the pressure to 270 or more tons. This is high tonnage, and the first few dies I made broke after squeezing only one token.

This looked like an insurmountable problem.

I had all the latest equipment: a 320 ton Mario DiMaio hydraulic press and the finest steel available, A-1 air hardening steel. I would draw the steel down, or heat to 800 degrees and place under a coffee can, so no draft of air would hit the dies, then let them cool on their own overnight. Still, I had the same unacceptable results.

Then it hit me. The dies were fine. The press itself needed modification.

The press was brand new and top of the line. I could have made my dies wider, longer, higher, of a different material, but these were concessions I didn't want to make. They would have been very heavy, and difficult for me to work with, even just to lift and place on the press. I was sure my dies could be perfected. It was just a matter of perseverance. I began looking at ways of improving or modifying the press.

In retrospect, everything I used I modified in one way or another. There was always the temptation to improve in anything I counterfeited. I used to say to myself constantly, "Don't improve them, just copy them, imperfections and all."

I found what I thought was a defective design in a critical part of the press. It was the part that held the dies, and it had a number of concentric cuts milled in it, to allow dirt and oil from the dies to escape into those recesses.

In the center of the part was a threaded hole in which you could screw a bolt to remove the part if necessary. This hole and the grooves weakened the part substantially, especially when used with my dies which were only about two and a half inches in diameter. Most dies were nine inches or more in diameter. Even if the working area, the design, was the size of my token, the die itself was large and heavy. I kept my pieces small, so I could lift them and change them easily.

I made another part for the bottom of the press.

The new piece would be made of S-2 oil-hardening steel, which is slightly softer than the steel used for the dies and a little more forgiving. There would be no grooves, as changing dies was a simple job and each die could be cleaned in seconds with a fast wipe of a cotton cloth. The threaded hold in the center was eliminated, and two smaller threaded holes were added near the outside edge of the part, for removal, if necessary.

This move in itself was a major improvement. I found it hard to believe that the company could be making these presses for years and not see such an obvious design flaw. These changes made all the difference in the world. No dies ever broke again.

Other simple improvements and additions to the press made it function even better. The hydraulic oil was cooled by water. But the inside, where the electronics were located, worked better with the addition of a $19 square fan.

None of these changes would have cost the factory more than $50 or so. The press cost $35,000, so it wasn't a matter of money. If I was a consultant to that company, I could show them any number of ways of improving their product which wouldn't cost any more money. In fact, they probably would be even cheaper to produce.

Everything I counterfeited, I always tried to make better. That's not the object in counterfeiting. The object is, of course, not to improve, but to duplicate something, including its flaws. But this was the press, not an item I was counterfeiting. This I improved.

When the coins are first made, they look brand new. The edges are sharp and crisp, and the design on both sides is unmarked.

Unless the casino had purchased their tokens the day I wanted to use mine, the ones I made would stand out immediately. Each casino's tokens had their own characteristics — apart from the design — which had to be duplicated perfectly.

Some tokens actually had rounded edges, not from normal wear and tear, but made on purpose as part of the token's design or functionality. This would be my first operation after the token left the press. It involved making a machine that would duplicate the token's edge when it was new. This process would have a degree of guesswork, because the casino's coins had wear on them. Within a short time, I could guess very accurately.

To get the exact look to the new tokens used in a particular casino, I took a polishing or finishing tub, which is a common item used in the jewelry and other industries. It resembles a cement mixer. I made a new barrel for it out of stainless steel, which is the metal used in a slot machine tray which the coins drop into. I made the drop in the barrel the exact height that a coin drops from a slot machine. Inside the barrel I welded a piece of steel to pick up the coins when it turned. When the coins reached the top, they would drop the same distance onto the stainless steel barrel. This system would be capable of doing several hundred coins at a time, and would duplicate the exact style marks found on a casino token.

In most cases, this would be the final step. Not for me. Some of the casinos used tokens with coloring, such as antique brown, or green, or were even gold- or silver-plated. Since I had an elaborate jewelry background, this wouldn't be a huge problem. It would just take a little experimenting. Once I had the correct formula, I wrote it down. Soon I could tell just what was needed by looking at the token. Most of the time I never needed my notes. But as with everything I did, I still fought my urge to improve the fucking tokens.

Maybe this sounds easy now, because I've already done it and overcome all the obstacles. So many factors, including the token's design, affected how the metal reacted to the tonnage the dies applied to it.

To give you an idea of how much pressure 320 tons is, the press weighed approximately 7,000 pounds. Most of the weight was on the top where the pressure was generated. The top had an opening about 16 inches wide by 26 inches high by about 24 inches deep. That was cut from one solid block of steel approximately

36 inches wide and 40 inches high and 24 inches deep. The sides were about 10 inches thick. The top was approximately 14 inches of solid steel.

Even with all of this mass of steel, each time the dies squeezed metal you could actually see the top of the press move upward slightly, maybe one sixteenth of an inch. You could just feel how powerful this machine was.

The dies were made from a piece of steel, about three feet long by two and half inches and cut to two and a half inch-lengths by an automatic band saw which sprayed a coolant onto the steel. When the piece was cut completely, the machine would stop automatically. The containment rings also were cut from a round piece of steel, about one and half feet long and about seven inches in diameter. From this, a slice of approximately one and a quarter inches was needed.

It was a long, deep cut, but one the saw handled with ease. It was cool to watch that saw cut such a large piece of steel so easily. The dies were placed in a large lathe and turned to the exact diameter of the tokens it would be making. Two dies were needed for each coin, and then a containment ring which fit over the dies when the material was being squeezed.

When the dies and containment rings were finished, it would be necessary to grind them slightly, so all surfaces were to exact tolerances and smooth. The center of the containment ring was given a two-degree bevel and polished to a mirror-like finish to allow the coin to drop after it was formed. If it were going to make a coin with a serrated edge, the edge would be part of the containment ring. The coin would be complete with one pressing when it dropped from the press. All the parts were then hardened.

I couldn't send them out after they had a design on them, so the design was put on the hardened die. This worked out quite well as I used an EDM (electronic discharging machine) to burn in the designs. It worked better with hardened steel. An EDM machine is like a welder in reverse. It removes material rather than adding it.

Size was my main concern in buying the EDM. Much better products were on the market, but they were big and heavy. I purchased mine from a company called U.S. EDM Corp., which has since gone out of business. The company sent a representative, an engineer, to show me how to use the machine.

It was grossly misrepresented to me when I purchased it. The engineer, in addition to showing me how to run the machine, was also going to make the necessary changes to include features that I was promised would be included with my purchase but were not.

One such change related to when the machine flushed — or moved the burnt metal from the dies it was creating. It was designed to use pressure from a stream of fluid. The dies, when being burnt, were completely submerged in a yellowish liquid called dielectric fluid.

I was promised it would have two methods of flushing, one being pressure, or shooting a stream of this fluid into the dies, and the second, vacuum, which would pull the burnt material from the dies.

The engineer was in a tough position because he knew the company promised me that both methods of flushing would be incorporated in the machine I bought. He also knew that it wasn't set up to do vacuum flushing with the current pumps and plumbing on the machine.

He studied it for two days, then made a number of notes and calculations. When he finally flew back to California, he promised me he would figure out exactly what was needed and send me all the parts along with instructions to install them. He apologized for the error.

On the second day the engineer was in Rhode Island, the owner of the company himself came by. You could see immediately that he was the financial part of the company. He knew almost nothing about his product.

As if this weren't enough, two other major problems existed with the machine. First, it didn't have enough clearance from the electrode, the part that would burn the design into the dies, to the dies themselves. It was misrepresented in their brochure. And this was with using my dies, which were only two and half inches tall. The second problem was the design of the ram, which travels up and down frequently and holds the electrode. In its down position, it burns the dies, and when it retracts to the up position, the flushing takes place. Their ram was far too flimsy and inaccurate for my standards.

I made several calls to the company over the next two and a half years. I was always told the same thing: "We're working on solving your machine's problems. It won't be too much longer."

I would call every two months or so, always to hear the same line. I had already made all the necessary modifications and improvements within a week or 10 days. If they were still around today, I'm sure they would still be working on it. Or better still, if they knew of my modifications, and how simple and easy and inexpensive they could have been incorporated into their machines in production, perhaps they would still be in business today.

With all the substantial modifications I made the machine performed exactly as I required it to do. It still was small and light enough for me to carry it in and out of my car. This was an important feature for me, because with the exception of the press and lathe, everything had to be as small and light as possible. The lathe, saw, a rolling mill — used to roll thick stock to the exact thickness I needed — the blanking out press, and the thousands of pounds of material used to produce the tokens were all kept at Vinny's house. He had a complete workshop there.

The EDM and the press were used at the 1860 Mineral Spring Ave. location. Lots of people came in and out of that spot, including insurance adjusters, electricians, the phone company repairman, even the fire department inspectors and the chief of police. Everything had to be hidden within a phony wall or closet.

The EDM was making dies while I would be talking to someone in the store. No one ever suspected that the largest casino token counterfeiting operation in history was taking place right under their noses, or the police department's, which was only a couple of blocks away.

The press was first located in Vinny's garage. I had an addition put on, doubling its size, then added heating and air conditioning. It was never kept clean enough to satisfy me, so I moved it to my shop and disguised it behind a wall. I'm a fanatic about cleanliness, especially with this type of machinery. Any little piece of dirt or dust could ruin or damage a die or the hydraulic pumps on the press.

I met Vinny Ricci when he was about 70 years old. He looked much younger than that. He was recommended to me by someone in the jewelry business and was practically my neighbor for years. He lived at the end of a short street called Asylum Road. We used to joke that the name was very appropriate. The project I was working on at the time was casino chips. Vinny made some small parts I needed. He never knew what I was doing.

This time would be different.

He would need to know everything about what I was doing. At first I was reluctant to reveal the entire plan to him including just how many casinos I was going to counterfeit. When he told me he hated all the casinos, that all he ever did was lose money, I knew he wouldn't have a problem with this.

Vinny worked for a friend of mine as a machinist. He had a bad attitude about everything. He hated his job, his family, everything. Then one day, he lost his job at Cora Manufacturing Corp. He needed money and I needed as much help as I could get. His father asked me if I would give him a job. He could do the more routine, easier work and would be a huge help. I agreed and gave him $1,000 in cash per week. That was twice what he was earning at his previous job.

Also, he offered to buy some of my equipment, especially the EDM, when I was done with my project. I told him he couldn't buy it. I would give it to him when I was finished with it.

For a year or so, everything was going fine. I was very successful with any new coin I made. They worked beautifully, and my plan was to counterfeit a lot of casinos, maybe 50 or so and take $500,000 or $600,000 from each one.

Most people would get greedy and try to rob one or two. I looked at it like the casinos were paying taxes — to me. Every family pays a little, and the total adds up to big money. I felt that taking too much from a casino was stupid and too risky. I thought my way was better, but there was a problem. Money was coming too slow.

Every week, I was adding a new casino to my collection. Little Vinny actually looked at me one day and said, "Not another casino?" I went real fucking wild. I called him an ungrateful asshole.

"How the fuck do you think I'm paying your salary," I screamed. "I'll make dies for another year or ten fucking years if I feel like it."

Things quieted down for a while, but I could see that every time I made dies for a new token, he felt as if I was using his machinery. I wasn't going to let this piece of shit make me feel uncomfortable, and at the same time, the work he was doing got progressively worse.

A year later, I was throwing away half of everything he did. The steel for the dies was expensive, but that's not what bothered me. I couldn't rely on his finishing a piece correctly and on time and I was running behind my schedule. Then one day I told him I needed a pair of dies and I didn't care if it took him a week to make them. I was going to Vegas and had to bring this new number with me.

Normally, each die should take four or five hours to complete, not counting the design, and die finishing which I always did myself. He had a week and I told him not to do anything else but these two pieces. I wanted them perfect.

When he finished them a few days later after spoiling at least two pieces, the base on one of them had a piece of metal from a coffee can wrapped around it. He had taken off too much base of the die while turning it on the lathe.

He said, "What difference does it make with the coffee can wrapped around the piece, its base diameter is perfect."

I took the piece, then I flung it at him and told him, "If I wanted a coffee can, I would go the supermarket and buy it."

The die missed him by only a couple of inches and he's lucky I let it go at that. I told him not to make anything else, that he was through. I told Vinny Sr. what had happened, and he said that Vinny Jr.'s behavior had been strange lately. He had just returned from vacationing on Block Island with his family and his youngest son had been diagnosed with Lyme disease. Vinny was actually accusing his father of injecting his son with this disease. Any idiot knows that Block Island was infested at that time with fleas and ticks carrying this disease.

I expressed concern that he might go to the cops, but Vinny said, "No, he's not that stupid."

Vinny and I continued with our project. By now, we had tokens for 35 casinos. I was finishing them at a rate of about one new token every week or 10 days. Lots of the tokens could use the same containment ring, so those I could finish faster than the ones I had to make containment rings for.

Depending on where I went and how long I stayed, I was handing envelopes to Vinny containing anywhere from $5,000 to $10,000 each. We were really cranking.

With so many casinos to choose from, my trips increased to at least two each month. Everyone was happy, everyone except Vinny Jr. He would come by, and I watched his father take him from the shop on several occasions. He didn't want his son to see any more of the operation.

In September of 1996 I suspected he called the Secret Service and told them what we were doing. I was told by a now retired secret service agent that they had received a tip, although he didn't say from whom. I believe it was Vinny, Jr.

Anyway, they were waiting for us in Bally's in Atlantic City. That didn't stop us. The coins they collected after we played came back from their lab as being genuine. So they waited almost two more weeks until we returned and the same thing. All the coins they bagged from several of the machines we played came back either genuine or uncertain. Four fucking labs came to the same conclusion. The retired agent said they were wondering if I was for real or not. They took a chance when they finally decided to arrest us.

One of the most difficult operations in this scheme was the electrode needed to burn the impression in the dies, using the EDM. The electrode is an exact duplicate of the token, only burned into the dies so that when the metal is squeezed into the dies' cavities, it produces the token.

The difficulty arose when trying to duplicate a token that is made from brass, nickel silver, bronze, or any other material that does not conduct electricity. In order for an EDM to function, the electrode must be a material that conducts electricity. Examples of good materials would be copper, silver, gold and carbon graphite. If the token could be sent out to a company that makes electrodes, they could duplicate the coin in one of those materials.

There were two problems. First, I could not send the token to any legitimate company for duplication. Secondly, even if I could, they would duplicate the token, as it was in its finished state. Dies made from these electrodes may not produce the same results as the finished token. It took me a long time to realize this. Who knows what the die that made a particular token looked like. It may have been higher in the center, smaller in diameter, or any one of dozens of other variations.

Metal reacts differently when squeezed under pressure. Sometimes I had to make adjustments to the electrode to duplicate the token. One common change was that the token's electrode be a couple of thousandths of an inch higher in the center. The finished piece would be thicker in the center than acceptable if the electrode was true to the token. Metal expands when put under tons of pressure, and all the metal expanded or behaved differently.

It was always a series of adjustments and modifications until the tokens were duplicated exactly in order to defeat the slot machine's anti-counterfeiting devices.

After time I could pretty much guess the amount needed to adjust the electrode, and I could sometimes make minor adjustments in the dies themselves. To produce the desired results, sometimes I would over polish an area to get the metal to flow, say into some deep design or lettering. When I finished the piece it could match the original token's characteristics perfectly.

Some of the tokens, like the $100 tokens from Mohegan Sun and other casinos, were made from pure silver. These were almost ready to use just the way they were. They already were made from a great conductive material and they were easy to do. Others, particularly the $25 denominations from many casinos, were also silver, so these were easy to do. All these electrodes needed was a little contouring of their shape, and I was getting proficient at knowing how silver would react.

The problem remained with the non-conductive materials. I found two methods to overcome this obstacle.

The first was to make an RTV (room temperature vulcanizing) silicone mold of the desired coin. Room temperature vulcanizing does not require heat to vulcanize the material. This is a silicone based product, using a two-part system consisting of silicone and a catalyst that acts as a hardener.

Vulcanized material hardens in less than hour, while this material takes overnight to harden.

Also, RTV does not shrink when it hardens. The coin is placed in a metal frame and the silicone is carefully poured over the coin and allowed to dry slowly, usually for around 24 hours. There is no measurable shrinkage using this method. Then, the cavity is filled with liquid wax and allowed to harden. You now have a perfect image of one side of the token, but in wax. Placing the wax back into the mold frame, and pouring casting material over the wax — then burning the wax out — leaves you with a cavity into which you can pour liquid silver or copper, This system, with practice, works beautifully.

I devised the second method for obtaining the necessary electrode. It was a system that produced better results, was quicker and a lot less work. I took an ordinary plating rectifier, which usually works in a range from one amp to 12 amps, at 12 volts, and put a rectifier on it. This split the one amp into 1,000 parts, or milliamps. This is necessary because one amp will plate a coin in a few seconds, either with copper, silver or gold. But, left longer than a few seconds, the copper or other metal being plated will have a tendency to distort its detail.

With my method you plate very slowly, with the part being plated turning at about one revolution per minute. The token is exposed to the plating electrode only a few seconds each minute.

It might sound complicated, but it really isn't. There are companies that make big, but light, earrings in this manner. It's called electroforming, and is the same basic principle as electroplating, except it works much slower and can plate much thicker without losing any of the item's detail. Machines that do this kind of work are terribly expensive, costing well over $150,000. I built mine at a cost of under $250 and it functioned flawlessly.

Doing this adds several thousandths of an inch to the token. A nickel silver token would receive a layer of copper. The copper will work in the EDM machine perfectly. But the token is still several thousandths of an inch larger than the original. This amounts to about three human hairs in thickness, and that's too much to be acceptable.

All EDM's has some electrode wear. A slow burning on the dies will produce much less electrode wear than a fast cutting, or roughing cut. I began with a fast roughing cut, which produces the largest part of the impression quickly. Then, I switched the cutting process to a very slow burn, which produces a fine finish. Since most of the copper plate on the electrode had worn down during the fast cutting, the coin was very true to size as I began the final finish.

With a little practice, it was possible to produce dies that need very little hand finishing and were highly precise in their dimensions. When I got to this stage, I was making dies very quickly and accurately. Every casino was vulnerable.

It was always fascinating to me to see the EDM machine doing its work. It would move the electrode down to the die quickly, then start to spark as it burned into the hardened steel. I shut off the light lots of times watching the sparks emitted from the electrode. I thought it was like the Fourth of July.

When the electrode burned a few seconds into the steel, it retracted to a position above the die, and contact was interrupted. The machine had to be cycled just perfectly, otherwise it would burn a hot spot, an unwanted hole, in the die. When the electrode was on its way up, the flushing took place, and blew fluid into the area the electrode just left. That would send a stream of black material out from the die, and that stream always reminded me of an octopus whose propulsion emits a sort of black stream of liquid. Remember, all of this action was happening in a tank filled with fluid.

The function of this machine must have fascinated me more that I realized. Whoosh, whoosh, whoosh, as it performed its miracle on the steel.

The sound was very important. It indicated to me whether I had a good reliable burn, with the proper time on, time off cycle. A good cycle meant the machine was functioning properly and could be left to do its work unattended. I set all the machines that took time to do their work on timers so I could leave the shop without feeling guilty about losing valuable time.

Can you imagine that? I felt guilty if I didn't have the machinery working night and day, but felt no guilt about what the fuck I was doing with that machinery. Boy, whenever that analyst does get around to me, he'll have his hands full.

***

We had spent a couple of hours playing black jack at Bob Stupek's casino. This was the last casino on the Las Vegas Boulevard across the street from the Little Angel's Wedding Chapel. It was a worn-out place, appealing mostly to old people that were on frugal tours. Still, it got its share of business.

Sometimes, it was actually quite busy. It was in the process of receiving a major facelift. The name was going to change to The Stratosphere Casino.

They were building a roller coaster on the roof. Supposedly it was going to be the highest roller coaster in the world. The building itself was pretty tall, and with the addition of the roller coaster it was the highest spot in Vegas.

Along with the roller coaster was another amusement ride — a straight free-fall of maybe 75 feet or more. It was almost like a bungee jump, again, being built on the top of the building.

Both were attractions that the casino hoped would attract younger people. Half the time, though, it seemed the attractions were closed because on a windy day they just weren't safe.

On the top floor of the building was a string of retails shops. One of them sold new and used genuine slot machines. I bought one for my own entertainment and had it shipped to Rhode Island. It cost about $2,500.

The casino had no large parking garage, no multi-level parking maze like the big casinos. I drove right in the parking lot and walked from there to the casino floor in minutes. After spending several months robbing this place, I got to the point where I would leave the car running outside the door, run in the casino, cash out a couple of thousand dollars' worth of chips and leave. Maybe five minutes elapsed at the most.

After having a great time playing blackjack for an hour or so on another occasion, I was sitting next to a high roller from India who had a $100 chip glued to his forehead. This guy was a bundle of laughs, but I decided I would check out. When I got to the cashier's window, a large man grabbed my arm. He had been our dealer until his shift was finished. I was startled by this action.

He said, "I'm sorry, I didn't mean to startle you. I only wanted to know where you purchased that great bracelet." I told him I made it years earlier. He asked that if I ever wanted to sell it, to please give him first chance at purchasing it. I told him I would, then I continued cashing out. I never wore the bracelet again in any casino.

Another day, I had more elaborate plans to play blackjack at Circus Circus, another casino on the strip. This was a much larger facility whose main attraction was all kinds of circus acts performed right above the casino floor.

There were two large casinos and each one had its own cashier.

The $25 casino chips were medium green with pink inserts and a funny red clown in the center label. Munzel green is the exact same color as the plastic cap used on a bottle of STP oil supplement, which could be found in any automobile store. There I go again. By now, it had reached a point where I would identify casino chips and associate them with products that were found in plastic bottles, newspaper advertisements and any other number of products.

I became so color conscious that I would look at something and say, "Wow, that's the exact color of a casino chip from the Pioneer or from Circus Circus or from MGM Grand or from whatever casino."

I think I know every casino's $5, $25 and $100 chips. I know their insert colors, labels, the amount of wear they have, the feel, the depth of the lines that cover the design, their security features or smart marks, their weight and anything else that has to do with any particular casino's chips.

To this day I associate colors with a casino's chips. I know it's crazy. Pistachio ice cream, for example, always reminds me of the Sea Breeze Casino in Laughlin.

I played a while and then cashed out of Circus Circus in a very short amount of time. Our plans included going to Laughlin, which is about a three- hour drive from the strip in Las Vegas.

In Laughlin, there were about 10 casinos. With the exception of one, the Ramada Inn, which is across the street, they all border the Colorado River which separates Arizona from Nevada.

Since Laughlin is quite a distance from Las Vegas, they are extremely anxious to get your gambling business. The hotel rates are absolutely rock-bottom cheap. The Hacienda — which is one of the most beautiful places you could stay anywhere — cost about $39 a night for waterfront rooms and as cheap as $25 for a regular room. It's like a vacation in and of itself and the food and the drinks are also ridiculously cheap.

We got there around 6 p.m. to find all of the employees — including the cashiers, pit bosses, stick men, dealers, security personnel, hostesses, everyone — dressed either as a ghost, a skeleton, a cowboy, Spiderman, or whatever type of costumes you can imagine. It was Halloween night and the atmosphere was one of lightness and fun and was very amusing. We began at the Sea Breeze, and worked our way to more than half of the casinos, playing at each and making money at the same time. We were staying at the Hacienda at the end of the strip.

It was going to be easy to move the thousands of chips I had sent there for this trip. Problem was, that the night before leaving for Vegas, I was still putting the finishing touches on one of Laughlin's casino chips and about 300 pieces from the Pioneer Casino. The chip that concerned me was dark green with maroon colored inserts. Everything was perfect, except the chips needed another 10 or 12 hours of tumbling in wax-soaked corn cob to get the exact finish on the label that I wanted.

I wouldn't have time to finish them, but I didn't want to leave them behind, so I tried various methods to speed up the process of finishing them. I finally discovered that a dab of Vaseline petroleum jelly produced the exact look and feel I wanted. I packed up the chips and put them in our luggage. I would finish them in Vegas or Laughlin.

The chips looked really good and with the festive attitude of the casinos personnel, I thought perhaps I would try to move some of them, maybe all of them, that night. They were a bit gritty, but behind every casino was a beach, with lots of sand, and people taking a break from playing had buckets containing their chips and coins with them. If anyone commented that they felt dry and gritty, I could say that I was playing with my chips on the beach. I took some beach sand and put it on the chips, then entered the Pioneer and decided to start playing.

Just to be on the safe side, I looked for the oldest blackjack dealer and sat down, placing a dozen or so greens on the felt table. This guy was so fucking old, I didn't think he could even see the chips. But, boy was I mistaken. Out of all the dealers I sat with, in all the casinos in Vegas, Reno, Sparks, Tahoe, Laughlin, Jean, Atlantic City and Connecticut, I picked the sharpest son-of-a bitch of them all. He spotted a defect immediately.

He picked up one of the chips. They were so perfect, except for the gritty feel, that he kept looking and looking. I apologized for the dirty chips. I said we had just come in from the beach area, and that I dropped the bucket they were in on the sand.

"I should have wiped them off for you, sorry," I said.

"Happens all the time," he replied.

We played a while, then left. I cashed out the few I had, after most of them were exchanged for either $100s or $5s as we played. I still had 300 or more to move.

There we were, ready to move thousands of chips on a busy Halloween night, and sitting on several hundred chips that needed only to be touched and wiped with Vaseline. It didn't look like much of a problem to me.

Have you ever tried to buy Vaseline in Laughlin? After driving in and out of every fucking store, Seven Eleven, gift shop, and anywhere else I thought I could find Vaseline, I came to a startling realization. Laughlin didn't know of the existence of Vaseline. I was forced to use a tanning lotion, which worked just as well, but had a strong coconut smell. We frantically began rubbing the chips with this fucking stinky lotion, until it got to the point where we couldn't smell it any longer.

The chips were now great, and we decided to cash out about half of them. We could no longer smell them, and assumed the odor had vanished, leaving perfect chips just waiting to bring us money.

The cashier had a nose longer that an elephant's trunk. She picked one up, smelled it and immediately said, "Been having fun with these chips, huh?" insinuating that we may have been rubbing ourselves, and our chips, with tanning lotion, in some sexual ritual.

I was quick to reply, "Yes, they're a great aphrodisiac. The cashier smiled, cashed me out. The next day I cashed in all the chips and headed for Vegas.

Chapter 15
'Silence Is Golden'

Pfft Pfft Pfft Pfft Bang.

On a warm, rainy, summer night I had my garage door wide open. I lived in a townhouse on a cul-de-sac at 43A Knoll place in North Providence's Louisquisset Condominium Complex.

The biggest problem living in a condo is storage. I solved this by putting a retracting staircase in my large, walk-in closet and finishing the attic where summer clothes could be stored in the winter and winter clothes could be stored upstairs in the summer. Anything that wasn't used often was always stored upstairs. The upstairs was complete with an elaborate shelving system.

The garage was heated , had hot and cold water faucets, and the floor was tiled. I could wash my Ferrari in either the summer or winter.

This night I wasn't washing the Ferrari. A friend and I were testing my latest creation, a silencer for a 22 caliber Ruger model Bulldog automatic pistol.

I took the gun apart and then, using my lathe, turned a thread on the barrel. Next, I took a piece of aluminum — about a quarter of an inch thick and an inch and a half round — and threaded it so it screwed onto the Ruger's barrel. It was a perfect fit.

I made another piece similar to the one screwed onto the barrel, but with a much smaller diameter hole — approximately one quarter of an inch in the center — where the bullet would exit. I took a round piece of thin, stainless steel tubing, which fit perfectly over the two aluminum pieces. The tubing was about five inches long by an inch and a half round.

Everything would fit so tight, it was necessary to use a Nylon hammer when I wanted to separate the parts without marking them up. Three small screws held the stainless tube to the aluminum parts.

Now I had a Ruger automatic with a five and a half by five and a half inch extension on the barrel.

What could I fill this with to muffle the bullet sound, I wondered?

I went to an automotive supply store nearby and started looking around. I spotted a gas line filter for a Chrysler engine. It looked like it was going to fit so I bought two of them.

When I got home I pushed them into the stainless steel tubing and they fit perfectly.

Next, I put the end piece on the tubing. I screwed the three little screws into the aluminum end piece and the silencer was ready.

I loaded the magazine of the pistol and aimed at the tree across the cul-de-sac. The tree was in a small wooded area bordering Lincoln and there was no danger of anyone getting shot — except maybe me if the silencer didn't work and the gun backfired.

It looked good. I didn't know how much noise it would make but I was pretty sure it would work. This was the moment of truth. With the garage door wide open and no one in sight, I pulled the slide back on the Ruger and chambered a round into the barrel. It was ready to fire. I took careful aim at the tree and squeezed the trigger. It sounded exactly like an air gun. Not dead quiet, but silent enough to use almost anywhere.

I squeezed another round, then a third. I knew that I was running the risk of a loud round because most silencers have a very limited life.

Unlike in the movies, the silencer is not something you could use endlessly. I would always laugh when I watched a silencer being attached to a revolver. Silencers don't work on revolvers. They work on automatics.

I also knew that my unit was holding up better than I imagined and I squeezed off another round. This was noticeably louder that the last one and sounded like an old steam engine on its exhaust stroke.

"OK," I told my friend, "I think that's it. Let's close the door and call it a night. The piece works great."

"Fire just one more round," he insisted. "I want to see if it stays at this sound level."

I insisted that it wouldn't and I didn't think it was a good idea to fire it any more. We were pushing the limits.

"It should be disassembled and the filters replaced," I said.

He persuaded me, reluctantly, into squeezing off yet another round from the 22 caliber long rifle ammunition.

"Bang."

I actually think it was louder than if it was shot without the silencer. The shot was not only loud, but the aluminum front of the silencer flew out the garage door and the filler inside the tubing also came out with the bullet so there were pieces of West paper like material that flew through the air more than eight or 10 feet from the garage door.

Frankie, my next door neighbor, ran out from his unit and saw me at the door holding an automatic pistol in my hand.

"You OK, Louis?" he asked.

"Yeah, Frankie, just trying out a new project."

"Okay, Lou, see you tomorrow."

My friend and I picked up whatever we could find of the debris that the gun had scattered on the driveway and went back into the house, closing the garage door behind us. The silencer had performed exactly as I had expected it to, maybe even better, because I figured it would only hold back noise for maybe one or two rounds, not four or five. The front aluminum piece would have to be replaced and made with a piece of steel , and new filters installed. Other than that, it was quite successful.

My neighbor Frankie was Nick Bruno's nephew. Nicky's dead now, but he was a major member of the Patriarca crime family. Nicky was a high ranking associate of Raymond's family and the New York Gambino family, but this man was loved by all five of New York's most powerful organized crime families. He was sort of a moderator who would settle disputes between New York's five families and those in Connecticut, New England and Rhode Island. Everybody loved Nicky Bruno and I can see Frankie had inherited his uncle's charm.

Frank was about 5 feet, 10 inches tall, maybe 210 pounds,. of which at least 10 pounds was his long, thick, brown hair ending in a ponytail. He was a handsome young man who attracted more girls than you could possibly count. He was the owner of a Replacement Hair Lines beauty salon franchise, which is a combination beauty salon and custom hair replacement center, in Warwick.

In reality, Frank earned his fortune because of his association with the Rhode Island mob.

***

I was outside the condo knocking on the pipes where the two gas meters were located. Inside the boiler room, Maureen had her ear on the pipe leading to the gas heater.

"Do you hear the tapping?" I asked.

"No," she said.

"OK, don't move, how about now?"

"I think so," she replied.

"All right, which pipe is louder? Let's try it once more." Tap, tap, tap.

"No, not this one, let's try this one." Tap, tap, tap.

"The second one is louder, I think," Maureen hollered.

"OK, then I'll shut the gas off on this one. I hope it's the right one."

At just that, moment Frankie's car pulled into the driveway and he came over to see if he could be of any help. Frankie wasn't a very handy guy so I really didn't rely on him too much for any kind of mechanical help. He didn't have the slightest idea what I was doing and who knows, maybe I didn't either.

Anyway, I told him that I wanted to install a remote control gas fireplace and that I wanted it in by Thanksgiving. The installer failed to show up.

"What I'm doing is tapping on the pipes and Maureen is listening on the other end to see which pipe seems to be making a louder sound and I'm relying on that to determine what pipe goes to my unit," I said. "We got at least a 50-50 chance of shutting off the right gas line."

"Well, as long as my daughter isn't home, don't worry Lou. I couldn't give a shit what you do to this place," Frankie said.

A few hours later the unit was installed and the fireplace lit up beautifully with the touch of a button. The condo hadn't blown up

Usually a neighbor comes over to borrow some sugar, maybe milk, a rake, a hedge trimmer, lawn clipper or some other household item. The relationship between Frankie and me as neighbors was a little different.

"Lou, I need some piss right away, take this bottle."

Frankie was always on probation and his probation officer would turn around and let Frankie come into my unit. He knew what he was doing. He was coming into my unit where I could pee in a bottle and Frankie would give it to him as a clean specimen. Not that Frankie was a drug addict, because he wasn't. He liked his weed and an occasional line or two and could probably never pass a random piss test.

If he wasn't asking me to urinate in a bottle for him, then he was asking me for a toss away because he had business in New York, mostly, but other states as well. A toss away is a gun without any traceable history. It's used for whatever reason and then dropped at the scene.

Frankie wasn't a violent person. I just think he felt powerful carrying the gun.

I was the perfect neighbor for Frankie and he was the perfect neighbor for me.

When he was dating a gorgeous young girl whose family owned the American Crayon Company and she had just passed the Rhode Island bar exam, Frankie used to say frequently, "How can I go to work, look at her, I can't leave her. How can I leave her?"

He would usually be in the driveway and we would meet when we were outside.

He'd say, "It's impossible for me to concentrate on my business. I'm going to have to marry her. I just can't leave her."

Then one day he came into my house and he said that he was going to get married.

I said, "So what else is new? That's all you fucking talk about is how much you love this girl."

With an embarrassed, almost childish look on his face, he said, "Yeah, but not to her. I'm gonna remarry Lisa, my ex."

I threw him out.

I said to him, "I have two kids and I have to listen to this kind of shit, but I don't need this stupidity from you."

I really liked Frankie. A couple weeks later the girl that he had been dating committed suicide. Frankie, myself, and my girlfriend at the time, Maureen, were absolutely stunned because this girl was a constant visitor in our home. She was gorgeous, she had so much to look forward to and we couldn't understand why she would do something like that.

It wasn't related to Frankie. She had had problems of another sort and decided to take her own life. It was devastating to all of us.

Chapter 16
Vegas Junkets

Rhode Island had lots of interesting people and many of them wound up in Las Vegas. I did business with several of them.

Junkets with Al Albo Vitelli, who owned Rocket tours, were a popular thing in our circle.

There were the wise guys, Skyball Scibelli from Hartford, Springfield Sam and his top aide Mario Fiore, from Connecticut. We would charter planes go to Vegas for free.

Through Jimmy Howard, a jeweler in North Providence, I made contact with his brother-in-law, Pat Pisano, who had jewelry stores in most of the larger Vegas casinos. Pat's brother, Mike, was the head of the culinary union in Vegas and could bring the entire city to its knees if he wanted. He introduced me to Sheriff Ralph Lind who was another powerful figure in the Las Vegas scene. Pee Wee Pisano, another one of Pat's brothers, was parking cars at that time at the Circus Circus and went on to become a powerful boss for the hotel workers union. Frank Londano owned Londano Provisions Company. He was another Rhode Islander. Every casino in Las Vegas, both then and now, would buy their meats through the Londano Provisions Company.

Bobby Rosati, from Providence, was connected to and financed by the Patriarca Family. He was a stockholder and the manager of the now defunct Dunes Casino He was a good looking, soft spoken man in his late 40s who used to shudder at the news that the Providence crew was coming to Vegas and would be staying at the Dunes.

Poor guy, he would beg us not to break into the hotel rooms, play slugs in the slot machines, rob old ladies' pocket books, pay the hookers with counterfeit money, or make trouble in ways only Providence guys knew how to. Bobby Rosati knew what we would do, but we were all connected with the same Family and there really wasn't anything he could do about it. Of course, he obtained his job through Providence sources and was obliged to take care of anybody that was from the Providence Family with free suites, comps, meals, and all the perks that go along with it.

I wasn't a gambler and technically the junkets were really limited for high rollers only. After all, you got free airfare, everyone stayed in their own suite, which was fully equipped with a bar, fresh flowers, fresh fruit, snacks, a Jacuzzi and all of this for the bubble. I mean, how do you think we paid for all of this?

I would go to the casino's cage, take out a marker for $10,000 or $15,000, and then act as if I were partners with big Al who was a real heavy gambler. I would pay back one or two of the markers every once in a while, then get back on the books a day or so later.

Of course, I had their money and could've paid them back at any time. But it looked better the way I did it, stretching it out and showing some action. Sometimes I actually left Vegas with $7,000 or $8,000 of the casino's money in my pocket and left my markers in the cage.

We would usually settle up on the airplane ride back home and I would say something like, "I'll write a check within a week. I had a bad trip and lost money."

Then, within a week or 10 days, I would take their money and put it in my checking account and send them a check to pay back my markers that I had left there. It really looked like I had gambled and lost.

One time Al was feeling lucky and was playing craps like crazy. In half an hour, he was down $25,000. Even the wise guys, Springfield Sam and his crew, told him to slow down. He had five days left and at the pace he was going, he'd be broke in no time.

As part of our usual scheme, I went to the cage and took out $10,000 in markers. I handed the chips to Al. About an hour later he had lost all of it and needed another $5,000. I'm into the cage now for $15,000. I signed another marker. Al's luck had changed a little bit and he was able to hold his own for several hours.

About 4 a.m., Al was still playing and was still down about $25,000. I wanted to go to bed. It had been a long day and I told him that I'd see him in the morning. Al went wild over this.

"Don't leave," he hollered, "What the hell is the matter with you? Don't you realize you're bringing me luck? You'll ruin my luck now if you take off."

I said, "Al, you're down some $25,000, you're barely holding your own, you can't fucking stand up, it's four in the morning. How the hell can I affect your luck? If you were on a winning streak, maybe I might go along with you and your superstition, but the way you're going, you'll be broke before morning comes."

I decided to go to bed. I could never understand a gambler's reasoning.

The following day I learned that he had gotten so out of hand that night that the pit boss told him to stop insulting his dealer. Al would throw dice so hard that it would wind up on the wood, then the dealer would have to make call, "Wood no good," and Al would start freaking out on him.

"Yeah, look at what came up, look at what came up. Now it's no fucking good?"

It went on and on like this until finally they told him to take it easy and stop playing for that night.

The next day Al wasn't in a very good mood. He decided to take a break from craps.

"I'm gonna take a break for an hour or two," he said.

Al was from the old school. He thought slot machines were for women only, yet here he is pumping dollars in a machine, and swearing when he didn't hit.

Five days later we were on the airplane and Al had left Vegas owing money to the cage. He also owed me $12,000 in markers that I had signed for him. I didn't know how exactly much he owed in the cage, but I'm sure it was substantial.

We used to tell Isabel, his wife that he broke even, or that he made $200 or that he lost $300 no matter what actually took place. I got my $12,000 back but I got it back in bits and pieces, $2,000 here, $3,000 on another occasion. It's a funny thing, when you're repaid money over a long period of time instead of all at once, it just seems to disappear and almost looks like it was never paid back.

One time I was having a brief affair with a young girl from Pawtucket. Her name was Arleen Conlon and she was very pretty. She had a young daughter. Because of her past drug problem, her ex-husband had custody.

Arleen was now clean and trying to get her daughter back. This custody battle was obviously an expensive affair for her. One night she told me she was going to go to Vegas to take up prostitution in order to get enough money to get a lawyer and fight for her daughter.

I thought she was kidding at first, but she actually showed me the ticket about a week later and it was a one way ticket to Las Vegas. I gave her a couple of hundred dollars, wished her luck and said I'd miss her.

Then a year and a half later, me and the guys were back in Vegas at the Dunes. We were there to see Bill Cosby. At that time, he didn't have the nice guy reputation he enjoyed for many years until the sexual assault allegations piled up.

Cosby was doing extremely risqué night club performances. Big Al was making the reservations. There was a little alcove off the casino floor which was lined with telephones and Al was on one of the phones there.

He said, "There'll be six of us, me, Al Picolli, Al Vitali, Pat Pisano, Gus Broccolo, Ray Monacchio, and Lou Colavecchio. In that little alcove where Al was making our reservations there was a girl using the next phone.

She approached him and said, "Excuse me. Is that Louis Colavecchio from Rhode Island?"

"Yes," Al said.

"Where can I find him?" she asked.

"He's staying here in the Dunes, Suite 2304."

Next thing I know me and Arleen were in bed, fucking and laughing that we should meet several thousand miles from where we used to meet and what were the odds of something like that happening. She stayed with me for a few days, then when I left for home, she asked me not tell anyone what she was doing in Vegas. She had a very good chance of getting her daughter back and this would ruin her chances. I told her not to worry. She wouldn't have any problem with me and she knew that I wouldn't tell anybody. Small world though, isn't it?

Chapter 17
Getting Caught

I went over to Vinny's house about 6:30 p.m.

We had tubbed several hundred coins the day before and put them in my mixture of chemicals which consisted of sulfate and other mild acid solutions to give the tokens an antique appearance. When they were all finished they looked great. Six of them were on one side of the table, a small gray workbench with a Formica top that we used to do finish work. Another six were on the opposite side of the table. Under each of the six coins was a three by five lined index card, turned upside down indicating which indicated which coins belonged to us and which coins were actually manufactured by the casino. The cards were marked "Us" and "Them". They should have read good guys, bad guys, but then I wouldn't know who the good guys were or who the bad guys were. Us and Them worked better.

The object was to see if I could tell which were genuine and which coins were counterfeit. I honestly didn't know. They looked exactly the same.

I carried them into the back and there I put them into six or seven mailing boxes and marked them SB-010. This was my code indicating that the coins were for the Showboat Casino and were of $10 denomination also marked on the outside of the boxes were the number of boxes that pertained to this particular casino and this denomination token. This box was one of seven. The next box would be two of seven, three of seven and so on. This way I could tell exactly what was left and what I had used up.

Since there were about 75 or 80 boxes, each weighing approximately 10 pounds, it was necessary to modify the trunk of my Honda. I removed the rug and flooring and anything else that was in the trunk's bottom surface. Using several pieces of cardboard, which I taped together, I made a template of the trunk's interior.

The template was placed on a piece of three-quarter- inch solid plywood and the plywood was cut to fit the trunk perfectly. The plywood was painted flat black, so anyone looking in the trunk would have seen nothing irregular. This additional support, just the three quarter of an inch plywood, allowed me to distribute 750 -

800 pounds evenly in front of and behind the car's rear axle. No other modifications to the car's suspension system were necessary. The car felt a little heavy, perhaps, and its acceleration wasn't quite as fast. No observer would see any signs that the trunk was carrying so much weight.

Donna and I had broken up just a few days earlier, and she moved back into her condo. She knew I was planning this trip, and came looking for me. She insisted on coming to Atlantic City with me and eventually persuaded me to take her. That may have been the biggest mistake she ever made in her life.

When all the coins were packed, I headed home. Donna stayed over. We would leave the next morning around 8 and take our time, stopping to eat the sandwiches she had prepared for the trip. We also had a new book on tape, John Grisham's *The Pelican Brief.*

When we reached the Hampton Inn on Blackhorse Boulevard just outside of Atlantic City, the audio book wasn't quite finished. I told Donna I wanted to hear the ending and catch the last few minutes of Darby's episodes. We must have looked like a couple of nuts, sitting in a parked car listening to the radio, but neither of us cared. We had to finish the book and I think we were probably there another 35 or 40 minutes.

The Hampton Inn has more than one location in and near Atlantic City, but this was the closest one to the casinos and was a very friendly place to stay. We were registered and decided to settle in our room and relax a couple of hours.

Our next move was to go to Bally's Park Place Casino which was the closest to Melissa's and the first casino located on the strip. I stopped the car and removed two boxes of $10 tokens from the trunk. I also had two dozen $20 tokens, which were genuine, that I had purchased a couple of weeks earlier. I wanted to study them and possibly counterfeit them, but I ultimately decided against doing this. The $20 token wasn't widely accepted and since I had so many other denomination tokens to choose from, I decided I would just play the few I had or cash them in after playing a couple of boxes of the $10s.

From Melissa's to Bally's was a short ride. With the exception of the quick stop to pull out the two boxes of coins, it was uneventful.

When I entered Bally's high roller area, I had an eerie feeling that my movements were being watched. There was almost no one there and I thought that was strange. It was a Friday night, around 7 o'clock or so and it should have been busier than it was.

Maybe it was just my intuition, but I told Donna not to play and I would cash out that few 20s I had. I said we should roam the casino a little and then leave. Donna was a bit surprised, but she was always able to pick up on my instincts and she went right along as if all went well in there. We cashed out the few 20s and left. All in all, I didn't think we were there more than 10 or 15 minutes.

The next planned stop would be Caesar's. Upon leaving Bally's parking lot I suspected we were being followed and contemplated turning around and head going back to the motel. This would bring us across a small bridge with about a 50 foot wide channel where boats would pass from one side to the other before going out into the ocean.

Going over the bridge I considered emptying the trunk of its contents, about 750 pounds of tokens or more than $100,000 worth of coins. Then, I figured what possible difference could that make if I was already being followed? After all, a diver could certainly retrieve them in a very short order and so there wouldn't be much advantage in being stopped with a full trunk or one that had been emptied in the river.

I decided that if it was just a matter of Bally's security watching me, perhaps it would be a good idea to get rid of the Bally tokens only. They were already in the front of the car and all I had to do was just drive over the bridge, open the window and throw them out.

I took a couple of side streets, lost what I thought was the car tailing me, reversed direction to return to the bridge and tossed them into the river. If Bally's had a beef, I had nothing from their casino in my possession. If it were more than Bally's, it wouldn't have made any difference at all. I didn't see anything suspicious in my rear view mirror. Maybe I was overreacting. Maybe I imagined the unusual atmosphere at Bally's or maybe I had drunk too much wine. It didn't matter at that point, I was going to go to Caesar's next and whatever would happen, I felt I couldn't change it.

It was busy on the strip and I had to park my car on the top level in Caesar's garage. I unloaded the 5s,10s and the $100 coins from the trunk. Donna and I walked into Caesar's and proceeded to the high rollers area. The atmosphere here was totally different than it had been at Bally's. There was a lot of action and everybody was frantically playing slots. We joined in immediately. I made several hits on the $10 machines but was about even on the $5 and $100 denominations.

One guy was playing two $100 machines at the same time. One of them was at the beginning of the row of about eight or 10 machines and the other one was at the very end. He was jumping from one end of the row to the other, and his mania intrigued me so much I couldn't stop watching him. The reels would still be spinning on the first machine that he had dropped two coins in and he'd be at the other end of the row playing, dropping two more coins in the second machine without the first having stopped spinning yet.

He was extremely fast and he never broke his pattern. First machine, then the end machine, two credits, the maximum that was allowed in each machine. One of the coins dropped through and it didn't register and he didn't get credit for it. His decision was to put in a second coin immediately rather than spin the wheels. That decision proved to be a good one for him because the machine hit on the three diamonds and his jackpot was $12,000. That one coin earned him an extra $6,000.

Funny thing about gamblers, they're compulsive but meticulous about how they play, whether they're winning or losing. After watching him about 45 minutes, I decided to cash out.

Donna and I went to the window. She arrived just ahead of me. I heard the teller count out $5,200 dollars. Not bad, I thought. She actually won money. Then I stepped up to the window and handed the cashier my coins. They were all mixed and she had to separate them into three piles which took her a minute or two. I kept about 10 of the $50 tokens and while she was getting me my money, I played the $50 machines located just behind me at the end of the $100 row.

I had purchased these coins a couple of weeks before, but, like the Bally's $20 tokens, decided not to manufacture them as they weren't very popular. Anyone wanting to play a $50 bet would use two $25 tokens. Someone who wanted to play $100 would use a $100 token and not two $50s. Besides that, there were only two machines that took these $50 tokens. I lost the few coins in a matter of seconds and was back at the window to collect my $4,500 in about a minute.

Moments later Donna and I began walking out of the casino. When we reached the exit, a big, well-dressed man tapped me on the left shoulder. He identified himself as Frank D'Agostino, the slots manager. He said there had been a slight mistake and would I mind returning for a moment.

I immediately replied, "Don't tell me, you counted wrong and you owe me another hundred."

He said, "I hope so."

I knew exactly what was going on.

On our way back into the casino, I told Donna that we would probably be arrested and not to say a word. Identify yourself, provide your license when they asked for it, but don't get into any conversations of any nature with anyone. These are not your friends, and even the most innocent sounding question had a purpose. I compared it to a car accident where both drivers were fighting and arguing who was right and who was wrong. These, and our types of cases are settled a couple of years later. The facts at that time get so convoluted that someone reading them would think you were referring to another incident.

As far as signing anything, she interrupted me, saying, "I know, I know, I would never sign anything without a lawyer."

"Good, you'll be fine."

"Donna, we're in here too long, way too long," I whispered. "They're having trouble finding any coins and I'll bet that they're going through all the machines we played, trying to find the counterfeits. They're having problems I'm sure."

She agreed. I told her that the next thing they had to do was start viewing the surveillance tapes to see if and when we brought anything in and when we began playing. This was going to be a big problem for them and I knew that eventually it would be to our benefit. I was right about that.

The room we were in was small, maybe 12 feet by 12 feet square with nothing but a cheap, small desk and four chairs. It was right off the casino's main floor, and we could hear people playing, laughing, talking, everything. It certainly wasn't soundproof, that's for sure. Looking around the room, I found nothing to indicate the room had any security cameras or other security devices. I tried turning the door knob, and it turned freely. I cracked open the door and could actually see the casino's main floor. I wondered why they would put us in this room without any security and without even locking the door. I could only guess that this was the first step in a procedure where the casino was not positive something illegal had taken place. I mean, supposing they were wrong. They could always say we weren't detained in a locked room with a security guard, and that they had forgotten we were even there. But, I knew this wasn't the case. They were having trouble finding evidence, nothing more.

It was around 11 p.m., and we had been in that fucking room more than two hours.

Then, a man entered the room and identified himself as a New Jersey state trooper assigned to the Division of Gaming Enforcement that oversees the New Jersey casinos.

I remarked to Donna in a loud voice, "Gee, maybe they didn't make a mistake in counting our winnings at the cashier's office."

He didn't respond, but asked that we please follow him. Another officer, who didn't identify himself, joined us, walking through the casino floor to a waiting unmarked police car. Our destination would be just a short distance away to an odd building. The cops parked in the back. We walked past a number of police cars, then entered a shabby building.

Imagine the opulence of Atlantic City's main street, with all its elaborate, elegant marble casinos, bright lights, and neon signs. Then move your eyes one block over, not toward the ocean, but to the slums that make up most of the rest of this area. That's where the police station was located.

We walked up a flight of stairs and found ourselves in a large room with a couple of wooden benches and some chairs, a broken soda and coffee vending machine and a table or two. We were not handcuffed, and were asked to each follow one of the troopers to a small, real shabby room with only a desk, phone and two chairs. They split us up immediately. I never saw the room Donna was in, but since it was right next door, I could only imagine that it looked about the same.

I was asked to empty the contents of my pockets and place them on the desk. I had several thousand dollars in cash, 20 or 30 $100 tokens, my hotel key, and a wallet on me. The tokens and money were placed in a bag, and after looking through my wallet, it was returned to me. He asked me if I was carrying a weapon, and I responded that I was not. He never checked to see if I was telling the truth.

"My name is Bob Schulte, and I'm with the New Jersey Division of Gaming Enforcement. You're being detained for passing counterfeit slot machine tokens," he said. "Now we know you're not the mastermind behind this scheme and we could wrap this thing up in no time."

I smiled.

"You think this is fucking funny," he shouted.

"No, I don't think it's funny," I replied, "but I have nothing at all to say, so move along with your investigation, I have nothing more to add."

He was really furious.

While this was going on, I heard another cop who was questioning Donna, scream, "Who's your fucking lawyer, Big Lou?"

Donna replied politely that she had nothing more to say. Both of us had been given the same pitch, like it's not you we want, so cooperate and everything will go away. Sure. And the Easter Bunny will bring you a nice, big basket of colored eggs next Easter.

When Donna's interrogator finally relented and accepted the fact that she wasn't going to give him any more information, he turned to very polite conversation, and just asked some bullshit questions about the weather, and other nonsense.

Then he said, "Boy, it must have been a long trip getting here from Rhode Island, because with all that weight in the car, the car must have been very slow."

Donna replied to this question. She said, "No, about three and a half hours. We made a couple of stops at a rest area."

I was later to explain the importance of that innocent appearing question. They now knew we had driven to New Jersey and that we had taken the tokens over the state line: that we had taken them from Rhode Island to New Jersey.

But it certainly wouldn't have taken a genius to determine that we drove the car from Rhode Island and later I told Donna not to be concerned. She didn't give them any big revelation. And with a trunk full of tokens and so much evidence, her statement didn't add much to their case that they didn't already know.

Bob Schulte told me he knew about my little red Honda. I just let him continue talking.

"Now, Lou, do you have a weapon in the car?"

No, I answer again.

"Well," he said, "the reason I ask is that if there is a gun in the car, it could be dangerous and we certainly didn't want anyone to get hurt."

This time I didn't answer.

"Do you mind if we search your car?"

This question I answered saying, "Certainly not, if you have a search warrant."

"What about your motel room?" he asked.

Knowing that I had nothing incriminating in the room, I said I would allow them to search the room, as long as I could get some of my medications and bring them back to the station. I explained that I suffered from a stomach ulcer and high blood pressure and could use my medications soon.

"OK", he said, "we'll go to the car first. Then the motel"

I said, "No, the motel only."

He knew I was going to be difficult. He also knew from Donna's interview that she, too, was going to be tough. They figured they had two amateurs, one a bank programmer and the other one, me, having no known police record, and that they would crack this case in very short order. By now they didn't think that any longer.

Within minutes, Donna and I were in a police car, and I explained to her I had made a tradeoff, which would allow them to search the hotel room without a warrant in exchange for my getting my medicines. I told her I knew there was nothing of value to their case in the room and that's why I was allowing it. But, the car was out of the question.

We arrived at the room about 20 minutes later and I got the two bottles of pills I needed and said, "All set."

They searched the room, but there was nothing there that was of any use to their case.

We were driven back to the police station. When we were back upstairs, the attitude had changed dramatically. Donna was placed in a locked cell with a sink, toilet, and a bed. She would be there a long time. I was taken to a small room, which was about five feet wide by maybe three feet deep. It was really a closet with a stainless steel table occupying the whole room. I couldn't imagine what they used this for, except maybe for prisoners to change their clothes in. But, I was soon to find out what they were going to use it for in my case.

I had just taken my pills, so they placed me in the room, clothes, jacket and all, and locked the door. If I were claustrophobic, I would have been dead. This room wasn't designed to be used with the door closed for more than 10 minutes at a time. I placed my mind in an almost trance like condition. I don't know why, but I knew I would be spending a lot of time in this room. Unfortunately, I was right.

About two hours later, the door to the room flung open.

"You ready to sit down again?" he asked me.

I replied, "No, I've said everything I have to say, thanks."

The door closed and I was trying to work the kinks out of my muscles. Being in one position for two hours was something difficult for me. So, I got an idea. Take off my shoes, and place them under my jacket and make a pillow. Actually, it wasn't too uncomfortable. I was determined to convince my captors that this room did not bother me. I decided to put on a big smile whenever they came back, and act as if I had been woken from a deep sleep.

Another three hours passed, and the door swung open. I had a big smile on my face and told the jerk, "You woke me up from the greatest sleep I ever had."

This pissed him off big time.

"I'll get that fucking smile off your face," he shouted.

He took my shoes, jacket, pants, belt and shirt. I had only my underwear and socks on, and it was cold.

"See how you fucking like this," he hollered, as he handcuffed my left hand to one side of the room and my right hand to the other side. The rings fastened in the cement blocks were about a foot above the steel table. I couldn't move from this position. This was cruel and unusual punishment, I remember thinking. But, it's all the ammunition he had to deal with me, and he was determined to solve this case by himself.

I don't know how long I was chained this way. I hadn't eaten in hours, and I was so cold my body was shivering uncontrollably. I'll die before they'll wear me down I swore to myself.

An hour or so later, the door swung open. It was another member of the state police, a Sgt. Pluffer. He was a small man for a state trooper. He was soft-spoken, and handed me my clothes back and said, "Put these on."

When I finished dressing he said, "Do you need to take your pills or use the toilet?"

I said, "Yes, my ulcer's bothering me."

He handed me back both bottles and said I could get water from a bubbler just a few feet down from the closet I was in.

I said, "Thanks," and tried not to show that I could hardly walk. I hadn't stood up in hours. I managed to make it to the bubbler and took both pills. When I returned, he asked me if I wanted a cup of coffee and a muffin or donut. I accepted the coffee and muffin and said to myself, "This guy's not so bad." I ate and drank in the small room, but now with the door open and my hands free.

Just when I thought my torture was over, this big asshole arrived. He was not alone. Standing beside him was a creep in a $20 suit. FBI, I said to myself. What the fuck does he want?

The man identified himself as an FBI special agent attached to the Atlantic City district. He pointed to a chair, and told me to sit in it. I did.

Then he said, "This is your last chance."

The other boob was very silent. They obviously knew each other and had discussed my case extensively. He went on to say to me that he had found my little gun in my car. It was a Freedom Arms five-shot, 22 caliber miniature revolver.

"You're looking at 5 years consecutive. This is your last chance," he repeated, "or we'll call the Secret Service."

This was the best news I had heard in a long time, because everything I had ever heard about the Secret Service was positive. The FBI was a bunch of publicity seekers and would do anything to get a bust. When they arrested someone, they always made sure the press was around. They thrived on publicity.

The Secret Service was just the opposite. They went out the back door and kept a low profile. I told the agent I had nothing more to say, and both he and the New Jersey cop left, calling me an asshole.

On his way out, Schulte remarked that the only thing that could have made this arrest better was if they had found some coke in my car.

I sat in the chair for about a half hour, when a big man, with a more compassionate looking face, and another $20 suit came over to me. He introduced himself.

"I'm Special Agent Edward Kitlas," and showed me his credentials He said, "Look, I know you're not in this alone. This is an organized crime activity, and we want some of the other members. I'll ask you only once to give me some cooperation, for your own good."

I told him that I had heard and been told that so many times it was getting stale. He grew angry, and looked at me straight in the eyes, and said, "This will be the last day of your life as you know it."

He turned around and left without saying another word. Looking back, he was absolutely right.

Shortly, the New Jersey trooper who was so obnoxious and another man from the Secret Service, came to me and said, "Stand up and put your hands behind your back."

I did as he asked and was handcuffed with my hands behind my back and the cuffs on far too tight. Then I was shackled around my waist and my feet.

The New Jersey cop said, "You're on your way to jail."

I thought to myself, finally I'll be out of this dump. We went down the back stairs, and sitting in a waiting car was Donna. I was happy to see her, but she was also handcuffed and shackled. She complained the cuffs were too tight, but otherwise, she was fine.

When we first arrived at Caesar's it was quite busy and the parking garage was almost full. We drove around and around the steep, winding parking garage ramp, with speed bumps every hundred feet or so, to keep the speed down. This twisty ramp with all these bumps posed no problem to my Honda, of course, because of the modifications I had made to the trunk to keep the car level and in balance when the trunk was loaded with my tokens.

Now, while we were in the police car, Schulte received a call from the Secret Service to meet them at the Honda, in Caesar's parking garage with the keys, as they were going to take the evidence from the Honda and transfer it to their car and later store it in their evidence room. Schulte helped the Secret Service agent pack his big Buick's trunk with almost 800 pounds of tokens. The Buick seemed to drop in the rear under the load of my coins, but when they were finished transferring the coins, the federal agent had Schulte sign a paper indicating that he had taken the tokens from the red Honda and transferred them to the Buick and another form indicating they were also going to take the red Honda and impound it. It was now a federal case.

Schulte backed his car up, and the agent backed the Buick up until it almost hit our front bumper. Everyone was leaving Caesar's parking lot. The Buick looked low, real low in the rear, but it continued down the twisty ramp without difficulty, until it came upon the first speed bump. Bam. Vroom, vroom, vroom!!! The muffler and suspension system hit the speed bump and the Buick's muffler and tailpipe dropped from the car immediately.

The Buick's rear end was hung up on the speed bump and the car wasn't going anywhere, its tires turning without any effect. It was loud, parts were all over the ramp, and I was laughing my balls off.

The fucking jerk didn't realize he didn't have enough clearance to pass over the speed bumps. Couldn't he feel the steering? It must have felt light as all hell. The agent called for assistance. He was tying up Caesar's ramp and looked like a real jerk. It took more than 20 minutes for another car to come and this time they loaded the tokens half in one car and half in the other. All they had to do in the first place was to put half in front and half in the trunk and they could have avoided this. You could see the surprise and anxiety in their faces as they waited for the second car. I overheard one of them say to the other, "Boy are we in some deep shit, they don't want to repair our broken antenna, imagine when they see this damage."

I have to admit it was funny. Even Bob Schulte was laughing. They held my car for six weeks, at a cost of $971 to Gunther's Mobile for storage alone trying to figure out what I had done to the Honda so it didn't do what the Buick did. They had experts examine the suspension, springs, axle, shock absorbers but no one noticed the three quarter inch piece of plywood lying quietly under the trunk's rug.

The New Jersey trooper, who had tried so hard to make my life intolerable, now had a whole different attitude.

He called his wife and said, "I'll be home late, honey, I'm with Big Lou." He turned around, and asked me if I would mind saying a few words to his wife.

He held the receiver to my mouth I and said with a smile, "How do you stand this guy?"

She hesitate a second, then replied, "It isn't easy." Schulte took the phone back.

From that moment on, I think he had a different feeling for both me and Donna. He asked me what kind of music I liked. I said jazz, so he turned the radio to a jazz station and said, "It'll be about an hour's ride, maybe a little more. Enjoy the music."

But the music was interrupted several times, as he kept calling to different friends of his and asking me to say a few words to them. As he was driving, he turned around and said he was just doing his job: "Nothing personal."

Chapter 18
Atlantic & Gloucester City Jail

The jail is just inside the town of Cape May. It's a quaint little town with gingerbread style houses — many restored to perfection — unusual shops, and the world's largest pretzels. It's a romantic and relaxing setting. I'm sure.

When Donna read the sign, "Welcome to Cape May," she felt the same way I did. This isn't going to be so bad, like a mini vacation after the torture we had just been through.

There were two rows of razor wire surrounding the cement block building. A wide gate slid open, revealing more razor wire. Another gate opened and we were driving toward the building. The building resembled something I saw once in a movie which showed scenes from a Turkish jailhouse, only this place was nowhere near as clean. A sign read, "No weapons beyond this point." There were several old wooden boxes nailed to the blocks, and the top lifted up for handguns to be placed in.

"OK, let's go in," one of the officers shouted as he opened the back door of our car.

Both officers removed their guns and placed them in the shaky wooden box, which tilted sharply to the left with the weight of the guns. We walked a few feet and two of the prison guards greeted us. They took us through another door to a small room with two wooden benches. One guard undid our handcuffs and shackles.

"Take your pants off," he said to me. "Leave your shirt on. We don't have any more tops."

Donna was escorted around the corner and I heard two women guards tell her to undress: "Leave just your panties, and put this uniform on."

We handed our belongings to a guard and he put them in a bag, placed a tag on the sack with a piece of wire, and said, "Sign this." It was a receipt for our belongings with only a number identifying each sack. He didn't feel like itemizing the contents. I heard him tell someone in the back, "Here's two more for you."

By now, both Donna and I realized this wasn't going to be like any of our previous visits to Cape May.

No one ever explains anything in a jail. I think there should be manuals published detailing the procedures involved in the various types of jails. It would certainly speed things up. But then, what's the hurry? Later we learned to say, "Hurry up and wait."

The next step was the processing room, a dirty, dimly lit room, with an old-fashioned ink pad, a roller, and cardboard pieces with lines and grids for inmates fingerprints and photos. The camera was an old Polaroid popular in the early 60s. This procedure is known as processing an inmate.

Donna and I were led into the holding tanks, as they are called. She entered the first one. It held women only. It was a combination of ninety-five percent blacks, four percent mixed and one percent unknown. Most were there on either drug charges or domestic violence crimes. I was in the next cell, with about the same combination of inmates, except my cell had one percent transvestites. The wives were locked up in Donna's cell, and their boyfriends, husbands, pimps, and so on were locked in my cell. They were all screaming and yelling at each other. Donna and I got to know several of them and exchanged stories about who was who and what they were in for. A couple of weeks later, when we were home, we had to admit some of it was funny as all hell. Nothing could be worse than this zoo. That was another mistake, because when we were put in the cellblocks downstairs, we realized then that this place we had just left was like a tiny piece of heaven.

Downstairs was something resembling the catacombs in Italy, except without the splendid history. It was only cement block construction, with some of the blocks painted yellow 40 or 50 years ago.

I was placed in cellblock C, and Donna in cellblock A. That would be the last time I would see her for the next seven or eight days. Her sister and brother-in-law had seen us on the news. Actually, it would have been almost impossible not to have seen us, as our arrest was broadcast worldwide, all day and all night long.

They drove down to Cape May, visited Donna, and put $50 in each of our commissary accounts. Now here's where the prison manual would have come in handy. I didn't know what the fuck a commissary account was. Not that it would have mattered anyway, because it took two weeks to process, and we weren't there that long. The doors going into cellblock C swung open if you placed all your weight against the edge. They were opened when inmates were let in or out for whatever reason, but they really didn't need locks, as the hinges were so rusted, they were almost frozen solid. A huge, disgusting woman-like creature sat up on a platform made from cement blocks, with a dirty glass window which had a hinged metal tray below it which swung in and out. If she wanted to pass you something, she placed it in this bin like tray and swung it into the inmates' area.

Inside the cellblock was like the Chicago commodities exchange.

"I have one ham and cheese I'll trade you for your two chocolate chip cookies," one inmate hollered while he held up his sandwich.

"I'll give you my Kool-Aid," which was 98 percent or more dirty water, "for a slice of bread."

Everywhere you looked, someone was making a deal for something or other. The room was big, maybe 150 feet deep and 75 feet wide. At the back left side was a metal stairway, leading to the top floor. To the upper right were some small cells with steel bars furnished with an upper and lower bunk. None of the toilets in the rooms worked, and the only place you could go that worked was on the first floor, below these cells. Two of the eight toilets in that room actually worked, but you had to plunge your waste to get it to go down.

The main room was lit up by two rows of lights, in which there were long fluorescent bulbs. Only about one third of the lights actually worked, so the room was very dimly lit.

Originally the facility had been designed to house some 60 or so inmates, but now it had over 200 in it. Mats were spread on every square inch of the upper and lower floors, and this is what you slept on. No mattress, no bed, no bunk, no pillow, just a filthy rubber mat — and none were available. An inmate brought me a mat and I placed it at the end of the room, near a shower that was always left on. It had no knobs to adjust it. The floor was pitched and led to a drain. I set my mat down and he told me to move, that I would get wet there. He asked a few inmates to put their mats closer and I snuck mine in between them. Since they had no shirt or shoes for me when I was processed, I still had on my Lorenzo Banfi handmade loafers. I used them as my makeshift pillow. I lay down and dozed off.

A couple of hours later, 10 or 15 inmates took their mats off the floor and the steel doors swung wide open. A cart was wheeled in. It was supper. The cart was crudely made from old wood with four casters on it. The food was so disgusting I refused my tray and took only a plastic glass with watered down Kool-Aid in it.

This was another time a manual would have come in handy. Never refuse anything offered you in jail. It's your bartering ammunition. A toothless bum named Joe said to take the tray, that they were serving chicken parmesan. I gave him my tray and he gobbled it down faster than my Airedale Terrier would a piece of filet mignon. I got to learn the ropes with him, and he turned out to be a very nice, intelligent person.

I wondered why everyone seemed to be so accommodating toward me. I soon found out.

My name was called over a scratchy, primitive old loudspeaker and I went up to the booth with a fat pig in it.

"Colavecchio?" she asked.

"Yes," I replied.

"Go to Room 137,"she snarled.

I asked where Room 137 was. She told me to follow the yellow line on the floor, and I would pass three or four rooms and then I would be there.

Before I left, Joe came over to me and said, "Lou, be careful. Keep to the right of the yellow line. If a CO (correctional officer) is coming the other way, put your hands and back to the wall until he passes." Violating this procedure would put you in solitary. By now I'm thinking about writing the fucking manual. I followed the yellow line, or what was left of it, and passed several rooms. One had a TV blaring out, with my picture and Donna's flashing every few seconds. We certainly were celebrities in that prison.

Room 137 was tiny with an old filthy desk and two wooden school chairs, the old-fashioned type that have a kind of tray that goes in front of you to write on, and one of the fattest women I had run across so far. There were needles and syringes in her desk drawer, and used ones thrown in an old brown waste paper basket. I wondered what the fuck I could be in for now. So far, no one has tried to stab me, but maybe my luck was about to run out.

She told me to sit down and came over to me, a needle in her hand. She said it was a shot for something or other. Most likely rabies, I thought. After sticking me with a horse size needle, she put an elastic around my arm and wanted to draw blood. I told her I had just had a complete physical a few days ago and my blood was fine. She insisted and I sat there while she poked around looking for a vein. After a few tries, my fucking arm looked like a piece of perforated sandwich steak.

Hell, she got enough blood just from my bleeding to fill a dozen vials. I asked her for ulcer medication.

She said, "No, it's not in your records."

I didn't even have any records yet.

On my way back to cell block C, the TV in the room I passed was still showing our photos. By now, the inmates had a copy of the local newspaper, and Donna and my pictures were on the front page. Anyone who didn't know who I was before today certainly knew now. Inmates were coming from everywhere.

"Wow, you're a rich man," one of them said. My orange pants were old, dirty, ripped and five sizes too large for me, and someone brought me a new pair, which fit great.

"What do you need?" someone asked me. I said I had an ulcer, and when I tried to get medication from the nurse, she said it wasn't in my medical records, so the answer was, no.

Now, every day, at 11:30 a.m. a cart comes by with medicine on it. They shout out your name and a fat slob hands you a cup with your name on it and your medication inside. One of the inmates asked if Tums or Rolaids would work.

I answered, "Better than nothing."

"I'll get them for you tomorrow, I've seen them on the cart," he said.

I slept on the floor that night. The prison is supposed to be smoke-free, but the smell of tobacco and weed was so strong, I was getting high on the second-hand smoke.

The following morning the meal cart came by. The food was on old gray plastic trays, with three or four recesses in it. There were 25 or 30 loose Cheerios in one recess, a chocolate chip cookie in another, and a small cardboard container of milk. I took the tray, ate part of the stale cookie and drank the milk. The food from the night before was still clinging to parts of the tray. It was disgusting, but I made a friend by giving my leftovers away.

Someone brought me an orange, a very rare and valuable commodity in prison. Instead of eating it, I peeled it, pushed my finger in it and began brushing my teeth with my fingers.

"Motherfucker," someone yelled out. I thought he was yelling at me, and he continued, "Didn't that fat whore give you a package when you came in."

I said, "No, what's a package?"

"It's a tiny tube of toothpaste, a toothbrush, soap and a pair of shower slippers. I'll get them for you today, don't worry, but don't go in that shower without some protection on your feet," he said.

"Some of these animals think the shower's a toilet," he added. It seemed that some inmates would actually shit on the shower floor.

"Thanks," I said. A few minutes later he checked the shower without me knowing it, and handed me his own shower shoes.

"Here, use these, the shower's clean now," he said. Of course, he meant it had no shit on the floor. That was the standard for cleanliness.

Everyone knew I had a commissary account, but it was just past the day you could order anything. Just the forms to order things like soap, shower shoes, peanuts, and a couple of dozen other items were like an endangered species. I wasn't going to be there long enough to use it, but they didn't know that and neither did I. They had all kinds of items ordered for themselves, and I told them I would get what they needed as soon as possible. If I stayed there longer, I would have. I took a fast shower and almost fell on my way out. The layer of scum was thick and slippery and I wasn't prepared for that. There were no towels, so you used your clothes to dry off. I never got my package, but I didn't need it. Someone was always around and happy to give me what I needed.

The CO was there to give the inmates what they needed. No real, factory-rolled cigarettes existed in this prison. It was a non-smoking facility. If you wanted a cigarette, you needed the tobacco, which cost $4 per cigarette, and newspaper to roll it in. Toilet paper in jail, any jail, is almost impossible to obtain. The best substitute was brown hand-wiping towels, but more often than not, a newspaper acted as toilet paper. Weed was prevalent and cost about the same as a cigarette. Cocaine, heroin, and pain pills were also sold by the COs. Almost anything illegal was available for purchase, if you had the money, but matches were non-existent.

I slept on the floor the first night, but the next morning, a couple of real tough guys approached me.

One of them said, "We'll have a room for you to sleep in tonight."

I felt like saying, "Sure, and I'm really home sleeping and dreaming this whole fucking nightmare," but I went along them. What else could I do?

Every morning, pink slips went into the fat fuck's cage, and guys would go up to her and shout out their name. If your name was on one of the slips, she put it in the drawer and passed it through to the inmate. That is, if she felt like it. Many times an inmate would spot a pink slip belonging to him and would ask for it. She pretended not to see or hear his pounding on the glass, almost making him beg for what he had coming. A pink slip usually meant either a bail hearing, court appearance, or other legal matter. But at least it got you out of this shit hole for a while. More likely than not, it was for making bail.

I went up to the window every day for exactly the same reason. But Joe told me not to waste my time or get disappointed when no slip was coming.

"This is a state facility," he said. "You'll be picked up someday soon and be held in a federal detention center."

The Secret Service had taken over my case, so I wouldn't be here long. He was actually happy for me, because, he said, "The food in the federal system is a much better quality."

I was just beginning to relax on my mat for the night, and the two who approached me earlier in the day tapped me on my shoulder.

"Come with us," they said. They were heading for the stairs to the second floor where the cells were located. None of the cell doors were locked because the toilets didn't work, and also, there wasn't anywhere you could go. The steel doors downstairs were bolted closed.

"What do you want, a lower or upper bunk?" one of them asked.

There wasn't an inch of space not used by someone sleeping on a mat and the rooms were all full. We were standing in front of a cell with two inmates sleeping in it. Where was I going, to levitation?

Still, I answered, "Bottom — I have an inner ear problem, and would prefer the bottom."

As if they gave a shit, I thought to myself. Then, in one fast second, the two musclemen pulled the guy sleeping in the bottom bunk and threw him out of the cell.

"Give him your mat," one of them said to me. The poor slob was flabbergasted but didn't say a word. He left quietly, looking for a spot on the floor big enough to put my mat. I spent the night in a lower bunk. This is something that inmates didn't get until after six months or a year. I had it in two days.

Jails are very cliquey places. The guys that got me the bunker were part of a tough gang. I wasn't worried about any reprisals from their gang. But I did have a run-in with a group of real tough guys from another gang the day before.

I was on my way to the toilet and they were sitting on the floor, talking and eating as if they were dining at Sardi's. When I walked past them, I let out a little gas. I had a long wait before there were any stalls free and what difference could it make, this shit hole smelled so bad anyway. In the toilet, I kept hearing someone yelling, "Mercy flush, mercy flush."

I had no idea they were shouting at me to flush the toilet before I was finished, and again after. When I left the bathroom, one of them blocked my way, and said, "Motherfucker, can't you see we're eating here."

Now I knew what he meant. Another chimed in, "Hey, rich boy, come over here."

Before I moved, several guys, part of the gang that got me the room, came to my rescue.

The next day my ulcer was really hurting. I hadn't had anything but the milk and two stale saltine soup crackers. One of the inmates asked me what I could eat that wouldn't upset my stomach.

"Anything packaged," I responded.

"Can you eat soup?" he asked.

"Absolutely," I said.

"I have noodle soup, will that be OK?"

"Yes, great," I said.

"OK, is 4:30 this afternoon a good time for you?"

Again I courteously replied, "Yes."

"I'll see you then," he said, and he walked away.

About 15 minutes later, I saw him carrying a peanut butter jar full with water. A couple of days before I was offered an empty peanut butter container and this time I took it. In jail, you take anything you can get. A plastic jar was filled with water, and around the neck of the jar was a string. I couldn't figure out what the fuck he had in mind. The next thing he did was remarkable. He held the jar in his right hand and with one smooth movement tossed the jar up in the air, some 18 or 20 feet high. It came to rest with a thud directly on top of the grate of one of the lights that was still working in the room.

The jar was resting on a light and the string dangled about six feet from the floor. This guy had done this before, I said to myself. He could have played for the Boston Celtics. His aim was perfect.

"4:30, your room," he said

I replied, "Yes."

While all this is happening, there's a CO sitting in the guard station at the end of the room, so this inmate's timing had to be as accurate as his pitch, or, on second thought, it really didn't matter. Nothing you could do would get any of those lazy COs to move from that station all day.

At 4:30, I was sitting on my bunk waiting to see what was going to happen next. I said I would meet him here, so I'm here. I didn't think he would show up. But if he did, I couldn't imagine what to expect. I waited in my room for another 10 minutes or so, then went out to the little balcony overlooking the main floor. I saw the guy jump up, grab the string, and the plastic jar slid off the light's grid. It dropped 18 or more feet and landed right into his hand. It seemed to almost slide effortlessly as if on a track. He made it look so simple. He disappeared for a few minutes, then came to my room.

The package said Lipton Cup of Soup, chicken flavor. He peeled back the lid on the package top and poured the hot water from the peanut butter jar into the soup container.

"How do you want it, soupy or thicker?" he asked.

I said, "You're the chef."

He said he liked it thicker, but there was lots of water if I needed it. He had a plastic spoon and fork, and handed them to me. In less than two minutes, I had the best meal I had eaten in several days.

"I have one left for tomorrow, but it's beef flavored. Is that ok?" he said.

I grabbed his hand, stood up, and gave him a hug.

"Thanks, man, you're fucking great," I said.

This was like dining at Sardi's, I thought.

I was aware that everyone who helped me had a selfish motive, still they were taking a chance. Those packages of soup, the container, the bunk bed, the orange, the pants, the shower slippers, toothbrush, toothpaste and everything else I received were like gold in there. They were, as far as I'm concerned, taking a risk by going out of their way to help me. I never forgot anyone who helped me while I was in that rat hole.

One CO was so fascinated by what I had done at the casinos that he handed me a slip of paper. It was a note from Donna. It read, "Hi, I'm great, smile, I love you."

One thing I couldn't understand was how inmates lit their smokes when there were absolutely no matches available. I found out that this is what made pencils so valuable a commodity. You could get almost anything you needed if you had a pencil to barter with.

"Here's how it works," Joe said. "You take a small piece of newspaper, and, using the pencil, mark it back and forth until the paper is fully covered with lead. Then you go over to an electrical wall receptacle and put one end in the negative side and the other end in the positive side. You short out the receptacle. The paper catches fire and your smoke is ready to be lit."

"No wonder all the receptacles are black," I thought. I wondered what caused that, since no one had anything to plug in these receptacles, like a radio or shaver or whatever. I never paid attention to why every few minutes the lights would go dim. But now I knew.

Joe continued, "If I had a pencil in here, I'd be a king. You can get two cookies just to light up one or two smokes. A pencil is a money maker, Lou."

I hadn't shaved in several days and my face began to itch. I asked Joe how I could get a shave.

"Well, Lou, they only have razors on Tuesdays, and even then, they have maybe a dozen for this whole place. You stand in line until they run out. Wait 'til Tuesday and stand in line. Then offer your next two meals for a razor. The C.O. doesn't care who the razors go to, as long as they write down who they went to and get them back within a half hour. Any longer than that, and they'll send guards to look for you."

"OK, Joe, I got the picture."

On Tuesday I'm standing in line. I'm probably the 18th person in line and knew I wouldn't stand a chance without Joe's suggestion. So, I hollered out, "Two full meals for a razor."

I got several of the first dozen inmates in line who would trade me their position in line for my meals and now I was probably third or fourth in a line. The CO asked my name and marked the time next to my name. The razors ran out a few inmates later, and the line disappeared immediately. Shaving cream was non-existent in this pit, but I had a bar of soap an inmate gave me, and this worked just fine. I felt like a new person, neat and clean-shaven. Nice. Real nice.

I promptly went to the CO's station, banged on the thick glass and held up the razor for the fat fuck to see.

"Colavecchio," I screamed. The tray slid open and I dropped the cheap Gillette disposable razor in the tray and began walking away.

"Get back here, inmate," she shouted with a vengeance. She was holding up the razor, pointing to the top, where the blade is. I didn't have the slightest idea what the fuck she wanted. I placed my ear toward a little round hole, with a rusted grate inside and she shouted, "Where's the plastic cover, Colavecchio?"

"What?" I said.

"The plastic cover, I need it now."

"I threw it away," I said.

"Well, find it Colavecchio, or it'll be your ass."

My vision of being neat, clean-shaven, and feeling good disappeared real soon as I crawled on my hands and knees in that filthy fucking bathroom looking for a clear plastic disposable razor cover. Where the fuck could it be? I'm thinking. Did I flush it down the toilet.

The 30-gallon, galvanized steel trash container was brimming over the top with garbage, so it would have fallen on the floor if I put it in there. I looked and looked but I never found it. I decided to ask Joe what I should do next.

"Nothing, Lou, nobody ever follows up on anything in here. It's just more work for those lazy bastards. Don't sweat it," he said.

Once again, Joe was right. Not another word was mentioned about it.

In prison they never tell you anything in advance. One morning two federal marshals came to transfer me to a federal facility in Philadelphia. Everyone was writing their names and addresses on pieces of newspaper and handing them to me. I hugged at least a dozen guys, and actually had tears in my eyes. Joe and I had become close and I had his name and number. I hugged him and told him I'd transfer my commissary account to his name.

He said, "If you can, Lou. If not, don't worry. Take care yourself."

"Thanks for everything, Joe, and good luck, kick their fucking asses in court!"

When I reached the processing room, my clothes were waiting for me. I was told to grab my pants and put them on. I signed that they had returned everything to me and I handed them back their pants. They took all my slips with everyone's names on them and told me my commissary account would be transferred to my next facility. I could not leave it to Joe. I felt I had let him down, but I knew he would somehow understand that I couldn't. He knew the system.

The two marshals were very busy talking to each other and weren't concerned about me and Donna in the back seat. We were chatting away, talking about our experiences in jail and trying to get the characters straight.

"Now, the fat girl with the tattoo was the girlfriend of the tall, black loudmouth in your cell," Donna said. "They were arguing because she caught him with her girlfriend doing drugs, but he denied fucking her, and she didn't believe him. That's why she cut him."

Donna went on: "Then, she felt bad, and blah, blah, blah."

We laughed as the stories continued. She asked me if I got her note. I told her I did, and it made my time go by faster and happier, knowing that you were doing fine. The drive went by so quickly, the next thing I know we're driving down a remote road to a little red building. It was no bigger than a good-sized farmhouse barn, and it looked like one.

"This is your stop, Donna. This is an accredited federal detention center, and you'll be here until your bail hearing," one of the marshals said.

Donna and I kissed goodbye and I said, "I'll see you in a couple of days."

She smiled and said, "I love you," then disappeared.

The ride to the men's federal detention center, in Gloucester, was about an hour . I fell asleep in the back seat and was awoken upon our arrival there. The building was a large, cinderblock structure, about the size of one of the larger supermarkets. It was in very shabby condition.

I was expecting something like Donna had, a nice rural setting, nothing resembling a jail. But, forget that. I was in another shit hole jail, only this one was just a small step above the last one. It had two rows of razor wire, exactly like the last place. It was actually another city jail, but for inmates with short terms. Part of the jail was set aside for federal prisoners.

Processing was much quicker, and I had a pair of trousers and a top that matched. Orange, of course.

The Gloucester City Prison Inmate Property Inventory Sheet dated Jan. 3, 1996, (the year was wrong, it was 1997) listed my items as follows: Money amount $57, 1 belt, brown, 1 pants, blue, 1 jacket, black, 1 fanny pack, black, 1 wallet, black, 1 lotion, 1 gum, Other Items: medication given to nurse. The bottom of the form was signed by me and dated by the guard, Jan. 3, 1997. This is how all prisons were run. I now realized that the fat fuck nurse at the last jail had my medicine but wouldn't give it to me.

As soon as the processing was completed, I was put in a small part of the building reserved for federal inmates awaiting bail hearings, parole violators, bail jumpers, child support delinquents and some work release inmates who went out all day, worked, and returned back to spend the night in jail. The main room was probably about 30 feet deep by 40 feet wide, and had locking steel doors which actually worked.

There were about 50 small cells with steel bar doors which were opened at 6 a.m. Lockup was at 11 p.m. In the main room, there was a shower that ran 24 hours a day and was a lot cleaner than the last one I left. There was no TV or any other entertainment, except for the inmates themselves.

I had a bottom bunk in a two-man room, and my cellmate was a hot shit. He was a young black man in love with a girl, and had heard advertisements urging young people to sign up for the Army National Guard and see the world. When he told her it was a great opportunity for her to travel and he would wait for her, she signed up. She was very much in love with him and they had a child together. They would get married after she saw Germany, which is where the Guard promised to station her for six months. He was soft-spoken, mild-mannered and bought the Guard's bait to travel hook, line and sinker.

"Fucking North Carolina," he moaned, "North Carolina, she's stuck in fucking North Carolina."

The Guard promised to send her to Germany, he said, but they really took advantage of her and sent her to North Carolina instead. Now, they would be apart at least six months, or, possibly, her whole term of enlistment — two years. He wound up punching the recruiting guard and was doing a year for assaulting a federal official.

The way he kept repeating the story was sad, but funny at the same time. He was a good-hearted slob who got taken advantage of in a big way. You couldn't help but feel sorry for him. His girl's away for two years, he's away for one year, and their daughter is living with her grandmother. No one would learn to speak German in that house.

Two days later, two marshals came to take me to Trenton, NJ, to a bail hearing. Sitting in a nice, clean cell, one of them asked what I'd like to eat.

I said anything and he suggested a Philadelphia steak sandwich. He knew a place that made a great one. When he returned about an hour later, he had a huge sandwich and a coke, and told me I could wash my hands with a small bar of soap he handed me. The sandwich was delicious.

The hearing lasted only a few minutes. Donna was there and we talked a little before the judge came in. The judge was the Honorable Joel B. Rosen, United States Magistrate Judge. He had a big smile on his face and said that due to the size of the token operation, and the overwhelming amount of evidence against us, the bail was set at $300,000 each.

Both of us were represented by Jim O'Neil, who drove from Rhode Island for this hearing. This was the first time I had ever met him in person, but I knew who he was by his reputation. He was tall, thin, man with a very compassionate personality, and we would become very close over the coming year and a half.

Jim objected to the amount of bail and asked if he could say a few words on our behalf. The judge granted his wish, and Jim went on to say that neither Donna nor I had previous criminal records and were first-time offenders, and we were not candidates to skip bail, as we both had strong ties to our families in Rhode Island. The judge was unimpressed.

"They have refused to cooperate, and this was a huge operation," the prosecutor stated, and he was positive we were hiding the identity of organized crime figures that were sure to be involved. The judge agreed with the prosecutor and stood firm at $300,000, but allowed Donna to place her condo as security. With me, he showed no mercy. He wanted cash, lots of cash, he said. I wasn't going to make bail that day, that's for sure.

So, Donna is home, and I'm in now in Camden, N.J. It took three days to scrape together the necessary cash to make my bail, but finally I had another hearing. The judge wasn't thrilled that I had a bail bondsman pledge 80 percent of the bail, which is double what is usually required. Jim told him that if it would help, he would chip in almost a thousand dollars, and pulled his checkbook out of his jacket pocket. My daughter and Donna were sitting in the back of the courtroom and it looked as if they would be returning home without me. I have the feeling that the judge was impressed with my daughter Susan, and he accepted my bail. On Jan. 7, 1997, I was released on bail.

The ride back to Rhode Island was great. We stopped at a McDonalds and I told the employee what I wanted. And they got it. It was like, how long has this been going on. I was like a kid with a new toy. It was called freedom.

The next day there were front-page headlines about our case, and Jim called and told us not to be upset. These newspapers would be trash the next day. Jim kept a nice, cool attitude throughout our long ordeal. I will call him my friend always.

That night, Susan and her boyfriend, Art Colburn, had us over Art's house for supper. The food, wine, cognac and expensive cigars were plentiful. A couple of friends of Susan's came by and we laughed and clowned.

"Just a case of mistaken identity," we repeated to each other.

Art was Mayor Buddy Cianci's chief of staff, and later would be the only defendant in the Providence corruption scandal called "Operation Plunder Dome" to be found not guilty. Everyone else, except for informants, is behind bars, with the ex-mayor doing almost six years.

Art called me aside and said, "Lou, take a ride with me."

He told everyone we were going to the laundromat to pick up his clothes. In the car, Art said, "I have an offer for you, Lou. It's from your friends. Two hundred and fifty thousand dollars and this whole thing disappears."

I told him no, that first, I didn't have $250,000 in cash. And I wouldn't give it up if I did.

He said OK and that he'd pass it along, and we returned to our party. I can't figure out to this day what the significance of that offer was. Was it a shakedown? Was someone connected enough to squash this case? I still don't have an answer. But I do have some ideas. They seem clearer to me now.

Anyway, we partied well into the night and smoked so many cigars that we set up a table in the hallway, outside Art's condo. Art owned the whole building.

Chapter 19
Fighting My Case

Life on bail wasn't any big deal. I went to report in once a week in the Providence office, was there a couple of minutes, and left. Everyone was very polite. Jim's office was on Benefit Street, the East Side of Providence and here we would plan our defense.

We needed a lawyer in Connecticut, since they were not going to consolidate their case into the federal mix. We also needed a lawyer in New Jersey. Jim began the search for the right people for my case. Donna would need her own lawyer, and I searched for her, and after interviewing with several defense attorneys, settled on Bob Mann.

Bob is a public defender, but also has a private practice called Mann & Mitchell. The Mitchell part is his wife. When we first sat down, I told Bob I thought we could fight this case because I was sure the New Jersey police searched my car before getting a warrant. I remember a cop saying they had found my little gun, but I didn't feel they had enough time to get a warrant signed by a judge, or even a telephonic warrant, when he made that statement. I thought the search of my car was illegal, and I wanted to use that as a basis for my defense and fight the charges against us.

Bob was cool. He said, "You're what we call an angel. A solvent client who wants to fight, it doesn't get any better."

Then he added, "I'll guarantee you two things: first, you'll be found guilty. Second, you'll do twice, maybe three times as much time in jail."

There was only one way out of this, and that would involve ratting on someone the government wanted to see in jail. They were looking for my friend, Louie Mansolillo. Since neither Donna nor I would put Louie on the plate, we could only hope to do damage control.

Next, I was introduced to Mel Scott, an old salt of an attorney, from Colchester, Connecticut. He had an office in New London and we met there frequently. Mel and I were on the same page from day one. Connecticut never brought charges against Donna, so Mel was the only attorney needed in that state. Jim's appearances in Connecticut were done under Mel's Connecticut bar license to represent me.

Our cases were both going to be heard in the New London courthouse.

At every appearance, Mel was late, sometimes to the point where I wondered if he was even going to show up. But he always did, and everyone knew and liked Mel. It took him 15 minutes just to get from the courtroom door to the front bench, saying hello and talking to everyone along the way. Even the judges had a tremendous respect for Mel.

The next state I needed a lawyer for was New Jersey. Jimmy knew the ex-Attorney General, Cory Edwards, who was a partner in the prestigious law firm, Edwards, Caldwell and Poff. The prosecutor in New Jersey was Kerry L. Menchen, who had vengeance against me, but even worse against Donna. I decided to have Cory represent Donna, to keep her sentence down to a point where she would do concurrent time with the federal sentence. In other words, I didn't want Donna to leave federal prison only to do time in a New Jersey prison facility. New Jersey is not a place you want to do jail time in. Nowhere is.

Jimmy would represent me in New Jersey, but again under the license of the home-state lawyer, this time Cory Edwards.

I had a huge advantage over Donna in New Jersey. I possessed knowledge and skills on how to either rob or help casinos from being robbed, and this technical knowledge would wind up being golden for me. I used it to help Donna to the fullest extent I was able, which would be difficult because as part of his plea bargaining, Vinny Ricci informed the government that Donna had full knowledge of the overall counterfeiting scheme, and accompanied me on various trips to casinos in order to "launder" the counterfeit tokens. He went on to say that Donna visited his residence where the tokens were being manufactured and that she played a significant role in the entire scheme.

The legal team was now in place. Jim would be the quarterback, and Mel Scott and Cory Edwards' firm would be the players. It was a nice combination. New Jersey went along with my bail agreement with the feds, but Connecticut didn't. I had to post bail in the amount of $10,000. Once I did, I was assigned to a probation officer, Ms. Robin Giardi, who was a wonderfully compassionate woman. She never hassled me in any way.

Several years later, however, she was taken off my case and I was assigned to a real prick, who began immediately busting my balls by issuing, without my knowledge, two warrants for my arrest, the implication suggesting that I had not complied with the first arrest warrant by turning myself in to the Connecticut State Police. The basis of both warrants was the same. My period of probation was completed, without any further criminal complications, but I hadn't paid much restitution in full.

The government prepared their case quickly and presented it to Jim. All the meetings with the Feds were combined with the New Jersey State Police, and were all held in Trenton. Donna was not needed at these meetings. Between our frequent visits to New Jersey and New London, Jim and I formed a close bond, especially with our urination schedule. We could just look at each other and knew when we needed to make a pit stop. At practically every stop we made along the way to either New Jersey or Connecticut, someone would recognize Jim and come up to him and say, "Hello, General" as he was a former attorney general for the state of Rhode Island.

The federal prosecutor handling my case was Patrick Rocco. The first time we met, he shook my hand, and with a smile, said, "Hi, I'm Pat Rocco, the man who's making your life so miserable."

On several occasions, we met him by chance in the elevator, and Jim would talk about sports and other topics with him, and it didn't take too long for them to get to like each other. Pat was just doing his job, and Jimmy had been a prosecutor many years earlier. They shared a significant, immediate bond.

The government's case against me was absolutely overwhelming. They had Vinny Ricci, who turned government witness against me, his wife Lorraine, and, if needed, Vinny Ricci, Jr., as well as his brother, Robert. I never held it against Vinny though, that he turned on me. He was in his 70's and had a burden with his son Robert, who was and would be a burden on him 24 hours a day for the rest of his life. I wouldn't want Vinny or Lorraine to go to jail.

The prosecution had all the physical evidence against me, including dies, machinery, and tens of thousands of pounds of metal to be used for manufacturing the tokens. The government could make a case on what I intended to steal, and with Vinny's cooperation, what I did steal. I was in a tough spot. But I did have some leverage. I decided to go with Jim's suggestion that we do a proffer, which is a legal term meaning that if I tell them what I had done, and, if I decided later to fight my case in court, they wouldn't use the proffer as evidence against me. But, in reality, that's a lot of bullshit. Hell, I had seen judges allow illegally obtained information used against defendants many times. When I gave the proffer, I had my eyes wide open. I wasn't buying the government's bullshit, like my roommate in prison's girlfriend. I knew I wasn't going to see Germany.

On the day of the proffer the people there were Pat Rocco, the prosecutor, a New Jersey State Police lieutenant, Edward Kitlas, a Special Agent for the Secret Service, Jim, myself, and a court stenographer. Donna was not present at this meeting.

The meeting began on a very sour note. The Secret Service agent shoved a photo in front of me. It was a photo of Louie Mansolillo.

He said, "This photo was taken in the parking lot of your shop."

Then he asked me if I knew who it was in the photo. I said, yes. He pulled out another photo. This one was Louie, but wearing a baseball cap.

The agent said, "Here he is coming into your shop wearing a disguise."

It was so stupid, I wanted to laugh, but I didn't.

"A disguise?" I said, "it looks like an ordinary baseball cap to me."

He demanded that I reveal Louie's role in the counterfeiting ring. I told him Louie was a casual friend, and Rhode Island is a small state, that it's almost impossible not to know someone, or a relative of someone of any prominence in the state.

"But this guy's not just anybody, he's the head of the Patriarca crime family and you needed his permission to do this scam, didn't you," he shouted.

My answer was simple, but it sure irritated the shit out of him.

I said, "Where are the pictures of the electric company's representative who came in the shop to see why I was only getting 104 volts, when the service calls for 115 volts? Where's the picture of the insurance inspector who examined the shop before issuing my insurance policy? Then, there should also be a photo of the chief of police, who qualified me for my gun permit."

I went on and on and finally I said, "You've been in my shop. You know everything was hidden behind false closets and panels. I ran this operation with customers, salesmen, neighbors, and lots of people coming in and out. Are they all part of some big conspiracy?" I asked.

"Sure I know Louie, so what, I know lots of people. Louie had no idea what I was doing."

In reality, the last couple of years, Louie watched the token business closely. We discussed what tokens to make and I asked him, more than once, if there was any casino he didn't want taken.

I had made a mistake years ago by not being clear on this point, and I sure wasn't going to make that same mistake again. Louie had no objection to me robbing any of the casinos.

He would say, "After you have a nice long run, let me in."

I had already had a nice run, but he wasn't aggressive. We talked about establishing a prices to sell the chips wholesale, and decided that because of their quality since they could go straight to the cashier, without even having to be played, the price would be sixty percent of the face value of the coin. Louie stopped in from time to time, just to see what casinos I was working on or to bullshit a while.

What I didn't know was that Louie was being photographed everywhere he went. The Secret Service was closing in on a major, $11 million credit card ring at that time and my shop was not a subject of their investigation.

The arrests of Louie, Joe Meglio, and others came almost the same time that I was arrested. The only evidence that was found linking Louie to the scam was a refrigerator that Louie gave his 90 plus year old mother. Louie received a year's probation. Joe Meg got a three- or four-year suspended sentence. This for an $11 million scam.

Next, the agent wanted to know how many tokens I had made and how many I had passed by myself, with Donna and others.

At this point, I asked to speak to Jim in private. I told Jim I didn't like the direction this meeting was going in, and that I thought we were going to limit my proffer to me and technical information only. I wouldn't answer any more questions about other people's involvement, or the amount of money I stole. I knew the risks involved even if the federal government did present an acceptable plea agreement; it wasn't binding on the other states involved.

So far, Vegas had said they never heard of me except through the media and denied I had counterfeited any of their casinos. I had embarrassed them and they didn't want others to know how vulnerable they were. Bally's Park Place and Caesar's didn't want to admit they were counterfeited, but the Secret Service threat-ened to shut down the high rollers slots area if they didn't cooperate and send every fucking token to a lab for analysis.

They were asking for things I wouldn't answer. Suppose Vegas decides to come after me. The Secret Service knew I shipped thousands of pounds of tokens to Vegas. They had the trucking company's bills of lading. They knew some of my drop points. Suppose they pressured Vegas to join in and press charges against me. I was digging my own grave and I was not going to dig any deeper. I told Jim to set the parameters for this meeting, limiting it to technical information only.

The government didn't like this restriction, and at first objected, threatening to add further charges to an indictment. I had not yet been indicted, but that didn't matter. They could always come up with more bullshit if they wanted. But the U.S. Mint had some specific questions concerning my skills, and they were very interested in knowing why my dies held up better than theirs, so I had some strong bargaining power.

Besides, nothing was going to bring me to involve other people, so finally they figured whatever they got was a plus. What I didn't know is that even New Jersey needed technical information, and that would be ongoing for the next year and a half. Actually, even at the day of my sentencing they had questions.

So, the proffer continued on my terms. The entire day went quickly, and when we were finished, everyone respected my position and I theirs. Jim and I had taken the train to this meeting, so we decided to go have a few drinks, then take a cab to the station. A big day had come to an end. I had admitted I committed this crime. Funny, that felt like I gave something up. With their evidence, Vinny and other witnesses and everything else, it wouldn't take much to convince a jury I had made these coins. Still, I had mixed emotions. As time went by, I realized that I did the best thing I could have done.

So, I'm on pretty good terms with the Feds and New Jersey, but that fucking prosecutor in Connecticut. You might think I stole his money. His name is David McShane. He's around 37 or 38, but looks a lot older with his hump back, wrin-kled skin and shabby, cheap clothes. Still, he was the most dedicated, relentless civil servant I ever met. Connecticut sure was getting their money's worth with him. This fucking jerk never missed a meeting, and believe me, there were plenty of meetings we had in Connecticut. He remained true to his character, even after I had done my time.

But now, Jim, Mel, and I are trying to convince the judge to make my sentence run concurrent with and equal to, any federal sentence I would be receiving. Jimmy and Mel were relentless and we must have made 12 to 15 trips to New London during this period.

I caught a break, I thought, when the judge turned out to be an alumnus from Providence College, having graduated in 1963, the year before me. He didn't dismiss himself because, as he said, "I don't think we ever met, did we, Mr. Colavecchio?"

"No, your honor," I replied. But he added, if we had any overlapping classes or anything indicating a connection at PC, he would have to excuse himself and find a replacement.

Now I have a friendly judge, but an idiot prosecutor. I figure I'm even at least, and up more than likely. We had settled with the Feds and New Jersey. I was to receive 27 to 33 months in the federal system and 7 years in New Jersey, with both sentences to run concurrently.

I remember when I first went in to Fort Dix, probably not more than six months had passed, when I got a letter from the New Jersey Parole Board that I would be receiving a parole hearing. It didn't matter to me, because in the federal system, you do 85% of your time. In the state system, you can be out in around 20 to 25 percent. Either way, the federal sentence was the only one that concerned me.

Mel called Jim and me. The judge agreed to sentence me to seven years, fully suspended, to run concurrent with the federal and New Jersey sentences. I wouldn't be doing any Connecticut time when I got out. Wow, what great news. The agreement was to be signed the following Tuesday, and Connecticut would be history.

When we arrived at the New London courthouse we were told the judge had cancelled all court appearances that day. We walked up the street to Mel's office. The phones were ringing off the hook.

"Nice work, Mel," I could hear someone shout through the receiver.

"Justice was served," Mel replied. "Nothing more than a terrible tragedy."

The phone never stopped ringing and Mel handed us a copy of the *Hartford Courant*. The headlines said, "Laotian Found Not Guilty in Hit and Run Deaths of Two Children." Mel was involved in a very high profile trial.

The two children were walking back from a play rehearsal for their school. They were 10 and 12 years old and the son and daughter of a prominent surgeon. The driver admitted to police that he took a sip of beer while driving his truck to Foxwoods, and that he must have taken his eyes off the road for a second or two. He admitted hitting something, but said he thought they were garbage cans.

A police officer at the trial testified, "Those garbage cans you hit were a 10 and 12 year old walking along the road."

The inference was that Mel had pulled some sort of a miracle in getting this guy off with a sentence of only a one year suspended license.

By now, Mel is off the phone, and can talk to us. He said that trial had put so much heat on himself and the judge, the judge figured it best to let things cool off for a little while.

Mel went on to explain that the driver, while he did sip on a beer, was several miles from the scene of the accident and the guy actually did hit two garbage containers on the side of the road. He didn't speak English, and the prosecutor's translator admitted that his dialect prevented him from understanding the defendant's statements. Another translator cleared up the story. The guy was an easy target for the police, but wasn't guilty. Mel did not let a murderer go free, as the papers had claimed.

The calls kept coming in. Mostly congratulations, and always Mel responding with the same answer, "Justice was served."

While all this is happening, we are in Mel's front office. There are several large glass windows looking out to the park across Williams Street. It was very picturesque, but the scene changed quickly.

Several calls came through from irate citizens stating they were going to machine gun Mel's office or blow it up, because he defended a mother-fucking piece of shit who killed two innocent children. There was one call after another. These were not his lawyer companions. These were very angry citizens.

"Perhaps we should continue in the back office," Mel suggested.

"Good idea," Jim replied.

Talk about shit ass luck. Here I was about to make a deal affecting my future and this fucking freak incident breaks just today. The judge thought two bites of the apple for Mel at this time was just too much. Jim and I drove home without any agreement in hand.

But, a week later, we quietly met in the judge's office and signed our deal.

The prosecutor was fucking furious.

"Judge, this guy stole at least $3 million, he should get a minimum of 10 years after he serves his federal sentence," he screamed.

The judge asked how he arrived at that amount. Did he have counterfeit tokens to back that charge up?

Then the judge asked another piercing question: "How could a casino, actually two casinos, be robbed at all when they had the latest, most sophisticated security systems in existence? Where is all this great security?"

"Your honor, Jim said, "may I show you a letter from the Mohegan Sun Casino to Mr. Colavecchio?"

"Yes, please do," he replied.

The letter was dated May 30, 1997, and went on to say, "Dear Mr. Colavecchio, based upon the authority of the Mohegan Tribal Gaming Commission and pursuant to Section 7(b)(11) of the Mohegan Tribe-State of Connecticut Gaming Compact, you are hereby barred from the Mohegan Sun Casino and the Tribal Reservation. This action is based upon a newspaper article dated May 14, 1997 wherein it is alleged that you were arrest (they spelled it wrong) for counterfeiting Mohegan Sun tokens. The Gaming Commission finds that your presence here poses a threat to the integrity of the Tribal gaming activities. You may appeal this decision in writing to Francis M. Mullen, Director of Regulations, Mohegan Tribal Gaming Commission, within seven (7) days of receipt of this letter. You may enter the Mohegan Reservation for the purpose of dealing with the Gaming Commission or to pursue any other matters related to an appeal. If you have any questions regarding this matter, you may contact the Commission at the above address. Sincerely, Edward F. Pickett, Jr. Assistant Director."

Can you imagine the judge's reaction to this letter from the head of security at one of the country's most modern, sophisticated casinos. The judge literally went into a laughing fit. He blurted angrily at David McShane that the casino, Mohegan Sun, didn't even know they were being counterfeited until they read it in a newspaper.

"So, let's be honest, Mr. McShane, you don't have the slightest idea what this defendant took from the casinos, if anything, do you?"

"Well your honor, we have tapes."

"No more," the judge interrupted. "You don't have the slightest idea what this guy did."

"Seven years suspended sentence, $30,000 restitution, no $15,000 restitution, sentence to run concurrent with federal sentence."

I was in like Flint. Connecticut was now a done deal.

While all these negotiations had been going on, I was consulting with both Foxwoods and Mohegan Sun casinos, as well as with the Philadelphia Mint, and this was exciting. If I went to Foxwoods, for example, everyone wanted to travel with me, because I received royal treatment.

"Would you like something to eat, Mr. Colavecchio?" the floor manager would ask me. "How about the people with you? Would anyone like food or a drink?"

We were treated with respect, and why not, I'm showing them how to tighten up their casinos. It's no different than the wise guys. If you earn them money, they'll love you.

Two important agreements I made in my plea bargaining were that I wouldn't contradict any article or casino's contention that I was caught by them because they found an overage of tokens in their machines. Hell, they didn't even know they were being counterfeited until I got caught and it made the news. The second major point was that I plead to a charge of interstate transportation of counterfeit securities, not counterfeit tokens, since they really couldn't detect which tokens were counterfeit. I had no problem with either of these requests. What's the fucking difference if I'm in jail for counterfeit tokens or counterfeit securities.

All that remained was waiting for the sentencing date, then jail.

One night, Donna and I had an argument. I had been drinking, and I'm not sure what we were arguing about, but I left the condo and drove to Ann's house. Ann had company, and they were drinking wine. I drank there also. By the time I left, it was around 2 a.m. Now the drive to Donna's condo was only about a ten-minute drive, but I was being very careful. I knew I was definitely drunk. Here I am going to jail in three weeks, and the last thing I need is another fucking beef. I neared the condo on Mineral Spring Avenue and slowed down to take a left into the condo complex. Bang. A larger vehicle slams into the side of my little red Honda and crushes it. Glass and parts from my car littered the road.

But the other vehicle had no visible damage. His bumper hit the side of my car, and the bumper was rugged. When I saw he had no damage, I told him, "This is your lucky day, go on."

He kept apologizing, then said, "I think I forgot to put my lights on."

He was a short, young kid and naive as all hell. He was actually apologizing to me. I cut in front of him and he's apologizing to me!

After he left, I backed the Honda into my parking space to hide the damage. I was going to take it to a market or mall the following night and call in the damage from there.

So, I'm back at Donna's, drunk but home. Not more than five minutes later there was a loud banging on the door, followed by shouting. "Police, open the door."

They had been parked in the parking lot of the Pizza Hut across the street and witnessed the incident. They finished their meals, then came to arrest me. The charge was leaving the scene of an accident. One of the cops was a real prick, but the other one knew my son, and knew who I was and that Jim was my lawyer. Jim had helped him get his job, and Jimmy knew most everyone on the North Providence Police force.

But I was an obnoxious asshole.

"We're on our way in," he said on the radio. "We got him."

I started to laugh at him. "What have you got you jerk. I ran the largest counterfeiting operation right under your fucking noses for years." I was smart-talking him all the way into the cell, when he finally said, "You know what we do with assholes like you?"

"No what, shoot me," I slurred.

"No, choke them."

I took off my belt and said, "Here, hang me you fucking jerk."

He grabbed my neck and began choking me, when the other cop stopped him. They left me in the cell and I fell asleep.

Donna had called Jim when I was first handcuffed in the condo and Jim called someone on the North Providence force. Two hours later, Donna was driving me home. I told her, "No, not home, I want to go to the hospital. I'm going to file a complaint against that asshole."

Donna said, no, but I insisted.

"Looks like a bruise," the doctor said. I told him what had happened. He took my information and sent me home. I didn't want to file a complaint against the cops. They never even asked me to take a breathalyzer test. The other cop was not looking to bury me. I just wanted some ammunition on file for Jim to use. The judge knew I was going to jail soon, so he heard the case immediately.

Jim said, "Your honor, he's going to Fort Dix in a week, and he's not going to the army."

The judge was Jim's friend and he smiled and said, "Case dismissed."

I'm sitting in my chair, and the adjuster makes himself comfortable on the sofa. The way he's looking at me, you'd swear I had something dripping from my nose. He knew who I was, and that I would be in jail before he paid the claim for my little red Honda.

The damage was $5,100, and I told him straight out, "Look, I rob casinos, not a lousy few hundred dollars from an insurance company. I pumped the claim up 500 bucks to cover my deductible, that's all, so you can pay $4,600 or $5,100. It's your call."

Now it's right out there. I'm the guy in the papers and I'm going to jail in a few days. He had half a smile on his face, and I got the feeling he really appreciated my honesty.

"Sign here," he said. I signed and he left. Two days later I received a check for $5,100.

"All rise, court is in session." Jim was ready to argue to lower my sentencing to 27 months instead of 33. When the judge entered the room, I wished I was on the other side of the podium, because I would have asked her out on a date. There was chemistry between us that you could cut with a knife. I loved her instantly and I haven't had this feeling too many times in my life. Her name was he Honorable Anne E. Thompson, and she was the Chief United States District Judge. When our eyes met I could feel the chemistry penetrate the distance between us. I was going to get the 27 months. Of this I was positive

"How do you plead, Mr. Colavecchio?" she said.

I wanted to answer, "In love, your honor," but instead I said "very, very guilty."

"Are you aware that if you plead guilty, you are giving up your right to a trial by jury, and that all 12 persons on that jury would have to find you guilty in order for you to be convicted?"

"Yes, your honor," I replied. "Are you under the influence of any drug or alcohol that would impair your decision this morning?" she asked.

Again, I wanted to say the only influence I'm under is that I'm in love with you, but, like a schmuck, I answered, "No, your honor, I'm not."

"Is there anything either you or your attorney would like to say to this court before being sentenced, Mr. Colavecchio?"

Jim began his pitch on how I was a great guy, never in trouble before this, and a whole lot of bullshit. I kicked him under the podium and whispered for him to stop.

"I do have something to say, your honor." I said, interrupting Jimmy's prepared spiel. "Your honor, I can be a very persuasive person, especially with a woman I'm involved in a relationship with. I don't want to ask anything for myself, but please take into consideration that Donna's only crime was to fall in love with a jerk like me. I ask your honor to add Donna's sentence to mine. She already paid a high enough price for loving the wrong person."

"Mr. Colavecchio, I admire your chivalry and commend you for living up to your responsibilities and your truthfulness to this court, but I must interrupt you and tell you how I feel. Donna is a mature, strong woman who knew what she was doing and I will sentence her accordingly. You may continue, if you wish, to address this court before sentencing, but nothing more about Donna."

I continued, "In that case your honor, I would like to take the opportunity to thank the New Jersey State Police, the prosecutor, Mr. Pat Rocco, and the Secret Service for the respectful and professional way I was treated throughout this whole ordeal. I'm truly sorry to have committed this foolish crime, not only because it was illegal, but for the shame and embarrassment it has brought to myself and my family. My actions were my own, a hundred percent. My mother and father brought me up in an honest, loving environment and my behavior can be blamed only on me, and no one else."

I would like to have added, "What are you doing later this evening," but I fought that urge. "I have nothing further to say, your honor, and will accept my punishment like a man."

"Well, Mr. Colavecchio, federal guidelines mandate your sentence. You have a point level of 18, which requires you to serve between 27 and 33 months in a federal correctional institution. I sentence you to 27 months, plus $90,000 restitution and 3 years supervised release, which is like probation. Will you need time to get your affairs in order?"

Yes, your honor, I replied.

"Is 3 weeks enough time?" she asked

"Three weeks is fine. Thank you, your honor."

"Good luck," she replied.

Three years later, I was to hear from her again. The letter was dated Feb.10, 2003, It read: "Dear Mr. Colavecchio, please be advised that your term of supervision, as ordered by the Honorable, Anne E. Thompson, Chief U.S. District Judge of New Jersey on January 14, 1998, expired on February 9, 2003. In as much as you have completed the term of supervision without further difficulty, it is my pleasure to forward a Notice of Discharge. I hope that you have derived some benefit from your association with our office and have gained insight into factors that led to your conviction and a desire to avoid further contact with the criminal justice system. While I have enjoyed our relationship, it is my sincere desire that we never have another opportunity to meet in an official capacity. As always please feel free to contact me if I can be of any assistance in the future. Best wishes, Brian Pletcher."

Along with this letter was a U.S. Treasury check in the amount of $75 for overpayment of restitution after my discharge by Judge Anne E. Thompson. Also enclosed was my passport, and a letter from the U.S. Dept. of Justice: "Dear Mr. Colavecchio, Enclosed is a filed copy of the Warrant For Satisfaction of Judgment filed in the U.S. District Court. The file is now marked 'Paid in Full' and closed on the records of this Office. Thank you for your cooperation."

A short time later, May 8th, 2003, I received yet another letter, from the U.S. Department of Justice, District of New Jersey. It read: "RE: United States of America v. Louis Colavecchio, Court No 97-599. Dear Mr. Colavecchio: Please be advised that the above captioned case has been satisfied. Please do not send any further payments. I am enclosing a copy of your Satisfaction of Judgment that was previously mailed to you. Please do not hesitate to contact me … if you have any questions. Thank you for your cooperation in this matter. Very truly yours, Christopher J. Christie, United States Attorney.

I had to pay $90,000 restitution as part of my plea agreement, but I only paid $75 per month. Since I was on suspended release three years and didn't begin paying until four months into the three-year period, I paid only $2,400 in total. Technically, that was a violation of my release, and I could have had my supervised release extended until the $90,000 was paid in full, or I could have gone to jail on a violation. Instead, Anne E. Thompson dismissed my supervised release and my restitution early, and sent me a refund saying that the court considered me paid in full the month before I sent the $75. No doubt about it, the chemistry was there.

Now Jim and I are outside the courtroom. Jim said, "Boy, did she like you." I told Jim I was sorry to have interrupted him, but I was confident I was going to get the minimum, 27 months. He said he was very worried when I asked to do Donna's time, that supposing she went along with that request.

I told Jimmy, "I'm sorry she didn't."

"How do you plead, Ms. Ulrich?" Donna's hearing only took a couple of minutes. Judge Thompson asked Donna if she knew she was giving up her right to a trial by jury, and that all 12 members would have to find her guilty, and then asked if she was under the influence of any drugs or alcohol or medication that could be affecting her ability to understand what was going on this morning. Donna answered abruptly, "No, I'm not under the influence of any drug, alcohol, or medication and, yes, I understand I'm giving up my right to a trial."

"Do you have anything to say to this court prior to your being sentenced?"

"No," Donna answered.

"Well, your agreement was for four months incarceration and one year supervised release. I see no reason to depart from that agreement."

Donna stood up and left the courtroom in an arrogant, distressed manner. Bob Mann was still standing. He was shocked. Later, he said, "Thank you, your honor."

***

"Lou, why is this coin so thick on this end and so thin on this side?" Bob Schulte asked me in the courtroom hall.

I said, "Bob, with all I've shown you, you should know the answer by now."

"I know how you like to sketch everything," he said.

I showed him the three or four obvious reasons and he turned to another trooper and said I think it's so and so, mentioning someone's name.

"That's what his press looks like."

He was referring to the fact that I mentioned a defect that a press could have, which would cause the coin to be uneven.

"Thanks, Lou," he said, like a little kid who was just handed a lollipop.

"Lou, you'll be out just when I'm retiring," Brian Murray, a Secret Service guy said.

"How does the idea of a partnership sound? We could run a security consulting firm for casinos."

I said I'd think about it. He wasn't kidding. I had another offer to set up a casino's high roller slots area in the Cayman Islands, but at the time I was on supervised release, and had to refuse it. They offered me $250,000, which seems like a lot, but I could easily take that much from them over a weekend if I wanted.

Donna and I arrived home and it was the end of a bittersweet day. Donna chose to begin serving her time at Danbury as quickly as possible. It was now strictly a women's prison and Donna made camp status immediately. Two weeks later, I drove Donna to Danbury. It was actually in a quite picturesque rural area of Connecticut. I was only allowed to go to the lower building, which was the processing center. There we said goodbye. Donna was more worried about how I'd do my time than she was about her four months. But, even so, she made me promise to write her every day while she was incarcerated, which, she said would help her in doing her time.

We kissed and she said, "I love you."

I said, "You'll be fine, I'll be OK. I'll write every day."

A week later, in February 1998, I boarded a train for New Jersey. Louis and Susan drove me to the station. I stayed in a motel overnight, and was due in Fort Dix before 12 noon.

Fort Dix is a big place located in the middle of McGuire Air Force Base. The cab driver couldn't find where the fuck to drop me off. The base is almost 15 miles long and we drove every fucking mile of it before I finally told him to drop me off at any building. I'd be late in another few minutes, and a warrant would be issued for my arrest. This would add two points to my sentence, as voluntary surrender reduces your total by that amount, and would have kept me incarcerated another six months at least. Turns out, we were at exactly the right building.

Chapter 20

Fort Dix

"19894-050. Remember that number. It's going to be the most important number in your life for the next couple of years," the CO said.

After he was finished with the processing procedure of finger printing, photographs, ID badge, etc., he said, "You'll be assigned to Building #52. It's at the very end of the compound, last building on the right side, across from the kitchen. Now, what's your number?"

I hadn't the slightest idea. I had no sleep the night before, and a very hectic, nerve wracking $50 taxi ride from the motel I stayed in to Fort Dix, wondering if I'd make my self-surrender time of 12 noon, or if a warrant would be issued for my arrest.

"I don't remember," I replied.

"Well look at your fucking ID badge," he hollered.

"19894-050," I responded.

"Wonderful, now remember it."

I'm walking along the middle of the complex, dressed in blue cloth slippers, khaki colored top and pants, carrying a plastic bag containing a small bar of soap, a disposable safety razor, one roll of toilet paper, a toothbrush and tube of toothpaste, a receipt for almost $600 for cash I brought with me to be credited to my commissary account, and a paper stating that I had a medical problem and would require a bottom bunk. I actually threw this away, then later went looking for it, because I had no idea how important it was or how difficult it would be to replace.

The walk to Building #52 was close to a mile long, and maybe more, because I missed finding it immediately. When I got just outside the large steel doors, somebody tapped me on my shoulder.

Now what the fuck did I do, I'm wondering

Is your name Louie?" he asked.

Yes. it is.

"My name is Robert, but everyone calls me Rob. You have some friends in here, and they asked me to keep a look out for you. I knew you were in processing, so I figured you'd be here pretty soon."

We shook hands and he said, "Follow me."

He had me set up in Room 212.

"It's a 12-man room, Lou, but you have the best spot in the room. Next to the window, and a lower bunk. You won't be there too long before we'll be getting you another one. An eight-man room is going to be available soon."

When I arrived at my room, there were only one or two inmates laying on their bunks. We shouted our names and I looked for my locker. There weren't any near my bunk. Lockers are like gold and if someone leaves, there'll be several people there to grab it. A locker with an inside shelf and a row of drawers is almost impossible to find. I didn't care much, as I had nothing to put in it even if I had one.

By 4 p.m. the room was full. It's a stand up count, the most important one during the whole day. If you're missing during this count, it's assumed you escaped, and if you don't or can't stand up, it's a fair assumption to say you're dead.

COs are not paid to think. I know one old man who had brain surgery and stayed in an outside hospital, not the prison infirmary, but a local hospital. When he was returned to his room several days later, he was in a wheelchair. He was expected to stand up at the 4 p.m. count. When he couldn't do so, he was issued a citation, and could have been sent to the hole. But later, after several of us protested at the lieutenant's office, they let it slide. The poor bastard was in a wheelchair, and had only a few weeks left on a one year sentence.

It was a very depressing day to say the least. Here I am with 11 criminals I don't know, and will spend the next two years of my life with. I lay on my bed, then realized I was lying on an old, gray mattress left over from World War II surplus. No sheets, no blankets, no pillow, nothing. The reality was setting in quickly.

"Lou, let's go eat," Rob said. I felt like he was like an old friend. "I have some sheets and a blanket for you, and tomorrow I'll take you to the laundry room. I have a friend there. We'll get you all new stuff. We'll also go to the commissary. You have a one-time only first shopper's privilege, and don't have to wait until Thursday, which is commissary day."

We went to the kitchen, and Rob knew everybody there.

"They're having some real shit tonight," he said. "I have no idea what it is. We'll get you a nice tuna sandwich and a salad, is that OK?"

"Yeah, great, Rob. I want to eat light. I don't have much appetite."

We left the kitchen just after 6 p.m., and I wanted to go back to my room. Rob followed me in, then said, "I'll be back with the sheets in a little while."

Half an hour later, I was lying on sheets with a blanket and pillow and had a huge bar of soap.

"Tomorrow we'll get you a locker and after that I'll take you to the laundry and commissary, I'll show you around."

"Thanks," I said, still lying down.

Rob was well known as a tough guy. Just to look at him, you knew he was a street fighter. He had several cuts that needed but never were stitched and just healed from the inside out, not fully covered with skin. He had been cut many times in his life, that's for sure. But his interest and in me brought me instant status in my room.

The first inmate to come over to me was Dennis Gazzo. He was a thin, good-looking, well-shaven man who was educated at the University of Connecticut, graduated as an English major, and was a health freak. He also was doing five and a half years for a marijuana sting set up by the government. It was a conspiracy, set up by a former friend and drug runner and the FBI. He owned a large parcel of land in Connecticut, just over the New York border, and had a huge house, barn, and horses as well. He had two kids and his wife was an attorney. We became very close friends, and at one point, I asked him why he would get involved with drugs again. He seemed to have everything he needed in life. His answer was witty and truthful. He did have everything, a beautiful wife, two kids, a horse farm, real estate in New York. The only thing that was lacking, as he put it, was the $2 million in cash that someone with all this needed or should have.

He was suckered back into a life he had left years before by an old friend who was facing a lot of time for a beef. He kept on Dennis's case until he convinced him to go along one more time. It was all set up by the FBI, and several people were now doing time, when actually no crime even took place. Before my sentence was completed, I had heard this same type of scenario many, many times. They are called 'he said, she said' laws by foreigners. We call them the conspiracy laws.

Dennis introduced me to the other members, my roommates of Room 212.

"This is William, but he likes to be called Young Buck," Dennis said. He was a young, maybe 21-year-old light-skinned, very good looking black kid, who wound up fucking one of the few female COs in our unit, and later, marrying her. He was a hot shit.

"Now, this is the famous Bob Harly," Dennis said. Bob was a 37, an old drug manufacturer from Philadelphia, an area known for crystal methamphetamine. He was doing 25 years and would be out in the year 2011. He was the ultimate inmate: sharp, a good card player, a braggart who liked to infer that they had millions stashed, whose locker was too full of earned wealth: tuna fish, toilet paper, snacks, juice, and water. You name it, Bob had it. To me, it seemed he wouldn't have earned all this stuff by playing cards if he had money. Then, there was also the risk of it being confiscated in a surprise inspection, when everyone had to leave the room while a CO or two went through everyone's locker looking for contraband. Hell, they found a quarter which I had hidden in my locker one time, but nothing was ever taken from his blatantly illegal locker. In jail, just having too many possessions constitutes contraband, even if you purchased them legitimately from the commissary. After every shakedown, he'd ask, "Did they take anything from my locker?"

The answer was always, no. Makes you wonder.

"And this is Big Bill, Lou," Dennis said. The Big Bill name was appropriate. He was a 350-pound black man who was winding down from a 13-year bit for drugs. He had huge fatty tumors on every part of his face, from his eyelids to his neck. I didn't know where to look and not appear to be staring. Big Bill was the most articulate, sharp witted, fastest thinking, soft spoken, and one of the smartest inmates I would meet in my two years at Fort Dix. He had passed a computer course and received Microsoft certification. He was so quick-witted that no one, not a single person, could match him at verbal sparring. His vocabulary was something to envy.

"And here's Peter," said Dennis. Peter's name was supposed to be Peter Horsely. He was very good looking, charming, witty, easy going, a good card and Scrabble player, and was also an FBI agent. Andy, whom I met a week and a half after I moved into this room, had warned me of him several times. I didn't need Andy's warning. Peter asked too many fucking questions under the guise of naivete and innocence. When he left abruptly one morning, one of my friends watched as he was picked up outside the compound by a federal vehicle. He knew everyone in the car. I don't remember the names of the others in the room. Twelve-man rooms change inmates frequently. New people come and go all the time in prison.

The next day, Rob came by and took me to the laundry.

"That's too big for you," his friend said about my shirt. He brought me out three brand new shirts, two long sleeved, and one short sleeved.

"Try these on," he said, as he handed me a new pair of pants.

"Perfect," I said.

The second pair was new, but too big. He handed them to Rob.

"Take these for now, there's nothing back here but shit."

Rob handed me the new pair of trousers that were big in the waist.

"We'll take them to the tailor tonight," he said. "He can really sew well."

No new shoes fit me, so I took a slightly used pair of a softer shoe, another very valuable commodity. They are only issued to inmates with a doctor's prescription. Next came all new, cotton sheets, a cotton blanket, which was very difficult to get, and two new pillowcases.

"Take this laundry bag for now, but you'll want to buy a new one. You can get them at the commissary," he said.

Our next stop was the commissary. No one would come to the window, even though I saw at least three assholes working inside. Rob pounded on the window. I thought it was going to shatter. An asshole lifted it up from inside and asked what the fuck we wanted. It wasn't commissary day.

"I have a first time shopper," he shouted. "Here's his list."

Rob had given me a blank commissary sheet, which I later learned was hard to come by, as every commissary sheet that went out had an inmate's number on it. I had filled out the things I wanted, and asked Rob if he needed anything.

"Black and Golds," he told me. These were cheap, five-to-a-box cigars. I bought him two boxes and he was fucking thrilled. I left my slip there and took a number, which represented my order. I was learning the ropes. I had a great teacher.

"OK, Lou, let's get you a phone and visitor's list. I'll take you to your counselor, Mr. Bridges. He's a fat, lazy fuck, so get these things in motion now. He won't work on them for a long time."

"Mr. Bridges, I have a phone list and a visitor's list," I said.

"Yeah, leave them in that tray," he said, as if I weren't even in the room. He was the laziest motherfucker I ran across in the whole system. He was a lying, deceptive piece of shit who only did anything for the inmates that ratted on other inmates, and there were plenty of them. I soon learned that one of the most valuable commodities an inmate possessed in jail was information. Ratting out a fellow inmate for a better room, a bottom bunk, another job, anything. Prison is full of sneaky little informants. A CO needs them to get information, and they get plenty of it.

Rob had spent the entire day with me, and we picked up my things at the commissary and headed back to our rooms. Rob was a few doors down the hall from me, and we just made it back on time for the 4 p.m. stand-up count. I didn't even notice it, at first. But, while I'm standing for count, I saw it. A nice, tall locker. Rob had it taken from a room on the third floor, and carried it to my room while we were out. When count was over, he came running into my room with a shelf and said tomorrow he'd have a chest of drawers for the inside. He would also have it cleaned up and painted. I now had a place for the items I had purchased from commissary. I removed them from the blue nylon mesh laundry bag I bought and put everything neatly in the locker.

It took me about a month to remember my numbers, 19894-050, but I didn't care. When I purchased my Timex at the commissary, they engraved my numbers in the back case. They do it with a hand-held, loud buzzing engraving machine, plugged in to a wall socket. The numbers are sloppy, but readable.

I was hanging with Dennis — or Gazzo, as I called him — most of the time. When I needed something Rob would come by to visit. I bought him a pack of Black and Gold's every week and it made his week. He would go to the mail room every day and wait until the mail call was over, then deliver me my mail. I tried waiting there once and was shocked to see a little piece of shit inmate doing the CO's job, calling out the mail on a pool table and tossing it to the inmate who it belonged to. Come to find out, the CO couldn't read. He wasn't the only CO who couldn't read, or who read so slowly that my two-year sentence would be over before mail call ended. I think it was a requirement that a CO be inbred and illiterate to get his job.

I had no idea what doing laundry was like, so I asked Gazzo to show me the procedure. The small 10 by 10 foot room had six washers and six dryers along two walls and a sink on another. Of the six washers, three worked part of the time, but not properly, so it was necessary to run everything twice.

On days when it was raining, you couldn't wash anything because the water was a shit brown color and would spoil your clothes. The dryers were worse than the washers. Only one or two worked, and you needed to run your clothes two or three times for them to be just slightly damp, not dry. The room was backed up with 50 or 60 laundry bags full of clothes always ahead of you. Six washers and six dryers, most of them not working, for 400 inmates.

Part of the reason the dryers didn't work was because of the inmates themselves. This included my crew. The dryers contain a large heating element and the inmates in the repair shop would remove these elements to make stingers. The stinger would be placed inside a 10 or 20 gallon empty mayonnaise container and when water was added, the stinger was plugged in, and it boiled the water in no time. The Spanish used it to cook rice. The Italians used it for our pasta. If you wanted to avoid having any problems with the Italians, just let them steal a little food and cook their pasta and sauce and they'd be happy. Doing laundry was an all day's job and I did it only once in my two years. Rob did my laundry, which also included doing my bed sheets, and making my bed the whole time I was on the East Side of the compound. Fat Vinny did my laundry when they moved me from the east side of the compound to the West Side.

Though I never liked him, and I'm sure he didn't care much for me, Bob Hartley respected my contacts and influential friends and actually gave me something of great value to me, a plastic ruler. I kept that thing hidden for two years and used it every day when I was drawing my eyeglass designs. That ruler survived countless shakedowns.

In the federal system, everyone, unless they're fucking dying, had to get a job. Everyone has to have, or attend classes to get a GED.

I had more trouble with the educational system and came close to losing my good time because of this. One day, my name appeared on a call sheet. A call sheet listed certain inmates who had an appointment that day, and the time and place where that appointment would be held. The several page memo was found outside the CO's office and was passed from inmate to inmate. Only one copy was available, so by the time you read it, unless you were near the beginning of the line, it was in pretty shabby condition. I soon depended on Rob and others to give me any information if my name appeared on the sheet.

I'm ordered to report to the education department. When I get there, I'm told to register for classes to obtain my GED.

"My GED," I said, "I'm a college graduate."

Fortunately I had my PSI with me, which indicated my level of education as a college graduate.

"OK," the jerk in the office said, "I'll take your name off the list."

"Thanks," I said and left. A week later, my name shows up again to report to the education department. When I reported I was told, "You need to get your GED. Class has already begun."

I went fucking furious.

"I was here last week and showed you my PSI. I graduated from Providence College, with a Bachelor of Science degree in Business Administration."

"Oh well, I just saw your name on our list. But I'll see that it's removed."

"Yeah, sure," I said, walking out angrily.

Another week went by and I was on that fucking list again. I went to the office and took the list off the asshole's desk and with a pen, crossed out my name on the list.

"This is the last fucking time I'm coming in this office," I screamed, "You people are so fucking incompetent, you should be taking the GED course."

I got called into the lieutenant's office for my action, but when I explained the situation, and told them I wanted my lawyer to write the head of the Bureau of Prisons, they were embarrassed and they let it go.

By now, I had a room with a view, a watch with my ID number engraved on its back in case I forgot it, a locker, possessions, a lock to lock the locker, money left in my commissary account, and, finally, I got that goddamn education department off my case. What the fuck else could I want.

"Lou, you're really pushing your luck now," Gato said. "Any one of these days, your name is going to be on the call sheet, and you'll be working in the kitchen."

He continued, "There's nothing worse than that, and you'll be there 90 days before you can get transferred. Get hold of Rob today, and find out what jobs are around. He'll know where to go so no one hassles you."

"I'm way ahead of you, Lou," Rob said. "I signed you up in plumbing. This is a no show job and my friend will sign you in and out on projects every day. You'll change jobs from time to time, because every once in a while, a new asshole gets put in charge of the department, and for a little while, puts the heat on. But you're good for now, I'm sure."

I headed over to the plumbing department to see where it was, and to let them see my face. It was in a wide building, maybe 200-feet wide, like a big garage with four doors. One was for electrical workers, another for plumbing, one for landscaping supplies and another for small appliance repairs. There was a raised concrete platform, and benches ran the whole width of the building. Little electric carts were everywhere. The COs used them to get around the compound. There wasn't a place on a bench in front of plumbing that wasn't occupied. No one was out on a job. No one did anything there, except for one guy whose name was constantly being called out on the compound's loudspeaker system.

Mike the plumber, Mike the plumber, report to the kitchen immediately. In the several months I would have this job, he's the only one who ever did anything. And, believe me, you wouldn't want any of these guys touching anything to do with plumbing, or anything else for that matter.

I entered the third door which led to the plumbing department. On the left side was a small room with tools hanging from the wall, and an outline around the tool, so that if it was missing, you'd know what it was and where to put it back. I never saw anyone working in this room, but if anyone did need a tool, he just helped himself to what he needed, then replaced it with a little tag that had his worker's number on it. If a tool was out, however, no one could go to lunch until it was replaced. That I learned the hard way.

Then there was a cement staircase that led down to an office on the left, one straight ahead and another to the right. The office to the right was the head of the department's office. I stood outside the open door until he finally decided to recognize my presence and asked what I wanted.

I said, "Sorry to bother you, CO."

I was cut short quickly and abruptly.

He hollered back at me, "Never call me CO. You call me Mr. Coughlin, asshole, or fuckoff, but never refer to me as a CO, you got that?"

I liked this guy. He didn't want to be associated with those assholes, and he made no qualms about telling anyone. He was a plumber employed by the BOP, not a cop, not a guard, but a plumber.

"Well, what do you want?" he asked.

"I'm your new plumber, I'm Colavecchio," I said.

"Do you know anything about plumbing, Colavecchio?" he asked.

Before I could answer, he pointed to a desk ornament that was a faucet on a wood base. His name was engraved on the base.

"Know what this is?" he asked, as he turned one of the knobs on the faucet.

"Sure," I said.

"OK, I guess you pass the test, Colavecchio. You're a plumber."

This was going to be a job I would like. I would also be making $16.35 a month.

Things were going smoothly now. I had met another inmate, Ronnie Nozolino, a dead ringer for Art Carney, who played Norton from the old Jackie Gleason show. Ronnie always had a joke or funny face ready. He was doing a one-year bit for a parole violation having just coming off an eight-year sentence for selling guns. His wife was a New Jersey cop.

Then there was Jack Porres, a small time thief who was doing a couple of years for not ratting out an accomplice. Jack was always lying on his bed dreaming about the life he'd have when he got out. His time was close to ending and he was getting ready for the "Good Life." He helped me a lot during the time we were together.

Every time a new inmate came in the room, Jack would remark on how low the FBI had sunk to have arrested some 18 year old black kid for selling an eight ball of coke. Thinking back, he was right. I remember a time when just being investigated by the FBI was prestigious. Now, here they were arresting the lowest of street dealers. Ronnie, Jack and I became close friends. My days were spent mostly hanging with the guys, and every day, weather permitting, walking the compound with Gato. I was losing weight and looking and feeling great.

Any mail leaving a federal prison is bar coded automatically, so if you try to send mail from one jail to another, they know immediately. I was writing to Donna every day during her four months at Danbury, but I had to mail the letters to a friend and he put them in another envelope with his return address on them and forwarded them to Donna. There wasn't much to say. It's not like I broke out of jail or something! But, she wanted me to write every day and so I did. When she got out, she wrote me every day, and every Friday I got what I referred to as my care package, which consisted of a letter, some tool and supply catalogs I had requested, and a magazine or two. Although I didn't like the idea, she insisted on visiting me every other month. This required special permission, as two felons, especially co-defendants in the same case, are prohibited from seeing each other. But, I had an advantage. The government still needed technical information from me, and I was taking full advantage of my bargaining tools.

One day, after I returned from supper, there was a new inmate who came into Room 212 to replace someone who had left. He was a big man, maybe 5'11", 275 pounds, but solid. He had the largest fists, fingers and lips of anyone I had ever seen. He actually was good-looking, but different. He had sideburns, which went from his temples to the bottom of his wide, square jaw. He was quick-witted, sharp-tongued and sarcastic.

"Hi, I'm Louie." I said to him.

"Yeah, I can see you're the boss around here," he remarked. "I'm Andy."

His name was Andrew Giannino, but was known as "the Sarge" as he had been a sergeant in the elite Army Rangers and was a trained assassin. One day, after we became very close friends, I Read his PSI. It was like reading a John Grisham or Dean Koontz novel. It told of how his training included instructions on killing two people in a maximum of eight seconds, by snapping their necks. He was a paratrooper, who, along with a crew of six or seven trained assassins, was dropped off in the jungle near Cambodia on a mission to kill Pol Pot. He was closely associated with the CIA, and had risked his own life to save other Rangers. He was reprimanded once, when the pilot of a helicopter landed to drop off Andy and his crew, and he overtook the pilot, then had his men remove the 50- caliber machine guns from the helicopter, and sent the pilot back home minus his powerful weapons. To hear him talk of the devastation these weapons caused was spellbinding.

On one occasion he was parachuted into enemy territory and immediately his closest friend slumped over and died in Andy's arms. He was shot in the head by a sniper. Andy convinced the pilot to land, knowing he was going to grab those machine guns. He and his crew set them up outside a small, known enemy village, then fired them until both guns ran out of ammunition. Absolutely nothing was left of any building, even if it were made of stone. Then he and his men went in and cleaned up the few remaining live enemies. He ultimately received a medal from the President himself.

Andy lived in Westchester, and he had numerous photos of his estate, his wife and family. During the end of our almost two years together, President Clinton and his wife purchased the house almost next door to his. Some of the trees in Andy's yard cost $35,000 and neighbors actually wanted to buy them from him throughout the years. They weren't for sale.

He surprised me when he said he grew up with his grandmother insisting he take music lessons, and that he could play the piano and drums. I couldn't imagine anyone with hands and fingers as large as his playing a musical instrument, but boy, was I wrong.

When he joined a band I went along as his supposed song writer. I did so because this was the only air-conditioned room in the whole compound. The second time and every time after, I went just to hear him play. He could play any type of music, from jazz to blues and was equally proficient at both the piano and drums. He amazed me.

"So you're Louie and you're the head man here. Well I guess I'll have to depend on you for my bit," he said.

"Where are you coming from," I asked.

"I was in Steubenville for a year and a half awaiting my appeal, then they decided to send me here because it's closer to my family. Why, you thought it was more."

Chapter 21
'You Thought It Was More'

"You thought it was more," I remarked.

"Where did you acquire this phrase?" I asked.

"From my friend in Harrison, New Jersey," he said.

"His name isn't Tony Miele, is it?"

"Yes, how did you know?"

"Because his brother Vincent was my uncle. "You thought it was more. "

He grabbed me and hugged me and I knew I'd be with him the rest of my bit. My life at Fort Dix would never be the same.

Up until now, I was eating tuna and lettuce for lunch and soup with saltine crackers for supper. I was exercising with Gato and walking four or five miles every night. My weight was down to 176 pounds, from 204 when I first went in. I was trying to get my waist to 34 inches, but 35 seemed to be the lowest I could go. Gato became a health nut, as do many people when they become incarcerated. I don't know why, but it's true. I wasn't too far behind him, but in a few weeks none of this would be important.

Andy was a very connected wise guy, in New York. His uncle controlled most of the docks in New York and New Jersey, and Andy had a lucrative construction business in New York City. His company was responsible for putting in more sidewalks in that city than all the other construction companies combined. We knew the same people, and we knew we needed to get over to the West Side of the compound. All the wise guys were on that side. The East Side was slowly turning into an immigration detention center, so it would only be a matter of time before we would be moved anyway. But, even here we would be great. Andy had already been in a year and a half. He knew the system well. Besides, he and his brother had done time in the past for bank give-ups, where armed guards faked robberies, and everyone had made millions before it fell apart a couple of years later. I introduced him to Rob, Ronnie Nozollino, Jack Porres, Gato and all the friends I had made. But Andy knew lots of people himself, and those he didn't know, knew of him.

What a fucking beautiful crew we had. It was non-stop laughter from then on. The next day I took him to the plumbing shop.

I said, "Andy, this is beautiful. It's a real joke. You can do anything with this guy, he doesn't bust balls."

"Great, let's go."

I already had Ronnie working with me at plumbing. Andy was to join us. When I took him to meet Mr. Coughlin, the first thing he said was, "Another godfather. Now I've got two working here."

Andy was in.

Right away, Andy finds a use for this job. We're going to use it to eat in the short line every day. That means we have to be in the kitchen every day at 10:45, then they lock the doors and no one is in there except the guys cooking. So, we find a pipe in the kitchen that we say needs tightening, go to plumbing, get a wrench, put my tag on the empty silhouette of the tool and we return to the kitchen. We get locked in, eat our own menu of grilled cheese sandwiches, fish, salads, whatever we wanted, then at 12 noon, when the kitchen officially opens, we go back to plumbing to return the wrench. Turns out the fucking wrench was due back before 11 a.m. and nobody could go eat until we returned it. All the workers, were released early to be first in line when the two kitchens opened at noon. So we had everyone pissed off at us. But we learned a good lesson. All we needed was something, anything, to take into the kitchen that looked like we were doing some work, but nothing that we needed to sign out for.

We found the perfect item. We told the CO in both kitchens that the hot and cold water pipes and the pipes leading to the soda machine needed insulating. The insulation was the perfect thing, small in diameter, light, about three feet long. We could put it under our carts or in our lockers without getting in trouble; after all, we were plumbers, and, best of all, we didn't have to sign it out.

We each carried a three-foot section of that fucking insulation everywhere. My uncle use to say that to get or keep a job in a hospital, you just had to carry something, anything, nothing more. He should have added jail to that statement. We carried the same insulation in and out of the kitchens for months.

Only once did one CO finally say, "I know what you guys are doing."

We figured our days of using the insulation gig were over.

He continued, "You guys are designing a whole new system back here, with a central manifold and all the smaller pipes to the pots and grill will feed off that manifold."

We all looked at each other. We were like a finely tuned orchestra, each member knowing his part.

"Wow," I said. "Andy, he knows his shit."

Andy elaborated on our plan to the CO and commended him on his insight.

"I know these things," the CO said. "That's why they pay me the big bucks."

We had two bocce courts on the east side, and the pipe insulation was always with us, even when we were playing. We had to hide the balls in a steel window grate that we had unbolted, but as plumbers, we had access to lots of tools. The bocce balls were ours. If we ever turned them in, we'd have to wait hours when we wanted to use them, and that's if you're lucky enough to find someone who would go looking for them. These COs couldn't care less about you or your fucking bocce balls.

"Everybody's different," my uncle used to say. Some of the smart-ass inmates refused to work and would hang around and do nothing. Andy and I couldn't understand this.

He would say things like, "I don't want to work for these assholes."

But we'd counter, "You're not working for them."

Working, is a good thing in jail, because a day in jail begins very early. Breakfast, for example, begins at 6 a.m. and ends at 6:45. Then, lights go out at the agreement of the inmates in the room, so generally a day went from before 6 in the morning, to around midnight. That's a long day if you don't get into something. I got into designing eyeglasses, and it was the perfect project for me to do at night.

Here you're in a jail, which if you removed all the drug dealers, would have only two inmates: Andy and me. Most of the drug dealers made thousands of dollars a week, some much more. They spent their money on cars, women, drink, clothes, and on expensive, handmade sunglasses. And, since there were 72 countries worth of drug dealers, I saw a lot of sunglasses.

My first designs were crude, but soon I had guys running up to me showing me their glasses. Many times I took a pair of one-of-a-kind glasses and brought them to the library, and made photocopies of the glasses. Then I would draw them, make some changes if I felt it was necessary and came up with my own designs. I was known to these inmates as the eyeglass man: I made some very unique designs. The photocopier was mainly to be used by the inmates who were allowed to file briefs and appeals and other jailhouse lawyers, some of whom knew the law more thoroughly than a defense attorney. I saw many a very professional document prepared by inmates. Some of them were once lawyers who were now doing time.

Some inmates are very clever, and I've seen some amazing things in jail. I'm very mechanical, but I could never figure out how the jailhouse tattoos were done until I saw it for myself. You stole a pair of electric clippers from the barbershop, removed the head and altered the unit to accept a needle. Now you had a tattoo machine.

In the same way you could sharpen your skills as a mechanic, you could sharpen your skills for criminal activities. Jail is the perfect place to get your Doctorate in Crime. You also can meet people for future plans. This, too, is the perfect meeting place. I saw so many guys get together and plan their future. What better place to meet than in jail.

The balance of power in jail is kind of like the Republicans and Democrats, and maybe an independent candidate. The Colombians were very united. They presented themselves as extremely polite and intelligent people. Then there were the American blacks. If you want to know what it's like to live as a minority member of society, a Caucasian just has to spend some time in jail and you'll get a first-hand lesson.

Andy would often be told by CO's to remove his hat when he was in the kitchen, and he inevitably remarked that the Muslims are allowed to wear their laundry bags on their heads everywhere, but someone like him, who fought and was wounded for this country, wasn't allowed to wear his gray, hand-knitted cap in the mess hall. The cap resembled one that would be worn by the Army Rangers and he never went anywhere without it.

The Italians couldn't care less about any group, including their own. To keep an Italian in jail happy, just give him his pasta. Actually, I did witness one time when the Italian population came together as a group. It was a dispute over the commissary's dropping pasta from the list of items they sold, while retaining beans and rice, which is the Spanish inmate's main dish. This was the only thing that brought them together and they got pasta back on the commissary sheet quickly. Nobody, from the lowly CO to the warden wants trouble in his prison.

Andy was the first to leave Room 212, the East Side He hurriedly packed his things in a few laundry bags and was on his way to the West Side. While he was packing, he said, "Lou, I got us a three-man room on the West Side, where all our friends are. You'll be in the room with me and Richard DiCenso . I'll get your transfer ready tomorrow and you'll be over the next day. You thought it was more."

This move caused big trouble, because three-man rooms, preferred housing as they are called, don't come until an inmate has been in the system at least four to five years. I was jumping ahead of a few thousand inmates.

A couple of days later, I was told to pack up my belongings, be downstairs by 2 p.m. and would be taking the bus to another location. They never mentioned where I was going, but I knew.

By 4 p.m. count, I was in a beautiful three-man room on the second floor. My roommates were Andy and Richard. Richard DiCenso was part of the Stamford, Connecticut crew, and I knew the Boss, Bill Sabia and most of the top level Stamford wise guys. Richard was a low level wannabe wise guy who sold drugs and refused to rat on the others, so he was doing seven fucking years for an eight ball of coke. He was around 38 or 39, very good looking, respectful and polite, a tough guy with manners. He had muscles on top of muscles. I felt embarrassed in the summertime to wear a short sleeve shirt around him.

This was like being in heaven, compared to the 12-man room I had just left, with guys who snored, farted, hollered at each other and argued over anything. Plus, I had my bed by the window. They gave me the best spot in the room. Soon after my arrival, Ronnie and Jack joined us on the West Side. The whole crew was back together, but not for long. Jack only had a few weeks left on his sentence.

Jack had a weekend orderly job, commonly referred to as a rich man's job, because there was no pay and almost no work involved. I wanted it because I was spending my spare time designing eyeglasses and I didn't want a job took more than 10 minutes work a day.

Jack and my friends were able to slide me into Jack's job when he left. Jack wanted to do things with me when I got out, and he thought he could convince me to go back to counterfeiting. Jack liked the good life and had a wardrobe that cost more than $100,000. Before coming into jail, he put his $100,000 wardrobe in storage and panicked one day when a letter arrived from the storage company that they had not been paid in two years and were going to auction off the contents of his storage room. He convinced one of his girlfriends to pay the bill.

The weekend orderly job was a plum, but I had no idea what I had to do. One Saturday morning I took a bucket, filled it with water, dipped one of two or three dozen filthy mops in the supply room and mopped the two floors I was responsible for. One was a small TV room with a Spanish station on 24 hours a day, and the other was a large room with a TV where we sometimes watched a movie or other event, like a fight. The floor was soaking wet when I returned the bucket and mop to the supply room. There were people waiting to use the equipment I was returning, so my timing had been great. I got there so early, no one was there to sign me in or out and a CO opened the door for me. I went back to my room, and fell asleep.

When I went into the large room, two inmates were leaving, complaining of the horrible smell. I almost threw up. I had to act quickly. I had fucked up two rooms and was going to be in real trouble, possibly losing my job.

"CO," I said, "the odor's coming from this vent, smell here."

He sniffed near the grate and said, "Yeah, I think you're right. It's spreading to the two rooms."

I told him maybe something had died in the wall or vent, and that I'd find out immediately. I was only bullshitting, but the jerk believed me and went back to his office. I ran to the stockroom and asked a friend what I could do to fix the smell. He told me that once you wet the mops, they smell of urine, or worse, and that you should always wash the mop with detergent in one of the two slop sinks before using them. Also, add Simple Green to the water. Soon, I'm back mopping the rooms, but this time they smell OK. I told the CO, "All set, I found the problem and fixed it."

He had forgotten what the hell the problem was. My job was safe.

Monday morning at 9 a.m. Andy said, "Lou, let's get going. Giovanni wants to see you."

Giovanni was the head man in a Mob-run drug organization referred to as "the Pizza Connection." It was one of the largest drug smuggling rings in the world and was run under via pizza parlors throughout Sicily, Italy and the United States.

Giovanni was the quintessential gentleman, soft-spoken and 70 years old. He commanded the respect of everyone on the West Side. For him to invite me to his room was considered a very big honor.

There were maybe six of us in the room. They were serving breakfast consisting of homemade biscotti, coffee with anisette, fresh juice, eggs, and toast. The anisette was from the lining of cigars they had smuggled in. I preferred my coffee without it, but this was the respectful way to drink coffee, and I was very respectful.

Through my association with Giovanni, I was to become friendly with Biaggio DiLeonardo, from Boston, who was caught on an FBI tape, along with Raymond Patriarca, Jr., getting initiated in a ceremony to raise him to the level of a Made Member of the Family. Ironic that the ceremony was taped and bugged, and that Raymond, Jr. would be doing time for making the same mistake his father had made years before: not believing the FBI was listening in.

Then, at 1 p.m., dinner. Always something homemade, and always something good to eat. Fucking Italians, all we do is eat. Supper was the same routine, but much more elaborate. Homemade tomato sauce, sausage, pasta, gnocchi, raviolis, pork, bread, mushrooms, and lots of other things, some that I didn't like, were also part of the menu. When I moved over to the West Side I weighed 175 pounds. When I was released in February, a little more than a year later, I weighed 214 pounds.

"How the fuck did you get through the system?" he asked.

The question came from Guido, a mobster who was part of a well-publicized shootout in the Olneyville section of Providence, where the FBI were actually waiting for them and shot everyone before the robbery even took place. Guido's uncle was killed, his father was doing time in another jail, and Guido lost part of his leg when he dared an FBI agent to blow his leg off. The agent was happy to oblige.

He was a very talented chef and he was trying to show me how to pinch the gnocchi without squashing them.

"Like this, Lou," he said. "Say you're being fingerprinted, right. Now roll your finger over slowly, then pick up the end and bend it over. But, not too hard. Then they become like sinkers."

"Boy, what a lot of fucking work. Why not just open one of our boxes of ziti and make that?" I asked.

"Because we had that last night and Giovanni wants potato gnocchi," he replied.

Cooking was not only too much work, but was taken far too seriously. I never volunteered again to help.

Besides Giovanni and Biaggio, I had met everyone I needed to know to make my life at Fort. Dix's West Side comfortable I had Fat Vinny doing my laundry, Eddie the barber cutting my hair, Rob, cleaning, buffing and waxing my room, Chuck Casserta, an enforcer from the Hells Angels, watching my back during the day, and John Shore, a boxer from South Boston, watching my back at night.

One night, I wanted to watch the fights on TV. I was the only one in a small TV room, when John Shore came in.

"Giovanni said you just finished eating and I'd find you here. Lou, what're you watching?"

"A fat fighter named Butterbean, John. I think he trained 30 minutes for this fight."

John laughed. He said Butterbean could have been a good fighter, but was eating his way through the divisions. Pretty soon, they wouldn't have a category heavy enough for him to fight in. The fight begins, and a minute into Round 1, a big, cocky gorilla enters the room, changes the channel and sits down in John's chair.

John had gone to go to the bathroom. When he returned, he politely asked this fucking gorilla to give him back his chair.

"I think that's my chair," is exactly how he put it "It's easy enough to mix them up."

Chairs are among an inmate's most valuable possessions. Everyone puts something on a chair, like their name, initials, or a photo to mark the territory. John was being very polite. The next thing John did was return the TV to the channel we had been watching. The gorilla made a remark, picked up the chair, folded it up, and began walking out of the room. John stood in front of him, blocking his way. The asshole actually took a swing at John.

John's about 5 feet 9 inches tall at most, and maybe 175 pounds. His left hand struck the gorilla on his chin and the second blow was so fucking fast, I only heard it land. The gorilla didn't move. I looked at John, as if to say, "John, let's get the fuck out of here, before we're both dead."

John knew exactly what I was thinking and said, "Just give him a few more seconds, Lou."

I thought John should have hit him again and then both of us would get the fuck out of there, but before I finished my thought, the guy went totally limp and fell back with no reflexes at all. He hit the floor solidly. He was out cold and he was hurt badly. John was put in the hole immediately and the gorilla was hospitalized, and never returned to the complex.

Within a couple of days, John and I were back watching TV. We missed the Butterbean fight, though.

The Italian respect thing was getting way out of hand. First, you shook Giovanni's hand, then Biaggio's, then Guido's, and all the way down the bench at each bocce court. The bocce courts here were serious, not like on the East Side. We had a guy whose only job was to keep the courts raked, dry, and clean. He got $300 a month to take care of the three courts we used and no one, I mean no one, who wasn't one of us, used these courts.

For the short period of time he spent on the West Side, Jack never did get the hang of Italian respect. He was respectful, all right, but kept on forgetting the order in which the respect had to be metered out. Every time we went to play, he'd ask me who to approach first. I'd point them out as inconspicuously as possible. One, two, no skip him, three, I'd whisper.

One day it was tournament time, and all the wise guys were out and partnered up. I was Andy's partner. Andy had a bocce court at his home and played like a pro. I knew the game well from my childhood, and I wasn't a bad player. I wasn't consistent, but when I was hot, I was really good. Andy tried to play the game without using the rails. This is the professional way to play, but I was good at determining angles and used the rails and backstop to my advantage.

Jack keeps repeating to himself, first, second, skip, then third. All of a sudden, he looks at me and says, "This is too fucking complicated for me. I'm afraid I'm going to fuck it up for you. I'm going back to my room to read."

Once, I actually fucked up big time. I didn't recognize a Boston mobster while I was walking. He didn't talk to me or Andy for two fucking weeks after that. Of course, he was also pissed that Andy and I had beaten him and his partner at the bocce tournament.

It takes a year to become a convict. The first six months, your thoughts are about equally divided between your home and jail. After a year, jail is your home. When Donna would come to visit, my thoughts temporarily turned to Rhode Island. But the minute she left, I couldn't wait to get back to my friends and my daily routine. I had an easy bit and the two years passed quickly. By the time I got out, I had over 1,000 eyeglass designs.

But, Louie the Coin, as everyone on the West Side was calling me, was going to get his balls busted. Right after I moved over to the West Side, I saw my name on the daily sheet.

It said, Colavecchio, 19894-050, hospital west, 10 a.m. This was a Tuesday and the hospital was closed on Tuesdays. Based on the quality of care an inmate received, you were probably better off getting sick when it was closed. I dressed up, because you weren't allowed in the medical facility unless you were in full dress uniform, including your shoes. I found no one there and the door locked.

Suddenly, someone opened the door, and told me to follow him quickly. In a small room, off the main corridor, was the FBI.

One agent identified himself, and said, "How would you like to get out of here today?"

I knew what he was after, and responded quickly, "Why, I like it here."

He had a plan in which I would involve inmates I was friendly with in a scheme to do a sting.

I told him, 'I'm too fucking old to become a rat now."

They were worse than the fucking inmates. Then came the threats, that I'd lose my three-man room, possibly my good time, any chance to get a halfway house, and no camp status. Every one of their threats came to be, except for losing my room. When the camp was finished, the building was so empty, it didn't make any difference anyway.

I lost my orderly job, and one asshole CO actually asked me to shovel snow.

I said, "Never."

I have a serious heart condition, and if he pushed me, I'd call my lawyer and file a complaint with the Bureau of Prisons. The asshole never bothered me again. Not only that, I never took another job. I said I was too sick to work.

There was a group of five or six guys that were part of a religious swindle, a case involving approximately $350 million. They were all gentlemen, with the greatest of manners, and were always smiling. We would be amazed by their answer when we asked how are you doing.

"Fine, just fine. The Lord has all our futures planned, God bless you," each would answer. Now, each of them were about two years into their 15 year sentences. Clinton's presidency was coming to an end. Take a wild guess, among all the people in the prison system, who he had pardoned during his last days? The entire group received presidential pardons. No wonder they were all smiles. Fuck, they got out before I did. How they worked it I'll never know.

The Jews made up the smallest population of all the ethnic groups, but by far, they were among the most powerful. During their religious holidays, a private room was dedicated for their use in a building that served as a worship center for all the religions. I went to church, but the priest was a money-hungry hypocrite who left another parish for a salary rumored to be around $65,000 yearly, plus housing. Hell, I'll bet the warden didn't get that much. The priest never had a single hair out of place, with his $30 or $40 razor cuts, and his impeccable clothing. I envisioned him as someone using his influence and position and taking his religion secondary

The rabbi, on the other hand, was a huge and fat but short man with a jolly disposition. He was an avid fan of the Three Stooges, and the only conversation I ever had with him consisted of three words, "Nyk, nyk, nyk." He began every conversation that way. He never missed a holiday, and he was always ready to help anyone, not just another Jew. He was a man of power, disguised as one of the Three Stooges. I liked that.

Toward the last couple of months on my sentence, I met my old friend Jerry DeThomas. I had known him the 60s and 70s when he owned Airway Cleansers in Providence. He did an eight-year bit for planning a fire in a nightclub he owned. Imagine if he had been sentenced a couple of years ago, when Rhode Island had one of the worst nightclub fires in history, with over 100 people left dead. Jerry was getting out the same time as I was and we visited almost daily. He owns Gerardo's, a gay club in Providence, and has a villa in Mexico.

About the same time I met Jerry, Eddy Latio, from the S&S, came in. He had been in the system about a year, but mostly at Wyatt, in Rhode Island. He was busted for his part in the gambling activities at our bar and would be doing a five-year bit. He had gained a few pounds and had snow-white hair, but still had that boyish look he always had. I asked him what he needed, and together we filled out a commissary sheet.

He made me laugh when he remarked, "Most people keep their money in banks. I got mine in three fucking commissary accounts."

I made life for Eddy easy, well, as easy as prison life gets. His commissary money came in right after his first time shopper's privilege was used up. Before a couple of days had passed, he had a nice room, a job in the library, and I introduced him to everyone.

"Andy, this is Eddy Latio, who I told you about. Eddy, this is the "Sarge." They hit it off immediately.

I was still working on my eyeglass project, and it would always make me laugh when I went into the library, and there was Eddy sitting behind a desk, his feet on the desk, with his eyeglasses halfway down his nose, and in full inmate dress uniform. What a change from those days in the S&S. Eddy made sure the photocopy machine was always in good order for me, because I was finishing this project and making duplicates several times a day. He would put a big sign, "out of order" on the machine and keep it unplugged to keep it ready for me.

He became part of our nightly eating schedule. We used to look out the window while we were eating our homemade lasagna, and laughing, loudly remark, "Look, look at all the big shots running for chicken."

Chicken, which was served once a week, brought everyone to the kitchen.

"The fucking chickens died of old age, but look at all the big shots standing in line."

In jail, you could be anybody you wanted to be, and any little asshole could pass himself off as big shot in his country, or state. But we had a way to look up everyone. We had access to any inmate's history, unless he was an FBI or other initial. For us, this was important, because the FBI was constantly planting agents as inmates, and we were always informed. You had to look out for everyone. Known rats actually had their own building, called the "Cheese Factory" and they got the best of everything, medical care, house visits, half-way houses. You name it, they got it.

In the joint there were drug and substance abuse programs, which alcohol and drug abusers could attend for a period of one year. Upon completion of their program, they would be given a sentence reduction of about a year and a half. But you needed proof of a pre-existing drug dependency, which would usually be noted in your PSI.

I've seen tough, high-level wise guys get an outside doctor to write the BOP. and then they would be allowed in the program when an opening became available. Andy and I used to laugh like hell. Some top-level wise guy begging to be placed in a substance abuse program.

What does he tell his family, we would say, "Your father's a wise guy, a criminal, an inmate, and a drug addict, too." What, the first three aren't enough. But, the government fucked them all. They let them get their statements from their doctors, get in the program, take fucking embarrassing classes. Then, when they graduated, they refused to reduce their sentences.

"So now you're a fucking drug addict, too," we would say. They got suckered and knew it.

***

Barry DePetrillo was associated with a New York' Colombo Family, and was a powerful, influential figure there. He lived in the room next to ours, another three-man room. The BOP liked using these rooms as leverage to get information from inmates, or to punish or bust balls of inmates they didn't like. Random inspections were held, just like shakedowns, and an excuse to throw someone out of their room could be found in any number of ways. Not that the action needed an excuse, but the idea was to bust balls, and losing a room over something trivial, like having the overhang on the sheets exceed six inches, even by a quarter of an inch, was sticking it up the inmates ass and reaming him out. And the BOP loved this.

The inspectors are in Barry's room, and he's pleading with them that the room is immaculate.

"This room is so clean, it's going to be on the front cover of next month's issue of Better Prisons and Gardens," he screams.

I mean, give me a fucking break. Here's a supposedly tough motherfucker practically on his hands and knees begging not to lose his room. Tough guys are few and far between in jail. The BOP is an autonomous entity that almost no one knows anything about.

To allow a private business like Unicor, which uses prison inmates for labor, is like giving China most favored nation status. It is a business owned by politicians, and in fact, all the BOP is political.

Our unit manager, Mrs. Cozza, was the daughter of a warden in another prison. They are like clones, mechanical devices that look like people, but who are manufactured in some warehouse, God knows where. She was a powerful person who actually controlled more than one unit on both sides of Fort Dix, and a stone cold liar. She'd make promises and think nothing of breaking them. She was a ruthless, hungry power-seeker married to a lieutenant in the system.

A lieutenant was a CO who rose up in the prison system and had ability to make minor decisions, like when to call a shakedown, coordinating a surprise piss test program, deciding if someone should do time in the hole, and for how long. But the unit manager made bigger decisions. Still, no one wanted anyone, inmates as well as outsiders, and especially lawyers with some political connections, to make waves.

The BOP was a sweet deal, and no one who was part of it wanted it fucked up. It was already fucked up. It couldn't stand outside scrutiny.

When Mrs. Cozza's husband got caught smuggling drugs and selling them to the inmates, she was first in line to testify against him. Her husband was incarcerated with us, and he was a pretty nice guy. I felt he was better off with us than living with her.

The BOP's dealings with a situation like this were mind-boggling. Because so much alcohol, cocaine and heroin were prevalent, the BOP came up with a brilliant idea. They stopped selling Visine eye drops in the commissary. That move, they rationalized, would allow COs to see whose eyes were bloodshot from drinking alcohol or doing drugs.

I have very sensitive eyes, and even if I didn't, the fumes and fuel dropping on us every day from the planes landing and taking off from McGuire, one of the largest military bases in the northeast corridor, was enough to make anyone's eyes cry with tears. So, I had to hunt down Visine, which now was considered contraband, and hide it. Getting caught possessing it or using it was a serious violation, punishable by who knows what the fuck a lieutenant decided.

Then it was dental floss. Someone must have watched a movie where an inmate wove dental floss into a rope to scale a wall or something. It didn't matter to the BOP that there were no walls or cliffs to scale, dental floss was now contraband.

Meanwhile, screwdrivers, wrenches, hammers, and a million other things ran rampant throughout the compound. No dental floss, no Visine. These people lived in their own little world.

They offered a class in carpentry, and I thought it would be great to take it because I like that kind of work. Andy and I took not only carpentry, but also electrical classes. In fact, he and I were appointed instructors in both classes. If we wanted to go play bocce, we got someone to substitute teach for us, just sit and keep the inmates quiet for an hour.

Richard Devereaux, was also a carpentry student. He was an insurance underwriter and multi-millionaire with a huge mansion in Newport, Rhode Island. His father had been Dean at the University of Rhode Island when my daughter was attending college there. Richard was a thin, 5 feet 9 inches tall, about 36 years old, who stole millions from his business and was doing a short popcorn bit for the IRS. He used to show us pictures of his 65-foot yacht, and every time he had a new girlfriend, which was quite frequent, he would have the main stateroom remodeled. The cost was around $45,000 each time.

After class one day, me, Andy, Mr. Gunn, the class instructor, and Richard were heading back to our units. Mr. Gunn was a nice guy, a thin, black man with a humble attitude. He was not a CO, but an instructor.

He puts his hand on Richard's shoulder and says, "You know, if you keep studying and increase your skills just a little, you'll be able to make, easy $8, maybe $9 an hour, and before too long, you'll earn $12 an hour, I'm sure."

Richard looked at Andy and me and said, "Wow, that much." Andy and I said simultaneously with a huge grin, "You thought it was more."

One night, the BOP really went nuts. Midnight and the fucking fire alarm goes off. It's 15 degrees outside and everyone's running out the exits. No fucking way the three of us in our rooms were moving anytime quickly. We put on our pants, shirts, jackets, hats, gloves and took our portable radios, and waited until the building was teaming with COs shaking down each room They discovered us in our rooms and we had to go outside in the freezing cold. At least we were dressed. Most of the others were in pajamas and were fucking freezing.

A half hour later, there were another 10 or 12 COs running into our building led by some stupid motherfucker screaming, "We'll shake this building down until there isn't a fucking toothpick that doesn't belong there. I don't care if it takes until spring."

Bear in mind, each unit had only two COs during the day and only one at night. If an inmate was in trouble, he was in real trouble because there was almost no security. I witnessed several stabbings. An inmate would have no problem doing it or fear of being stopped by a CO. He would, of course, be ratted out the next day by a line of rats looking for a piece of cheese.

There weren't enough COs in the whole compound to conduct a shakedown of this magnitude. This asshole lieutenant called COs in from their days off. This was costing the BOP money and the BOP doesn't spend a fucking dime on anything it didn't have to.

The final result was they found one of our stingers and maybe a hundred pounds of ziti. The next day the lieutenant was transferred to another facility. He was in deep shit. We replaced the stinger the following morning and the 100 pounds of ziti didn't put a dent in the supply we had hidden in the air conditioning ducts and the grates. You name the spot, we had a hiding place nearby.

Sometimes, when our supplies were running low, we would go into the mess hall and stand in line like the rest of the inmates. We picked our time carefully. We wanted a particular CO who was running the line that day.

You're allowed two packets of salt, two peppers, and one packet of Equal or whatever sweetener they had gotten a deal on that week. A group of us would go through the line piling up all three items on our tray, four or five packets of salt, three or four peppers, three or four Equals. She would fucking freak out. If she was in a good mood, she would just confiscate your whole tray, and send you back to the end of the line. By then, the food would be cold, or you'd be too late to eat it. Now, if she had a feather up her ass, which was more likely than not, she would fling the whole tray, food and all, on the floor.

She had been in the Army before working for the BOP, but was definitely BOP material. But while we had her occupied with flinging trays and having inmates clean up the mess, our guys were in the kitchen supply room robbing 50 pound slabs of bacon, canned tomatoes, turkeys, chickens, and everything we needed to stock up on. Hell, we weren't going to eat the shit on the tray anyway. I'm surprised we didn't get the gas grill and cooking utensils.

What the kitchen didn't have, our guy who ordered for the commissary could buy and we'd rob it from there. But a lot of the things we got, I didn't like. Squid, calamari, tripe. The only fish I really liked was the anchovies. If the guys wanted a sauce with calamari or tripe, or mushrooms, knowing that none of these things appealed to me, they'd make a small pot just for me, then add all the other things to their sauce. Two hundred and fourteen pounds came real easy. I haven't been able to take it off yet.

My days were getting short now. The name "Louie the Coin" was being replaced by "Shorty," an inmate whose time was almost completed.

I noticed a change in Andy. His granddaughter was now a year and a half old and he had nine or ten years more to go. Camp status is given only to inmates with two years or less time left, and for non-violent, first-time offenders. I fit this profile to a T, but I couldn't get camp, as I wouldn't cooperate.

The camp at Fort Dix was almost complete. There was no razor wire, no gates, no butt hut used for anal inspections, no security, no nothing. And many of my friends were putting the final touches on the buildings and getting the place ready for occupancy. They started moving inmates into the facility to live there and get the bugs out of the plumbing and electrical hook ups before moving all the eligible inmates in.

Andy had an appeal going on while we were together. He had a high priced Washington attorney who published a small magazine telling of cases she represented, the sentences of some of her clients, and the reductions she got them. I knew an inmate who had retained her only to blow about $35,000 before he let her go. She was nothing but a charlatan who preyed on rich inmates with long sentences, giving them false hope of significant sentence reductions. Andy was beginning to feel that this might be his case.

He talked all too frequently of giving her one more year, one last hearing, and if it produced no results, he would plan a way out. I told him to keep his plans to himself, because he was starting to talk about it too much.

Week after week, his name appeared on the daily sheet. Giordano, hospital west, 10 a.m. Sometimes twice in a week. He said they had found a polyp on his bowels, but I knew they couldn't give a shit what they found.

Then, Andy makes camp status. Ten years left to go, a previous bank robbery conviction, and he makes camp. Within two weeks, building #42 was empty, except for 10 or 12 inmates in a 400-man facility. I had not only the whole room to myself, but practically the whole building.

Andy insisted they needed him there because of his construction skills, but he wound up being the camp's cook. Eddy Latio was still in low security, which is below minimum and much more restrictive. Ten minute moves, more surprise shakedowns, more counts, less freedom to move about the compound. We would meet in the library. I told him to be careful.

"The Sarge is losing it and if he can't get out one way, he'll get out another."

This is the first time I ever called Andy the Sarge. I don't know what he did to get outside the gate, but I had an idea. Eddy was sharp and said, "Don't worry, Lou, I'm very careful around him. When you get out, tell Our Friend I'm fine."

I spent two years in prison at Fort Dix. I'm out now. I'm broke, I'm a felon. Not much of a bright job opportunity awaits a 60 year old ex-convict. But, like my uncle Vincent used to say about me, "I've never seen anyone with the resilience you have. Your ability to bounce back never fails to amaze me."

Well, now I'm much older than when he said that, but still I have a plan.

Supposing I write a book, and let's say it makes lots of money, then suppose I can sell the Louis Bene Casino Collection of fine eyewear, and supposing I can stay out of jail, and live until I'm 100.

I know I'm asking a lot, but Paula once said to me when I was first sentenced to 27 months — that, as a former math teacher, at my age, middle 50s, 27 months was around four percent of my life. That's a small percentage to pay for living as well as I did. If I can make it to 100 years old, I will have lived my lifestyle and spent only two percent for doing it my way.

Cool, huh. "You thought it was more."

Epilogue

The History Channel decided to do a series of one-hour segments about people who cheated Vegas out of large sums of money.

My case so interesting to them that I was given a show devoted solely to my misadventures. The series was called "Breaking Vegas," and my particular segment was called "The Counterfeit King." Breaking Vegas is a real naive statement. Sure, some smart cheats come in to a casino and beat them of hundreds of thousands, even millions of dollars, but that doesn't put a dent in the mystique called Vegas. Vegas was, and is, built on gambling, and in gambling, the house always has the edge. Given enough playing time, Vegas will always triumph.

I did break Vegas. In fact, I changed gambling throughout the entire country, even though that wasn't my intention. The Vegas I knew and loved was long dead, even before I began robbing them. I remember the days of wise guys carrying money in paper bags used to purchase a small percentage of a casino. Days of Teamsters Union Pension Fund monies building and expanding the Vegas Strip. Days when someone like me, who took a casino's money, would more than likely wind up dead and his body left in the desert, or the trunk of a stolen car.

Today's Vegas was built on junk bonds, issued by stock underwriters and sold through brokers to private individuals, investment institutions and mutual funds, among many others. Yes, the Old Vegas has been replaced with a Disney Land façade. The major portion of their revenue still comes from gambling. They invite you to bring your family, then post a sign in the casino's floor that no one under the age of 21 is allowed in the casino. Have you ever tried to register in a casino's hotel without passing through the casino itself? Hotels have a path to their check-in desks that brings you through the casino itself. They are preparing the next generation of marks to become accustomed to a casino's environment, and this is smart marketing on their part.

One thing is missing, and I robbed that from Vegas. I broke Vegas, and most every other casino in the country of something that myself, and most casino patrons loved. That something was the unique sound of metal dropping from the hopper in a slot machine. The cling, cling, cling of metal tokens hitting the stainless steel tray of the machine was exciting. It made your adrenaline flow when someone hit big. That sound can't be duplicated and it's gone.

It has been replaced with a recording of the sound of metal hitting metal. The payoff is a paper ticket with a bar code printed on it and redeemable at another machine, if you can locate one that is working. Machines transform payout tickets to currency. The fewer people handling money, the fewer chances for a slip up.

No more dirty, bulky tokens. No more moistened wipes, to clean your hands after playing the machines. I miss the old days, and I suspect lots of others do, too. If I changed the way slot, or slot-less machines are played, then I apologize. It wasn't done on purpose.

As I look back on my life, I see things much clearer, but I'm not sure how that makes me feel. Sometimes sad, I guess. I packed so much into my 70-some years, and there isn't a lot I would change, or without everything else changing, could change. If only I had been more careful with money, for instance, then my actions would have changed as result. Maybe I wouldn't have done so many things that I now value. Do I feel guilty that what I did was wrong? No, I don't.

How about my kids? Did I leave them with a name they have to be ashamed of? I don't know. Maybe.

But I'm not a priest, or some psychiatrist, or any one of the numerous other predators who commit abominable crimes against some young patients by using their twisted father figure to haunt them for the rest of their lives. How about money? Did I rob my children of a possible inheritance by selfishly indulging myself with my lifestyle and material possessions and not giving a damn about the consequences of my behavior?

I was considered a stand-up guy all my life, but I've seen many of these same people crawl and bow under pressure when faced with prison terms. They, too, were called stand-up guys. So much betrayal, lies, and deceit. Does having a reputation as a stand-up guy make any sense anymore, considering where it's coming from, those people who live on treachery and deceit.

Yes, I lived the good life, but I was selfish. My word was always my bond, and I still think that's a worthwhile quality even though today I'm not sure who, if anyone, will appreciate it or recognize it for what it is. Looking back is always hard, because there is nothing you can do about it. The past is permanent. You live with past as best you can.

I don't blame for anyone of my mistakes, except myself. I believe that there is some sort of predestination which makes us do the things we do, but once done it's too late to do anything about them. Sometimes, as I read my own book, I forget it's me I'm reading about and I don't like what I see. But, there's not a fucking thing I can do to change that.

No time machine exists to take any of us back to alter the past. If there was, wouldn't it be like changing a paragraph in a story, only to find that everything that comes after the changes also moves?

One isolated change affects the whole. All my life I tried to act tough and cold. Invincible. But why? How could I not let people close to me see my weaknesses? I'm a fucking human being, not a piece of steel. It's just a matter of how you deal with your influences, and the choice is purely yours. How many times have you heard someone say: "Look at the shit I have to put up with?" But that's just my point; you don't have to put up with shit. We have choices. I chose not work for anyone all my life. I didn't want anyone's shit. Am I better off for that? I don't know the answer. I traded a beautiful lifestyle when I was young, for a struggling one now. I gave the government two years of my life, but, I got back experiences that make it more than worth the two years I lost.

I watch mature young people carefully plan out their lives. Sometimes, I envy them. They won't bob like a cork on the water, up and down, like I did. But what price will they pay for such a structured life? I couldn't do it. We each live our own life, and the thing that means were success will vary from person to person.

Look at this example. If an average person were to ask an old successful person, someone who had legitimately earned prestige, "What do you think are the ten most important things in a person's life?"

I think he would probably answer something like this: "Well, first, a person must have an appreciation of the fine arts, music, painting, literature, architecture, and so forth. Second, a person must be well traveled and understand other cultures. This is very important. Third, we should be interested in human rights, or lack thereof, here and in other countries and become involved in instituting changes." This could go on all the way down to number nine or ten where he finally makes mention of money. Or puts money so far down that it doesn't even appear on the list.

Now, ask someone who is struggling and has a rent or mortgage payment due, children to feed, medical and other bills to pay. Someone whose every penny is spent before it's earned. What do you think he might reply to that same question?. What do you think he'll place in the number one position? "Fucking money, you dope," would probably be his answer. Would the struggling parent be wrong in saying that money for rent basis necessities is his number one concern. I don't think he'd be wrong, do you?

As my life comes to a close, did I achieve success? I guess the answer is a qualified "yes." Most of my life I possessed happiness, but only now I realize what price I paid for it. I did learn from my mistakes, and that's part of being successful, I suppose.

Besides, I still have some possibility to change the ending, the final chapter. The matches are pretty much burnt out now, but maybe I'll get one more light, just one more chance.

That would be nice. "You thought it was more."

About the Authors

Louis Colavecchio, known to many as Louis "The Coin", began a life of entrepreneurial adventure as a youngster.

Along the way he got to know many characters on all sides of the law, throughout the United States and Europe.

His father arrived in Providence from Italy in 1903. As an established businessman, Benedict Colavecchio and his wife Theodora encouraged young Louis to gain an education.

While working fulltime, Louis Colavecchio earned a degree in business administration from Providence College.

Colavecchio's talents as a jeweler, manufacturer, and man of romance are part of the historical record — as seen on The History Channel and The BBC. It might be an understatement to say Colavecchio changed the face of casino gambling forever.

Colavecchio was such a great counterfeiter — *The Providence Journal* reported — that after he spent more than two years in federal prison for his handiwork, he was paid $18,000 by the feds as a consultant to explain why his manufacturing dies outlasted those at the U.S. Mint.

They say he was a hero in Providence as well because The Coin did not rat out any of his friends.

Now, he applies all those talents and his imagination in a new venue — storyteller.

***

Franz Douskey is the author of *Sinatra and Me: The Very Good Years*, with Tony Consiglio, and *Elvis is OUT There*. In 2011, Douskey was nominated for a Pulitzer Prize for his book of poems *West of Midnight*. His work has appeared in hundreds of publications including *Rolling Stone, The New Yorker, Cavalier, The Nation, USA Today, and Yankee Magazine*. Douskey is Professor of Humanities at Gateway Community College in New Haven.

***

Andy Thibault, author of "more COOL JUSTICE" (morecooljustice.com), teaches basic news writing and investigative reporting at the University of New Haven. Thibault was a research consultant for the HBO series Allen V Farrow. He covered the Boston Marathon bombing trial gavel to gavel for the NBC News Investigative Unit. Thibault was honored by the Connecticut Council on Freedom of Information in 2014 with the Stephen Collins Award for his "many contributions to the cause of open and accountable government and a free and vigorous press."

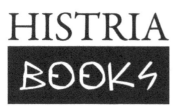